Swahili

lonely planet

phrasebooks
and
Dr Martin Benjamin

Swahili phrasebook
4th edition – July 2008

Published by
Lonely Planet Publications Pty Ltd ABN 36 005 607 983
90 Maribyrnong St, Footscray, Victoria 3011, Australia

Lonely Planet Offices
Australia Locked Bag 1, Footscray, Victoria 3011
USA 150 Linden St, Oakland CA 94607
UK 2nd Floor, 186 City Rd, London EC1V 2NT

Cover illustration
Safari Swing by Daniel New

ISBN 978 1 74104 705 9

10 9 8 7 6 5

Printed by China Translation and Printing Services Ltd
Printed in China

Editor Branislava Vladisavljevic would like to acknowledge the following people for their contributions to this phrasebook:

Dr Martin Benjamin for the translations, cultural information, and writing a concise guide to Swahili grammar. Martin is an anthropologist who has lived and worked in Tanzania for many years as a researcher and consultant on issues of development, health and gender. In addition to teaching Swahili and Anthropology at Wesleyan University, he is the founder and editor of the Kamusi Project Internet Living Swahili Dictionary at Yale University. Readers who wish to advance their Swahili can use the online lessons that he is developing in the Learning Guide at www.kamusiproject.org, and all travellers to East Africa are invited to visit the How to Help page of this site to learn how to contribute photos to the cause of Swahili education.

Martin wishes to thank Charles Mironko and Anne Geoghegan for their work on the previous edition of this phrasebook – many of their words have found their way into the current edition. Thanks also to Ben and Branislava for all their work preparing and editing this book. My deepest thanks for making it possible for me to (almost) meet my deadlines go to my wife Veronica, who yielded me to this project in the weeks right after our wedding.

Lonely Planet Language Products

Publishing Manager: Ben Handicott
Commissioning Editors: Rachel Williams & Karin Vidstrup Monk
Editor: Branislava Vladisavljevic
Assisting Editors: Meladel Mistica, Jodie Martire, Francesca Coles & Laura Crawford
Layout Designers: Margie Jung & Katherine Marsh
Managing Editor: Annelies Mertens
Layout Manager: Adriana Mammarella
Series Designer: Yukiyoshi Kamimura
Cartographer: Wayne Murphy

make the most of this phrasebook ...

Anyone can speak another language! It's all about confidence. Don't worry if you can't remember your school language lessons or if you've never learnt a language before. Even if you learn the very basics (on the inside covers of this book), your travel experience will be the better for it. You have nothing to lose and everything to gain when the locals hear you making an effort.

finding things in this book

For easy navigation, this book is in sections. The Tools chapters are the ones you'll thumb through time and again. The Practical section covers basic travel situations like catching transport and finding a bed. The Social section gives you conversational phrases, pick-up lines, the ability to express opinions – so you can get to know people. Food has a section all of its own: gourmets and vegetarians are covered and local dishes feature. Safe Travel equips you with health and police phrases, just in case. Sustainable Travel, finally, completes this book. Remember the colours of each section and you'll find everything easily; or use the comprehensive Index. Otherwise, check the two-way traveller's Dictionary for the word you need.

being understood

Throughout this book you'll see coloured phrases on each page. They're phonetic guides to help you pronounce the language. Start with them to get a feel for how the language sounds. The pronunciation chapter in Tools will explain more, but you can be confident that if you read the coloured phrase, you'll be understood. As you become familiar with the spoken language, move on to using the actual text in the language which will help you perfect your pronunciation.

communication tips

Body language, ways of doing things, sense of humour – all have a role to play in every culture. 'Local talk' boxes show you common ways of saying things, or everyday language to drop into conversation. 'Listen for ...' boxes supply the phrases you may hear. They start with the phonetic guide (because you'll hear it before you know what's being said) and then lead in to the language and the English translation.

social ... 107

food 153

safe travel 179

sustainable travel – safari 195

dictionaries 199

index 255

swahili

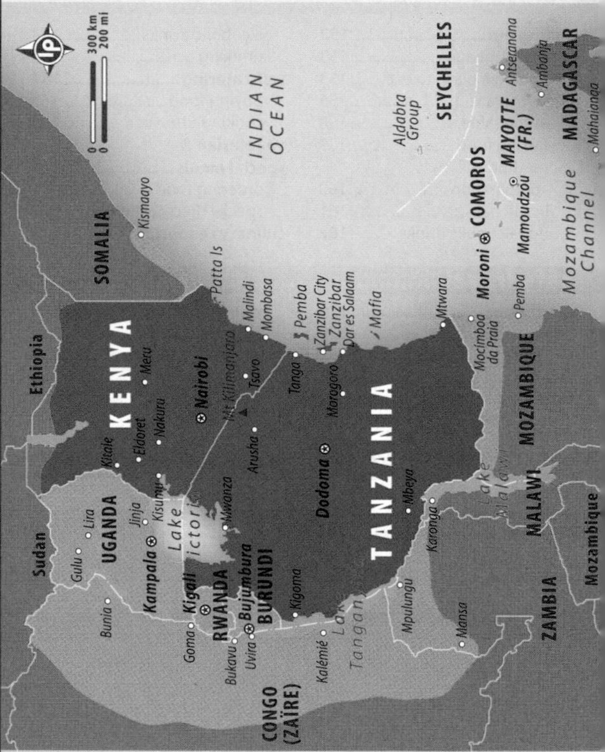

national language

widely spoken

For more details, see the **introduction**.

INTRODUCTION

utangulizi

Swahili is one of the most widely spoken African languages and is internationally recognised as the key language of communication in the East African region. It belongs to the Bantu group of languages from the Niger-Congo family and can be traced back to the first millenium AD. This Bantu origin is clearly visible in the distinctive grammar and sound system of Swahili.

Although the number of speakers of Swahili throughout East Africa is estimated to be well over 50 million, it's the mother tongue of only about 4–5 million people, and is predominantly used as a second language or a lingua franca by speakers of other African languages. Swahili is the national language of Tanzania and Kenya and is widely used in Uganda, Rwanda and Burundi, as well as in the eastern part of the Democratic Republic of Congo and on the Indian Ocean islands of Zanzibar and the Comoros. There are speakers of Swahili in the southern parts of Ethiopia and Somalia, the northern regions of Mozambique and Zambia, and even on the northwestern coast of Madagascar.

at a glance ...

language name: Swahili

name in language: *Kiswahili* kee·swa·*hee*·lee

language family: Niger-Congo

key countries: Tanzania, Kenya

approximate number of speakers: 4–5 million as first language, over 50 million as second language or lingua franca

close relatives: Bantu languages (eg Pokomo, Mijikenda, Comorian)

donations to English: safari, simba (lion)

The development of Swahili through time is an interesting story of contact between nations, reflecting many political and social changes in this part of the world. Originally spoken by indigenous people along the coast and on the islands, it was the main language of coastal trade, and therefore from the 7th century heavily influenced by Arabic, principally in the vocabulary – the word 'Swahili' itself comes from an Arabic word for 'coastal'. With the arrival of European explorers and colonisers and the rise of the slave trade in the 19th century, Swahili spread inland. Apart from Arabic, there are influences from Persian, Portuguese, and of course, English (words like *baisikeli*, *penseli* and *kompyuta* have only been adapted slightly to reflect Swahili pronunciation).

It's hardly surprising that in an area as vast as East Africa many different dialects of Swahili can be found, but you shouldn't have problems being understood if you stick to the standard coastal form, as used in this book. Standard Swahili developed from the urban dialect of Zanzibar City, dominant from pre-colonial times. The missionaries and colonial governments in Kenya and Tanzania used it first to communicate with the locals and later encouraged its use in administration, which led to its official status in the post-colonial period.

Even though Swahili grammar can seem a bit daunting, you should find the pronunciation pretty much straightforward. The writing system is based on the Roman alphabet, which will make using this phrasebook and learning Swahili much easier.

So wherever you go throughout the East African region, you'll find Swahili greatly useful and attempts to communicate with locals in the language will be greatly appreciated. This book gives you the practical phrases you need to get by, as well as the fun, spontaneous phrases that lead to a better understanding of East African people and their culture. Local knowledge, new relationships and a sense of satisfaction are on the tip of your tongue. So don't just stand there, say something!

abbreviations used in this book:

a	adjective	**n**	noun
adv	adverb	**pl**	plural
f	feminine	**prep**	preposition
Ken	Kenya	**sg**	singular
m	masculine	**Tan**	Tanzania
lit	literal translation	**v**	verb

The pronunciation of Swahili is relatively simple, since most of the sounds in this language are also found in English. Once you learn a few basic rules you won't have any problems reading or pronouncing it, but we've included a pronunciation guide throughout this book to make it even easier.

vowel sounds

Vowels are short and each one is pronounced clearly, even when not stressed. There are no diphthongs in Swahili (ie vowel sound combinations, like in English 'how' or 'day').

symbol	english equivalent	swahili example	transliteration
a	father	*dada*	*da*·da
ay	may	*wewe*	*way*·way
ee	bee	*sisi*	*see*·see
oh	role	*moja*	*moh*·ja
oo	moon	*duka*	*doo*·ka

consonant sounds

Most consonants in Swahili have equivalents in English. The only one that might be a bit unusual for an English speaker is the sound ng. It can be a bit tricky at first, but with a little practice it should come easily – try saying 'sing along' a few times and then dropping the 'si', and that's how it sounds at the beginning of a word.

The sounds th and dh occur only in words borrowed from Arabic.

Swahili speakers make only a slight distinction between r and l. Instead of the hard 'r', try pronouncing a light 'd'.

symbol	english equivalent	swahili example	transliteration
b	**b**ig	***b**etri*	*bay*·tree
ch	**ch**illi	***ch**akula*	cha·*koo*·la
d	**d**in	***d**uka*	*doo*·ka
dh	**th**is	***dh**ambi*	*dham*·bee
f	**f**un	*su**f**u*	*soo*·foo
g	**g**o	***g**ari/**gh**ali*	*ga*·ree/*ga*·lee
h	**h**at	*tare**h**e*	ta·*ray*·hay
j	**j**am	***j**iwe*	*jee*·way
k	**k**ick	*u**k**uta*	oo·*koo*·ta
l	**l**oud	*u**l**iza*	oo·*lee*·za
m	**m**an	***m**wana**m**u**m**e*	m·wa·na·*moo*·may
n	**n**o	***n**u**n**ua*	noo·*noo*·a
ng	si**ng**	***ng'**ombe*	ng·*ohm*·bay
ny	ca**ny**on	***ny**asi*	*nya*·see
p	**p**ig	*chu**p**a*	*choo*·pa
r	**r**un (but softer, more like a light 'd')	*di**r**isha*	dee·*ree*·sha
s	**s**o	*ki**s**u*	*kee*·soo
sh	**sh**ip	***sh**ida*	*shee*·da
t	**t**in	***t**ochi*	*toh*·chee
th	**th**ing	***th**ela**th**ini*	thay·la·*thee*·nee
v	**v**an	***v**umbi*	*voom*·bee
w	**w**in	***w**azo*	*wa*·zoh
y	**y**es	***y**o**y**ote*	yoh·*yoh*·tay
z	**z**oo	***z**iwa*	*zee*·wa

regional variations

Being used over a huge geographical area, Swahili has many dialectical variations, which can be grouped as northern, central and southern dialects, with a further basic distinction between urban and rural dialects. The form of Swahili in this phrasebook is the standard form which is based on Kiunguja, the coastal dialect spoken in Zanzibar City. When you travel across East Africa, you should be understood using this book, as all the regional variations are generally mutually intelligible and also increasingly influenced by this standard form, which is used in all the media.

word stress

In Swahili, words are almost always stressed on the second-last syllable. There are only a handful of words that break this rule, and these are mostly loanwords. In our pronunciation guide, the stressed syllable is always in italics.

stressing the point

- Changing the stress in a word can sometimes make a whole lot of difference. Make sure to get the stress in the right place on *barabara* ba·*ra*·ba·ra (amazing). If you say ba·ra·*ba*·ra, you're simply saying 'road'!

- Many words in Swahili come from English, but the pronunciation changed slightly. Be sure to stress the second-last syllable in the word *tiketi* tee·*kay*·tee (ticket), rather than the first syllable (*tee*·kay·tee) as you would in English. *Tikiti* tee·*kee*·ti is used instead of *tiketi* in many areas – listen to the locals' pronunciation and follow their lead.

reading & writing

Swahili was traditionally written in a modified Arabic script (used mostly for writing epic poetry). The Roman-based alphabet, in use since the mid-19th century, was formalised in the 1930s. It consists of 24 letters (all the letters of the English alphabet except 'q' and 'x').

The correspondence between the written language and the pronunciation is consistent. As a general rule, every written letter is pronounced. When two vowels appear together, each one must be pronounced separately. For example, *kawaida* (usual) is pronounced ka·wa·*ee*·da. However, if the same vowel is repeated twice at the end of a word, it's pronounced as one syllable and the stress falls on that (last) syllable, rather than the second-last one: *sikukuu* see·koo·*koo* (holiday).

There are only a few two-letter combinations in written Swahili that don't follow the general rule of pronouncing every letter separately: *ch, dh, gh, ng, ny, sh* and *th* all represent single sounds (see **consonant sounds**, page 12). Our coloured pronunciation guides indicate the correct pronunciation so don't worry if you can't remember these rules.

The symbol ' which appears in written Swahili after the letter combination *ng,* as in *ng'ombe* ng·*ohm*·bay (cow), is called a glottal stop, which is similar to the tightening of the throat that happens when you cough. You can also hear it in the word 'bottle' when the double 't' is swallowed. It's not represented in the pronunciation guide, as it only serves to show in writing that *ng'* should be pronounced as one syllable. Without it, these two letters belong to separate syllables, as in *changu chan*·goo (finger).

alphabet					
A a a	*B b* bee	*C c* see	*D d* dee	*E e* ay	*F f* ayf
G g jee	*H h* *ay*·chee	*I i* ee	*J j* jay	*K k* kay	*L l* ayl
M m aym	*N n* ayn	*O o* oh	*P p* pee	*R r* ar	*S s* ays
T t tee	*U u* oo	*V v* vee	*W w* *dab*·al·yoo	*Y y* *wa*·ee	*Z z* *zayd*·ee

a–z phrasebuilder

tengeneza sentensi

contents

The index below shows the grammatical structures you can use to say what you want. Look under each function – listed in alphabetical order – for more information on how to build your own phrases. For example, to tell the taxi driver where your hotel is, look for **giving directions/orders** and you'll be directed to information on **location**, **prepositions** and **requests**. A glossary of grammatical terms is also included at the end of this chapter. The label 'survival Swahili' used after some forms in this chapter means that the form won't be fully correct, but will generally be understood. You can find detailed explanations and grammar exercises in the Learning Guide at www.kamusiproject.org.

adjectives & adverbs

describing things

Adjectives always come after the noun they describe.

good news	*habari nzuri* (lit: news good)	ha·*ba*·ree n·*zoo*·ree

Many adjectives in the **dictionary** have a hyphen in front. The hyphen indicates the space for a prefix, which varies depending on certain qualities of the thing being described. The rules are complicated and there are many exceptions, but the basic groups are listed here.

noun qualities	prefix	swahili example	english example
person or animal sg	*m-*	*mtoto* ***m****zuri* m·*toh*·toh m·*zoo*·ree *tembo* ***m****kubwa* *taym*·boh m·*koo*·bwa	**good child** **big elephant**
person or animal pl	*wa-*	*watoto* ***wa****zuri* wa·*toh*·toh wa·*zoo*·ree *tembo* ***wa****kubwa* *taym*·boh wa·*koo*·bwa	**good children** **big elephants**
object sg&pl (survival swahili)	*n-* or *j-* or no prefix	*habari* ***n****zuri* ha·*ba*·ree n·*zoo*·ree *pikipiki kubwa* pee·kee·*pee*·kee *koo*·bwa	**good news** **big motorcycle**

Many Swahili nouns can become adjectives by using the word 'of' before them. The word used for 'of' changes depending on the qualities of the thing being described, as shown in the table on the next page. The word 'of' is also used to express possession. (For more details on the forms for 'of' see also **possession**.)

noun qualities	'of'	swahili example	english example
person or animal sg&pl	wa	*tembo **wa** kijivu* *taym*·boh wa kee·*jee*·voo	gray elephant
		*mbu **wa** jioni* *m*·boo wa jee·*oh*·nee	evening mosquitos
object sg (survival swahili)	ya	*baisikeli **ya** kisasa* ba·ee·see·*kay*·lee ya kee·*sa*·sa	modern bike
object pl (survival swahili)	za	*boti **za** mbao* *boh*·tee za m·*ba*·oh	wooden boats

Adverbs also go after the verb they're modifying. Often, the word *kwa* appears before the adverb – in that case, *kwa* resembles the English suffix '-ly' (eg 'nicely').

I walked a lot.
Nilitembea sana. nee·lee·taym·*bay*·a *sa*·na
(lit: I-*past*-walk much)

She speaks in a hurry.
Anasema kwa haraka. a·na·*say*·ma kwa ha·*ra*·ka
(lit: she-*present*-talk with hurry)

articles

describing things • naming things/people

Swahili doesn't have articles (a/an, the). To refer to a specific object (ie 'the' thing), use a demonstrative pronoun ('this' book) or a possessive pronoun ('his' book) (see **demonstratives & possession**). To refer to 'a' thing (ie an unspecified thing in a generic sense), use the adjective *-moja* for 'one' (preferably with the appropriate prefix – see **adjectives & adverbs**):

a flower *ua moja* oo·a *moh*·ja
(lit: flower one)

'Some' is expressed with the phrase *baadhi ya*, which is used before the noun, or *kadhaa*, which comes after the noun.

some people	*baadhi ya watu* (lit: some people)	*ba*·dhee ya *wa*·too
	watu kadhaa (lit: people some)	*wa*·too ka·*dha*

be

doing things • making a statement • negating

In the present tense, the verb 'be' (*kuwa*) is incredibly easy. No matter what the subject, the word for 'am/is/are' is *ni*.

I am English.
Mimi ni Mwingereza. — *mee*·mee nee mween·gay·*ray*·za
(lit: I am English)

We are Africans.
Sisi ni Waafrika. — *see*·see nee wa·a·*free*·ka
(lit: we are Africans)

It's just as easy to form negative statements – the form of 'be' is *si* for all persons in singular and plural.

I am not a doctor.
Mimi si daktari. — *mee*·mee see dak·*ta*·ree
(lit: I am-not doctor)

We are not students.
Sisi si wanafunzi. — *see*·see see wa·na·*foon*·zee
(lit: we are-not students)

However, many things that you can 'be' in English are things you can 'have' in Swahili (see **have**).

In the past and future tenses the verb 'to be' has a different form for each person, as shown in the next table.

past tense			
I	was	*nilikuwa*	nee·lee·*koo*·wa
you sg	were	*ulikuwa*	oo·lee·*koo*·wa
he/she (person)*	was	*alikuwa*	a·lee·*koo*·wa
it (object) (survival swahili)		*ilikuwa*	ee·lee·*koo*·wa
we	were	*tulikuwa*	too·lee·*koo*·wa
you pl		*mlikuwa*	m·lee·*koo*·wa
they (person)*		*walikuwa*	wa·lee·*koo*·wa
they (object) (survival swahili)		*zilikuwa*	zee·lee·*koo*·wa
future tense			
I	will be	*nitakuwa*	nee·ta·*koo*·wa
you sg		*utakuwa*	oo·ta·*koo*·wa
he/she (person)*		*atakuwa*	a·ta·*koo*·wa
it (object) (survival swahili)		*itakuwa*	ee·ta·*koo*·wa
we		*tutakuwa*	too·ta·*koo*·wa
you pl		*mtakuwa*	m·ta·*koo*·wa
they (person)*		*watakuwa*	wa·ta·*koo*·wa
they (object) (survival swahili)		*zitakuwa*	zee·ta·*koo*·wa

* or animal(s)

demonstratives

naming things/people • pointing things out

When you want to point something out (eg 'this thing' or 'those things'), remember that in Swahili the demonstrative comes after the noun it refers to:

this child	*mtoto huyu* (lit: child this)	m·*toh*·toh *hoo*·yoo
those giraffes	*twiga wale* (lit: giraffes those)	*twee*·ga *wa*·lay

noun qualities	this/these	that/those
person or animal sg	*huyu hoo*·yoo	*yule yoo*·lay
person or animal pl	*hawa ha*·wa	*wale wa*·lay
object sg (survival swahili)	*hii* hee	*ile ee*·lay
object pl (survival swahili)	*hizi hee*·zee	*zile zee*·lay

have

doing things • making a statement • possessing

In Swahili, the verb 'have' (*kuwa na*) is very similar to the verb 'be' (*kuwa*) – essentially, it translates as 'to be with'. Many things that you 'are' in English are things that you 'have' in Swahili:

I am hungry.
Nina njaa. — *nee*·na n·*ja*
(lit: I-have hunger)

She is cold.
Ana baridi. — *a*·na ba·*ree*·dee
(lit: she-has cold)

In the present tense, the verb is irregular, but not difficult, as you can see in the tables that follow. In the past and future tenses, simply add the word *na* after the correct form of the verb 'be' in the table on page 20.

I	have	*nina*	*nee*·na
you sg		*una*	*oo*·na
he/she (person or animal)	has	*ana*	*a*·na
it (object) (survival swahili)		*ina*	*ee*·na
we	have	*tuna*	*too*·na
you pl		*mna*	m·*na*
they (person or animal)		*wana*	*wa*·na
they (object) (survival swahili)		*zina*	*zee*·na

I	don't have	*sina*	*see*·na
you sg		*huna*	*hoo*·na
he/she (person)*	doesn't have	*hana*	*ha*·na
it (object) (survival swahili)		*haina*	ha·*ee*·na
we	don't have	*hatuna*	ha·*too*·na
you pl		*hamna*	*ham*·na
they (person)*		*hawana*	ha·*wa*·na
they (object) (survival swahili)		*hazina*	ha·*zee*·na

* or animal(s)

location

giving directions/orders • indicating location

To say that something is 'here' or 'there' requires two parts – variations on the verb 'be' and a locative suffix (ie a verb ending that indicates location). Swahili divides location into three general areas – 'here', 'there', and 'inside', with these corresponding suffixes:

here	*-po*	·poh
there	*-ko*	·koh
inside	*-mo*	·moh

I will be at the market at noon.
*Nitakuwe***ko** nee·ta·koo·*way*·koh
sokoni saa sita. soh·*koh*·nee sa *see*·ta
(lit: I-*future*-be-there market-at hour six)

In addition, if something is at a specific place, the word for that place will often take the suffix *-ni*:

store *duka* *doo*·ka
at the store *duka***ni** doo·*ka*·nee

In the present tense, the locative suffixes are used with the subject prefixes in the table below, depending on the person or thing whose location is pointed out:

subject prefixes used when making statements			
I	*ni-*	we	*tu-*
you sg	*u-*	you pl	*m-*
he/she (person)*	*yu-*	they (people)*	*wa-*
it (object) (survival swahili)	*i-*	they (objects) (survival swahili)	*zi-*
subjects prefixes used for negating			
I	*si-*	we	*hatu-*
you sg	*hu-*	you pl	*ham-*
he/she (person)*	*hayu-*	they (people)*	*hawa-*
it (object) (survival swahili)	*hai-*	they (objects) (survival swahili)	*hazi-*

* or animal(s)

Is she at school?
*Yu**ko** shuleni?* — *yoo*·koh shoo·*lay*·nee
(lit: she-there school-at)

She is not here.
*Hayu**po**.* — ha·*yoo*·poh
(lit: she-not-here)

For past and future tenses, use the forms of the verb 'be' from page 20 and attach the suffix directly to the verb. Adding the locative suffix will always change the stress of the verb to the syllable immediately before the suffix. Swahili speakers often change the final *-wa* to *-we* before adding the locative suffix.

Was he at the hotel?
*Alikuwa**ko** gestini?* — a·lee·koo·*wa*·koh gay·*stee*·nee
(lit: he-*past*-be-there hotel-at)

We won't be here tomorrow.
*Hatutakuwe**po** kesho.* — ha·too·ta·koo·*way*·poh *kay*·shoh
(lit: not-we-*future*-be-here tomorrow)

negatives

Negative verbs are formed in a similar way to positive verbs (see **verbs**), but with different subject prefixes and different tense markers.

negative subject prefixes			
I	*si-*	we	*hatu-*
you sg	*hu-*	you pl	*ham-*
he/she (person)*	*ha-*	they (person)*	*hawa-*
it (object) (survival swahili)	*hai-*	they (object) (survival swahili)	*hazi-*

* or animal(s)

Negative tense markers for past and future tense are *-ku-* and *-ta-* respectively:

I didn't know.	*Si**ku**jua.* (lit: not-me-*past*-know)	see·koo·*joo*·a
It won't rain.	*Hai**ta**nyesha.* (lit: not-it-*future*-rain)	ha·ee·ta·*nyay*·sha

In the present tense, however, no tense marker is used, but there's a twist – if the verb ends in an *-a*, that final *-a* changes to an *-i*.

know	*-jua*	·*joo*·a
I don't know.	*Sijui.* (lit: not-me-know)	see·*joo*·ee

For negative forms of the verb **be**, see page 19.

nouns

describing things • naming things/people

Nouns in Swahili are divided into groups with similar qualities or characteristics called 'noun classes'. What noun class something belongs to determines many other things in a sentence – for example, the subject prefix or object infix of the verb, the prefix of any associated adjectives, and the demonstrative and possessive pronouns to use.

Although Swahili has 16 noun classes, you can get by with the basic sets of rules shown in all the tables of this chapter. The others cover concepts you can explore if you're inspired to study Swahili in greater depth. Most noun classes come in pairs for the singular and the plural (with a different prefix for the two forms). The prefixes for noun classes that will allow you to get by are given in pairs below:

noun classes

prefix sg	example	prefix pl	example
m- (person or animal)	***mke*** *m*·kay wife	*wa-* (person or animal)	***wake*** *wa*·kay wives
m-	***mto*** *m*·toh river	*mi-*	***mito*** *mee*·toh rivers
no prefix	***embe*** *aym*·bay mango	*ma-*	***maembe*** ma·*aym*·bay mangoes
ji-	***jicho*** *jee*·choh eye	*ma-*	***macho*** *ma*·choh eyes
ki-	***kiatu*** kee·*a*·too shoe	*vi-*	***viatu*** vee·*a*·too shoes
ch-	***choo*** choh toilet	*vy-*	***vyoo*** vyoh toilets
u-	***ukuta*** oo·*koo*·ta wall	no prefix	***kuta*** *koo*·ta walls

Many nouns are the same in the singular and the plural – the only way to tell whether a speaker is referring to one or several things is by looking at the associated grammatical elements within the sentence:

This bird flies.
Ndege huyu anaruka. n·*day*·gay *hoo*·yoo a·na·*roo*·ka
(lit: bird this it-*present*-fly)

These birds fly.
Ndege hawa wanaruka. n·*day*·gay *ha*·wa wa·na·*roo*·ka
(lit: bird these they-*present*-fly)

personal pronouns

doing things • making a statement

Personal pronouns in Swahili have just one form for both subject (eg 'I', 'they') and object ('me', 'them') in a sentence.

I/me	*mimi*	*mee*·mee
you sg	*wewe*	*way*·way
he/she/him/her/it	*yeye*	*yay*·yay
we/us	*sisi*	*see*·see
you pl	*ninyi/nyinyi*	*nee*·nyee/*nyee*·nyee
they/them	*wao*	*wa*·oh

Personal pronouns are often not necessary as subject of a sentence, as the form of Swahili verbs already indicates who that is. Using the personal pronoun in such a case often has the same effect as putting an exclamation point at the end of your sentence:

I want food.
Ninataka chakula. nee·na·*ta*·ka cha·*koo*·la
(lit: I-*present*-want food)

I want food!
Mimi ninataka chakula. *mee*·mee nee·na·*ta*·ka cha·*koo*·la
(lit: I I-*present*-want food)

You can sometimes, however, use the personal pronoun instead of a verb construction in answer to a direct question:

Who wants food?

Nani anataka chakula? — *na*·nee a·na·*ta*·ka cha·*koo*·la

(lit: who *third-person-sg-present*-want food)

I do.

Mimi. — *mee*·mee

(lit: me)

possession

naming things/people • possessing

To say that a thing belongs to someone or something, you can either use the word 'of' with the name of the possessor, or you can use a possessive pronoun. The possessive pronouns have a prefix and a suffix, which change according to different patterns. The suffix changes according to who or what is the possessor:

english equivalent	pronoun suffix	
my	*-angu*	·*an*·goo
your sg	*-ako*	·*a*·koh
his/her/its	*-ake*	·*a*·kay
our	*-etu*	·*ay*·too
your pl	*-enu*	·*ay*·noo
their	*-ao*	·*a*·oh

This is our camera.

Hii ni kemra ***yetu****.* — hee nee *kaym*·ra *yay*·too

(lit: this be camera our)

Both the possessive pronoun prefix and the word 'of' change according to the noun class qualities of the thing being possessed:

noun qualities	pronoun prefix	'of'	swahili example	english example
person or animal sg&pl	*w-*	*wa*	*mtoto wangu* m·*toh*·toh *wan*·goo	**my child**
object sg (survival swahili)	*y-*	*ya*	*pikipiki yako* pee·kee·*pee*·kee *ya*·koh	**your motorcycle**
object pl (survival swahili)	*z-*	*za*	*nyumba* ***zetu*** *nyoom*·ba *zay*·too	**our houses**

If you use the word 'of' instead of the pronoun, this word and the name of the possessor always go after the thing being possessed:

today's news *habari za leo* (lit: news of today) ha·*ba*·ree za *lay*·oh

prepositions

giving directions/orders • indicating location

Prepositions always come before the word they go with:

since yesterday *tangu jana* *tan*·goo *ja*·na

across from, opposite	*ng'ambo ya*	ng·*am*·boh ya
after	*baada ya*	ba·*a*·da ya
at	*kwenye*	*kway*·nyay
before	*kabla*	*ka*·bla
from	*kutoka*	koo·*toh*·ka
in	*katika*	ka·*tee*·ka
on	*juu ya*	joo ya
since	*tangu*	*tan*·goo
to	*hadi*	*ha*·dee

questions

asking a question

To ask a question in Swahili, use the word *je*. It essentially means 'hey, I'm asking a question' and can go either at the beginning or the end of a sentence:

What's your name?
Jina lako ni nani, je? — *jee*·na *la*·koh nee *na*·nee jay
(lit: name your be who *question*)

The word *je* has one other function – if you attach it directly to the verb in a sentence, it serves as the question word 'how?':

How do you say ...?
Unasemaje ...? — oo·na·say·*ma*·jay ...
(lit: you-*present*-say-how)

You can also turn most statements into questions simply by raising intonation at the end of a sentence.

For question words, see the **dictionary**. To answer a direct question, see **personal pronouns**.

requests

giving directions/orders

Basic requests are very easy. To tell one person to do something, simply use the verb stem (dictionary form of a verb). To tell more than one person to do something, add the suffix *-ni* to the verb stem (if the verb stem ends in an *-a*, it changes to an *-e*).

english	verb stem	request sg	request pl
run	*-kimbia* keem·*bee*·a	*kimbia* keem·*bee*·a	*kimbieni* keem·bee·*ay*·nee
return	*-rudi roo*·dee	*rudi roo*·dee	*rudini* roo·*dee*·nee
speak	*-sema say*·ma	*sema say*·ma	*semeni* say·*may*·nee

A few verbs have irregular request forms:

english	verb stem	request sg	request pl
come	*-ja* ·ja	*njoo* n·*joh*	*njooni* n·*joh*·nee
go	*-enda* ·*ayn*·da	*nenda* nayn·da	*nendeni* nayn·*day*·nee

there is/are

making a statement • negating • pointing things out

The word *kuna* corresponds to both 'there is' and 'there are'. The word *hakuna* is used for 'there isn't' and 'there aren't'.

There are two passengers.
Kuna abiria wawili. — *koo*·na a·bee·*ree*·a wa·*wee*·lee
(lit: there-are passengers two)

There isn't any toilet paper.
Hakuna karatasi ya choo. — ha·*koo*·na ka·ra·*ta*·see ya *choh*
(lit: there-are-not paper of toilet)

verbs

doing things

Most verbs in Swahili follow a very regular (although often quite complex) set of rules. The Swahili verb has slots for different elements. A basic verb consists of a subject prefix, a tense marker and a verb stem. The table below shows these and other slots (such as object infix and suffix) that can be filled within the structure of a verb:

verb slots				
subject prefix	tense marker	object infix	verb stem	suffix
a-	*-na-*	*-tu-*	*-pik(a)-*	*-ia*

He is cooking for us.
Anatupikia. a·na·too·peek·*ee*·a
(lit: he-now-us-cooks-for)

As you can see in the table below, the subject prefix changes depending on the noun class of the subject ('he'), while the object infix depends on the noun class of the object ('us').

noun qualities	subject prefix	negative subject prefix	object infix
I/me	*ni-*	*si-*	*-ni-*
you sg	*u-*	*hu-*	*-ku-*
he/she (person or animal – often begins with *m-*)	*a-*	*ha-*	*-m-/-mw-*
it (object) (survival swahili)	*i-*	*hai-*	*-i-*
we/us	*tu-*	*hatu-*	*-tu-*
you pl	*m-*	*ham-*	*-wa-*
they (person or animal – often begins with *wa-*)	*wa-*	*hawa-*	*-wa-*
they (object) (survival swahili)	*zi-*	*hazi-*	*-zi-*

As the example below shows, both the direct object ('the book') and the indirect object ('me') use the same set of infixes, although if you have both a direct and an indirect object in the sentence, only the indirect object will be marked in the object slot within the verb.

He gave the book to me.
Alinipa kitabu. a·lee·*nee*·pa kee·*ta*·boo
(lit: he-*past*-me-give book)

He gave it.
Alikipa. a·lee·*kee*·pa
(lit: he-*past*-it-give)

The following are the most common tense markers that you'll come across:

tense	tense marker	swahili example	english example
present	*-na-*	*ninasoma* nee·na·*soh*·ma	**I am reading**
past (completed action)	*-li-*	*nilisoma* nee·lee·*soh*·ma	**I read**
past (recent or ongoing action)	*-me-*	*nimesoma* nee·may·*soh*·ma	**I have read**
future	*-ta-*	*nitasoma* nee·ta·*soh*·ma	**I will read**

If you take one subject prefix, one tense marker, and one verb stem, you can make a basic verb:

He said ... *Alisema ...* (lit: he-*past*-say) a·lee·*say*·ma ...

If your sentence has an object, put the appropriate infix between the tense marker and the verb stem.

I will marry you. *Nitakuoa.* (lit: I-will-you-marry) nee·ta·koo·*oh*·a

For information on negative verbs, see **negatives**.

word order

making a statement

Swahili sentences are usually constructed in the order subject-verb-object, just like in English:

The elephants eat grass.
Tembo wanakula nyasi. *taym*·boh wa·na·*koo*·la *nya*·see
(lit: elephants eat grass)

For word order in questions and negative statements, see **questions** and **negatives**.

glossary

adjective	a word that describes something – 'a **long** journey'
adverb	a word that explains how an action was done – 'he walked **slowly**'
article	the words 'a/an' and 'the'
demonstrative pronoun	a word like 'this/these' or 'that/those' used to point something out
infix	syllable(s) inserted in the middle of a word, eg to show what the object in the sentence is
locative suffix	syllable(s) added to the end of a word to indicate location
noun	a thing, person or idea, eg 'table'
object	the thing or person in the sentence that has the action directed to it, eg in 'Please bring me the menu', 'the menu' is the direct object and 'me' is the indirect object
possesive pronoun	a word that conveys the meaning 'mine', 'yours', 'ours', 'theirs', etc
prefix	syllable(s) added to the beginning of a word, eg to show who the subject in the sentence is
preposition	a word like 'from' or 'after' in English
pronoun	a word that means 'you', 'she', etc

subject	the thing or person in the sentence that does the action – '**I** took the train'
suffix	syllable(s) added to the end of a word to modify its meaning, eg **-ly** is added to 'happy' to make 'happily'
tense marker	*infix* in a verb which shows the time an action takes place, ie past, present, future
verb	the word that tells you what action happened – eg 'I **saw** the book'
verb stem	the dictionary form of a verb, which doesn't change – 'search' in 'searched' and 'searching'

language difficulties

matatizo ya lugha

Do you speak (English)?
Unasema (Kiingereza)? oo·na·*say*·ma (kee·een·gay·*ray*·za)

Does anyone speak (English)?
Kuna mtu yeyote kusema (Kiingereza)? *koo*·na *m*·too yay·*yoh*·tay koo·*say*·ma (kee·een·gay·*ray*·za)

Do you understand?
Unaelewa? oo·na·ay·*lay*·wa

Yes, I understand.
Ndiyo, naelewa. n·*dee*·yoh na·ay·*lay*·wa

No, I don't understand.
Hapana, sielewi. ha·*pa*·na see·ay·*lay*·wee

I understand.
Naelewa. na·ay·*lay*·wa

I don't understand.
Sielewi. see·ay·*lay*·wee

speaking sheng

While travelling around Kenya, you might come across Sheng, a mixture of Swahili and English with a fair sprinkling of other local languages. It's spoken almost exclusively by young people. Unless you're reasonably fluent in Swahili, you probably won't even realise Sheng is being spoken, so listen out for *sassa sa*·sa (distinctive greeting between friends). The response can be either *besht* baysht, *mambo mam*·boh or *fit* feet (all variations of 'hello').

I speak (English).

Nasema (Kiingereza).	na·*say*·ma (kee·een·gay·*ray*·za)

I don't speak (Swahili).

Sisemi (Kiswahili).	see·*say*·mee (kee·swa·*hee*·lee)

I speak a little.

Nasema kidogo.	na·*say*·ma kee·*doh*·goh

What does *'asante'* mean?

Neno 'asante' lina maana gani?	*nay*·noh a·*san*·tay *lee*·na ma·*a*·na *ga*·nee

How do you ...?

pronounce this	*Unatamkaje?*	oo·na·tam·*ka*·jay
write *'asante'*	*Unaandikaje 'asante'?*	oo·na·an·dee·*ka*·je a·*san*·tay

Could you please ...?	*Tafadhali ...*	ta·fa·*dha*·lee ...
repeat that	*sema tena*	*say*·ma *tay*·na
speak more slowly	*sema pole pole*	*say*·ma *poh*·lay *poh*·lay
write it down	*andika*	an·*dee*·ka

knock knock!

The word for 'stranger' in Swahili, *mgeni* m·*gay*·nee, is also the word for 'guest', and many East Africans enjoy welcoming strangers as guests not only to their countries but to their homes too.

You'll always be greeted with *karibu* ka·*ree*·boo (welcome). It's an all-purpose word, used to welcome visitors to the home, the business or even the country. It also means 'you're welcome' (when someone thanks you).

When entering someone's home or office, you should always announce your presence and your intent to come in by calling out *hodi hoh*·dee (Hello, may I enter?) before crossing the threshold. It can be accompanied by knocking on the door. Even if you're being escorted in by the inhabitant, it's polite to pause at the door and say *hodi.*

numbers & amounts

namba na kiasi

cardinal numbers

namba kamili

0	*sifuri*	see·*foo*·ree
1	*moja*	*moh*·ja
2	*mbili*	m·*bee*·lee
3	*tatu*	*ta*·too
4	*nne*	*n*·nay
5	*tano*	*ta*·noh
6	*sita*	*see*·ta
7	*saba*	*sa*·ba
8	*nane*	*na*·nay
9	*tisa*	*tee*·sa
10	*kumi*	*koo*·mee
11	*kumi na moja*	*koo*·mee na *moh*·ja
12	*kumi na mbili*	*koo*·mee na m·*bee*·lee
13	*kumi na tatu*	*koo*·mee na *ta*·too
14	*kumi na nne*	*koo*·mee na *n*·nay
15	*kumi na tano*	*koo*·mee na *ta*·noh
16	*kumi na sita*	*koo*·mee na *see*·ta
17	*kumi na saba*	*koo*·mee na *sa*·ba
18	*kumi na nane*	*koo*·mee na *na*·nay
19	*kumi na tisa*	*koo*·mee na *tee*·sa
20	*ishirini*	ee·shee·*ree*·nee
21	*ishirini na moja*	ee·shee·*ree*·nee na *moh*·ja
30	*thelathini*	thay·la·*thee*·nee
40	*arobaini*	a·roh·ba·*ee*·nee
50	*hamsini*	ham·*see*·nee
60	*sitini*	see·*tee*·nee
70	*sabini*	sa·*bee*·nee
80	*themanini*	thay·ma·*nee*·nee
90	*tisini*	tee·*see*·nee
100	*mia moja*	*mee*·a *moh*·ja
1,000	*elfu*	*ayl*·foo
100,000	*laki*	*la*·kee

ordinal numbers

namba ya mpango

For persons and animals, use *wa* wa. For objects, use *ya* ya before the cardinal number – '1st' and '2nd' are irregular though:

1st	*wa/ya kwanza*	wa/ya *kwan*·za
2nd	*wa/ya pili*	wa/ya *pee*·lee
3rd	*wa/ya tatu*	wa/ya *ta*·too
4th	*wa/ya nne*	wa/ya *n*·nay
5th	*wa/ya tano*	wa/ya *ta*·noh

fractions

sehemu

a quarter	*robo moja*	*roh*·boh *moh*·ja
a third	*theluthi moja*	thay·*loo*·thee *moh*·ja
a half	*nusu*	*noo*·soo
three-quarters	*robo tatu*	*roh*·boh *ta*·too
all	*jumla*	*joom*·la
none	*hakuna*	ha·*koo*·na

useful amounts

kiasi zenye manufaa

How much?	*Kiasi gani?*	kee·*a*·see *ga*·nee
How many?	*Ngapi?*	n·*ga*·pee
(Please) give me …	*(Tafadhali) nipe …*	(ta·fa·*dha*·lee) *nee*·pay …
less	*chache zaidi*	*cha*·chay za·*ee*·dee
(just) a little	*kidogo (tu)*	kee·*doh*·goh (too)
a lot	*kingi*	*keen*·gee
more	*zaidi*	za·*ee*·dee
some	*kiasi*	kee·*a*·see

time & dates
saa na tarehe

telling the time

kusema saa

The word for time, *saa* sa, also means 'hour', 'watch' and 'clock'. Time and hours are distinguished by different noun classes, so *saa mbili* sa m·*bee*·lee (lit: clocks two) means '2 o'clock Swahili time/8 o'clock European time' while *masaa mawili* ma·*sa* ma·*wee*·lee (lit: hours two) means 'two hours'. (For more on noun classes, see the **phrasebuilder**.)

What time is it?	
Ni saa ngapi?	nee sa n·*ga*·pee
It's (ten) o'clock.	
Ni saa (nne).	nee sa (*n*·nay)
Five past (ten).	
Ni saa (nne) na tano.	nee sa (*n*·nay) na *ta*·noh
Quarter past (ten).	
Ni saa (nne) na robo.	nee sa (*n*·nay) na *roh*·boh
Half past (ten).	
Ni saa (nne) na nusu.	nee sa (*n*·nay) na *noo*·soo
Quarter to (ten).	
Ni saa (nne) kasarobo.	nee sa (*n*·nay) ka·sa·*roh*·boh
Twenty to (ten).	
Ni saa (nne) kasoro ishirini.	nee sa (*n*·nay) ka·*soh*·roh ee·she·*ree*·nee

what's the time?

The Swahili time system starts six hours later compared to the international one. It begins at sunrise which occurs at about 6am all year round. This system causes endless confusion for visitors to East Africa, especially as many people set their watches using the international system and then try to read them according to the Swahili system. Your best bet is to verify which system is being used – international time, *saa za kizungu* sa za kee·*zoon*·goo, or Swahili time, *saa za kiswahili* sa za kee·swa·*hee*·lee. Since people usually specify what period of the day they're talking about, you can determine which time system they're using from context.

International time	Swahili time	
midnight	6	*saa sita usiku*
1am	7	*saa saba usiku wa manane*
2	8	*saa nane usiku wa manane*
3	9	*saa tisa usiku wa manane*
4	10	*saa kumi alfajiri*
5	11	*saa kumi na moja alfajiri*
6am (sunrise)	12	*saa kumi na mbili asubuhi*
7	1	*saa moja asubuhi*
8	2	*saa mbili asubuhi*
9	3	*saa tatu asubuhi*
10	4	*saa nne asubuhi*
11	5	*saa tano asubuhi*
noon	6	*saa sita mchana*
1pm	7	*saa saba mchana*
2	8	*saa nane mchana*
3	9	*saa tisa mchana*
4	10	*saa kumi mchana*
5	11	*saa kumi na moja jioni*
6pm (sundown)	12	*saa kumi na mbili jioni*
7	1	*saa moja jioni*
8	2	*saa mbili usiku*
9	3	*saa tatu usiku*
10	4	*saa nne usiku*
11	5	*saa tano usiku*
midnight	6	*saa sita usiku*

morning	*asubuhi*	a·soo·*boo*·hee
afternoon	*mchana*	m·*cha*·na
evening	*jioni*	jee·*oh*·nee
At what time ...?	*... saa ngapi?*	... sa n·*ga*·pee
At (ten).	*Saa (nne).*	sa (*n*·nay)
At (7.57pm).	*Saa (mbili kasoro dakika tatu jioni).*	sa (m·*bee*·lee ka·*soh*·roh da·*kee*·ka *ta*·too jee·*oh*·ni)

the calendar

kalenda

days

Monday	*Jumatatu*	joo·ma·*ta*·too
Tuesday	*Jumanne*	joo·ma·*n*·nay
Wednesday	*Jumatano*	joo·ma·*ta*·noh
Thursday	*Alhamisi*	al·ha·*mee*·see
Friday	*Ijumaa*	ee·joo·*ma*
Saturday	*Jumamosi*	joo·ma·*moh*·see
Sunday	*Jumapili*	joo·ma·*pee*·lee

months

Swahili has two systems for counting months: one consisting of English soundalikes that foreigners like to use and the one that Swahili speakers commonly use. It's best, however, to use the second system, which simply counts months as ordinal numbers starting with January. At a pinch, though, many people will understand the English version.

January	*mwezi wa kwanza*	*mway*·zee wa *kwan*·za
February	*mwezi wa pili*	*mway*·zee wa *pee*·lee
March	*mwezi wa tatu*	*mway*·zee wa *ta*·too
April	*mwezi wa nne*	*mway*·zee wa *n*·nay
May	*mwezi wa tano*	*mway*·zee wa *ta*·noh
June	*mwezi wa sita*	*mway*·zee wa *see*·ta
July	*mwezi wa saba*	*mway*·zee wa *sa*·ba
August	*mwezi wa nane*	*mway*·zee wa *na*·nay
September	*mwezi wa tisa*	*mway*·zee wa *tee*·sa
October	*mwezi wa kumi*	*mway*·zee wa *koo*·mee
November	*mwezi wa kumi na moja*	*mway*·zee wa *koo*·mee na *moh*·ja
December	*mwezi wa kumi na mbili*	*mway*·zee wa *koo*·mee na m·*bee*·lee

dates

What date is it today?
Leo ni tarehe gani? — *lay*·oh nee ta·*ray*·hay *ga*·nee

It's (18 October).
Ni (tarehe kumi na nane, mwezi wa kumi). — nee (ta·*ray*·hay *koo*·mee na *na*·nay *mway*·zee wa *koo*·mee)

seasons

The seasons in East Africa don't correspond to those of other parts of the world. They vary greatly depending on altitude and latitude. *Kiangazi* kee·an·*ga*·zee (lit: dry-season), which roughly corresponds to June, July and August, can be cold in the southern highlands of Tanzania, pleasant on the coast and hot in the northern regions of Kenya. People may refer to the following seasons but have different times of year in mind:

… season	*kipindi …*	kee·*peen*·dee …
cold	*cha baridi*	cha ba·*ree*·dee
harvest	*cha kuvuna*	cha koo·*voo*·na
hot	*cha joto*	cha *joh*·toh
rainy	*cha mvua*	cha m·*voo*·a

present

sasa

now	*sasa*	*sa*·sa
today	*leo*	*lay*·oh
tonight	*leo usiku*	*lay*·oh oo·*see*·koo
this…		
morning	*asubuhi hii*	a·soo·*boo*·hee hee
afternoon	*mchana huu*	m·*cha*·na hoo
week	*wiki hii*	*wee*·kee hee
month	*mwezi huu*	*mway*·zee hoo
year	*mwaka huu*	*mwa*·ka hoo

past

iliyopita

day before yesterday	*juzi*	*joo*·zee
(three) days ago	*siku (tatu) zilizopita*	*see*·koo (*ta*·too) zee·lee·zo·*pee*·ta
(three) months ago	*miezi (mitatu) iliyopita*	mee·*ay*·zee (mee·*ta*·too) ee·lee·yoh·*pee*·ta
since (May)	*tangu (mwezi wa tano)*	*tan*·goo (*mway*·zee wa *ta*·noh)
last …		
night	*jana usiku*	*ja*·na oo·*see*·koo
week	*wiki jana*	*wee*·kee *ja*·na
month	*mwezi uliopita*	*mway*·zee oo·lee·oh·*pee*·ta
year	*mwaka uliopita*	*mwa*·ka oo·lee·oh·*pee*·ta
yesterday …	*jana …*	*ja*·na …
morning	*asubuhi*	a·soo·*boo*·hee
afternoon	*mchana*	m·*cha*·na
evening	*jioni*	jee·*oh*·nee

future

mbeleni

day after tomorrow	*kesho kutwa*	*kay*·shoh *koot*·wa
in (six days)	*baada ya (siku sita)*	ba·*a*·da ya (*see*·koo *see*·ta)
until (June)	*mpaka (mwezi wa sita)*	m·*pa*·ka (*mway*·zee wa *see*·ta)
next …	*… kesho*	… *kay*·shoh
week	*wiki*	*wee*·kee
month	*mwezi*	*mway*·zee
year	*mwaka*	*mwa*·ka
tomorrow …	*kesho …*	*kay*·shoh …
morning	*asubuhi*	a·soo·*boo*·hee
afternoon	*mchana*	m·*cha*·na
evening	*jioni*	jee·*oh*·nee

during the day

wakati wa siku

afternoon	*mchana*	m·*cha*·na
dawn	*alfajiri*	al·fa·*jee*·ree
day	*siku*	*see*·koo
evening	*jioni*	jee·*oh*·nee
midday	*saa sita mchana*	sa *see*·ta m·*cha*·na
midnight	*saa sita usiku*	sa *see*·ta oo·*see*·koo
morning	*asubuhi*	a·soo·*boo*·hee
night	*usiku*	oo·*see*·koo
sunrise	*macheo*	ma·*chay*·oh
sunset	*magharibi*	mag·ha·*ree*·bee

How much is it?
Ni bei gani? — ni bay *ga*·nee

It's free.
Ni bure. — nee *boo*·ray

It's (500) shillings.
Ni shilingi (mia tano). — nee shee·*leen*·gee (*mee*·a *ta*·noh)

Can you write down the price?
Andika bei. — an·*dee*·ka bay

There's a mistake in the bill.
Kuna kosa kwenye bili. — *koo*·na *koh*·sa *kwayn*·yay *bee*·le

Do you accept ...?	*Mnakubali ...*	m·na·koo·*ba*·lee ...
credit cards	*kadi ya benki*	*ka*·dee ya *bayn*·kee
travellers cheques	*hundi ya msafiri*	*hoon*·dee ya m·sa·*fee*·ree

I'd like to ...	*Nataka ...*	na·*ta*·ka ...
cash a cheque	*kulipwa fedha kutokana na hundi*	koo·*leep*·wa *fay*·dha koo·toh·*ka*·na na *hoon*·dee
change a travellers cheque	*kubadilisha hundi ya msafiri*	koo·ba·dee·*lee*·sha *hoon*·dee ya m·sa·*fee*·ree
change money	*kubadilisha hela*	koo·ba·dee·*lee*·sha *hay*·la
get a cash advance	*kupata hela ya awali*	koo·*pa*·ta *hay*·la ya *a*·wa·lee
withdraw money	*kuondoa hela*	koo·ohn·*doh*·a *hay*·la

Where's …?	*… iko wapi?*	… *ee*·koh *wa*·pee
an automated teller machine	*mashine ya kutolea pesa*	ma·*shee*·nay ya koo·toh·*lay*·a *pay*·sa
a foreign exchange office	*foreks*	*foh*·rayks

What's the …?	*… ni nini?*	… nee *nee*·nee
charge	*gharama yake*	ga·*ra*·ma *ya*·kay
exchange rate	*kiwango cha kubadilisha hela*	kee·*wan*·goh cha koo·ba·dee·*lee*·sha *hay*·la

I'd like …, please.	*Nataka …, tafadhali.*	na·*ta*·ka … ta·fa·*dha*·lee
a refund	*unirudishie hela*	oo·nee·roo·dee·*shee*·ay *hay*·la
a receipt	*risiti*	ree·*see*·tee
my change	*chenji yangu*	*chayn*·jee *yan*·goo
to return this	*kurudisha kitu hiki*	koo·roo·*dee*·sha *kee*·too *hee*·kee

coast, island or town?

The Swahili name for Zanzibar Island is Unguja. It's often used locally to distinguish the island from the Zanzibar Archipelago (which also includes Pemba), as well as from Zanzibar Town (called Mji Mkongwe or Stone Town).

The word 'Zanzibar' comes from the Arabic Zinj el-Barr (lit: Land of the Blacks). It was used by Arab traders from the 8th century to refer to both the archipelago and the adjacent coast. Now, the name refers exclusively to the archipelago.

getting around

kutembea

Which … goes to (Mbeya)?	*… ipi huenda (Mbeya)?*	… *ee*·pee hoo·*ayn*·da (m·*bay*·a)
Is this the … to (Mombasa)?	*Hii ni … kwenda (Mombasa)?*	hee nee … *kwayn*·da (mohm·*ba*·sa)
boat	*Boti*	*boh*·tee
bus	*Basi*	*ba*·see
ferry	*Kivuko*	kee·*voo*·koh
minibus	*Daladala/ Matatu* **Tan/Ken**	da·la·*da*·la/ ma·*ta*·too
train	*Treni*	*tray*·nee

When's the … bus?	*Basi … itaondoka lini?*	*ba*·see … ee·ta·ohn·*doh*·ka *lee*·nee
first	*ya kwanza*	ya *kwan*·za
last	*ya mwisho*	ya *mwee*·shoh
next	*ijayo*	ee·*ja*·yoh

Is the … going today/tomorrow?
… itaenda leo/kesho? … ee·ta·*ayn*·da *lay*·oh/*kay*·shoh

What time does it leave?
Itaondoka saa ngapi? ee·ta·ohn·*doh*·ka sa n·*ga*·pee

What time does it get to (Kisuma)?
Itafika (Kisumu) saa ngapi? ee·ta·*fee*·ka (kee·*soo*·moo) sa n·*ga*·pee

How long will it be delayed?

Itachelewa kwa muda gani?	ee·ta·chay·*lay*·wa kwa *moo*·da *ga*·nee

Is this seat free?

Kuna nafasi hapa?	*koo*·na na·*fa*·see *ha*·pa

That's my seat.

Hiki ni kiti changu.	*hee*·kee nee *kee*·tee *chan*·goo

Please tell me when we get to (Moshi).

Niambie tukifika (Moshi).	nee·am·*bee*·ay too·kee·*fee*·ka (*moh*·shee)

Please stop here.

Simama hapa, tafadhali.	see·*ma*·ma *ha*·pa ta·fa·*dha*·lee

How long do we stop here?

Tutakaa hapa kwa muda gani?	too·ta·*ka* *ha*·pa kwa *moo*·da *ga*·nee

I'm sorry, I've changed my mind.

Samahani, nimebadili nia.	sa·ma·*ha*·nee nee·may·ba·*dee*·lee *nee*·a

hop on, hop off

The most common word people call out to get a bus to stop is *shusha shoo*·sha (drop off). It's also considered slang. Pay attention to the way East Africans deliver the line. If you casually call *shusha* the same way when you want to get off, you can sometimes bring an entire bus to laughter.

On the other hand, if you're standing by the side of the road and you want to get a local bus to stop, simply extend your arm fully and flap your hand like a whale's tail.

tickets

tiketi

A … ticket to (Iringa).	*Tiketi moja ya … kwenda (Iringa).*	tee·*kay*·tee *moh*·ja ya … *kwayn*·da (ee·*reen*·ga)
1st-class	*daraja la kwanza*	da·*ra*·ja la *kwan*·za
2nd-class	*daraja la pili*	da·*ra*·ja la *pee*·lee
child's	*mtoto*	m·*toh*·toh
one-way	*kwenda tu*	*kwayn*·da too
return	*kwenda na kurudi*	*kwayn*·da na koo·*roo*·dee
student	*mwanafunzi*	mwa·na·*foon*·zee
I'd like a/an … seat.	*Nataka kiti …*	na·*ta*·ka *kee*·tee …
aisle	*jirani ya njia*	jee·*ra*·nee ya n·*jee*·a
nonsmoking	*kutovuta sigara*	koo·toh·*voo*·ta see·*ga*·ra
smoking	*kuvuta sigara*	koo·*voo*·ta see·*ga*·ra
window	*jirani ya dirisha*	jee·*ra*·nee ya dee·*ree*·sha
Is there (a) …?	*Kuna …?*	*koo*·na …
air conditioning	*a/c*	*ay*·see
blanket	*blanketi*	blan·*kay*·tee
sick bag	*mfuko wa kutapikia*	m·*foo*·koh wa koo·ta·pee·*kee*·a
toilet	*choo*	choh

Where do I buy a ticket?
Ninunue tiketi wapi? — nee·noo·*noo*·ay tee·*kay*·tee *wa*·pee

Do I need to book?
Ni lazima nifanye buking? — nee *la*·zee·ma nee·*fa*·nyay *boo*·keeng

How much is it?
Ni bei gani? — nee bay *ga*·nee

How long does the trip take?

Safari huchukua muda gani?	sa·*fa*·ree hoo·choo·*koo*·a *moo*·da *ga*·nee

Is it a direct route?

Njia ni moja kwa moja?	n·*jee*·a nee *moh*·ja kwa *moh*·ja

Can I get a stand-by ticket?

Naweza kununua tiketi kutumia kama nafasi ikipatikana?	na·*way*·za koo·noo·*noo*·a tee·*kay*·tee koo·too·*mee*·a *ka*·ma na·*fa*·si ee·kee·pa·tee·*ka*·na

Can I get a sleeping berth?

Naweza kupata kitanda?	na·*way*·za koo·*pa*·ta kee·*tan*·da

What time should I check in?

Ripoting ni saa ngapi?	ree·*pot*·eeng nee sa n·*ga*·pee

I'd like to … my ticket, please.	*Nataka … tiketi yangu tafadhali.*	na·*ta*·ka … tee·*kay*·tee *yan*·goo ta·fa·*dha*·lee
cancel	*kufuta*	koo·*foo*·ta
change	*kubadilisha*	koo·ba·dee·*lee*·sha
confirm	*kuhakikisha*	koo·ha·kee·*kee*·sha

listen for …

dirisha la tiketi	dee·*ree*·sha la tee·*kay*·tee	**ticket window**
hii	hee	**this one**
hiyo	*hee*·yoh	**that one**
imeche leweshwa	ee·may·chay lay·*waysh*·wa	**delayed**
imefutwa	ee·may·*foot*·wa	**cancelled**
imejaa	ee·may·*ja*	**full**
mgomo	m·*goh*·moh	**strike**
ratiba	ra·*tee*·ba	**timetable**
stendi	*stayn*·dee	**platform**
uwakala wa safiri	oo·*wa*·ka·la wa sa·*fee*·ree	**travel agent**

luggage

mizigo

Where can I find …?	… *iko wapi?*	… *ee*·koh *wa*·pee
the baggage claim	*Sehemu ya kuchukulia mizigo*	say·*hay*·moo ya koo·choo·koo·*lee*·a mee·*zee*·goh
the left-luggage office	*Chumba cha kuwekea mizigo*	*choom*·ba cha koo·way·*kay*·a mee·*zee*·goh
a luggage locker	*Sanduku la kuhifadhia mizigo*	san·*doo*·koo la koo·hee·fa·*dhee*·a mee·*zee*·goh
a trolley	*Kigari*	kee·*ga*·ree

My luggage has been …	*Mizigo yangu …*	mee·*zee*·goh *yan*·goo …
damaged	*imeharibiwa*	ee·may·ha·ree·*bee*·wa
lost	*imepotea*	ee·may·poh·*tay*·a
stolen	*imeibwa*	ee·may·*eeb*·wa

That's mine.
Ni yangu. — nee *yan*·goo

That's not mine.
Si yangu. — see *yan*·goo

Can I put my bag here?
Naweza kuweka mzigo wangu hapa? — na·*way*·za koo·*way*·ka m·*zee*·goh *wan*·goo *ha*·pa

Can I have some coins?
Nataka sarafu. — na·*ta*·ka sa·*ra*·foo

plane

ndege

Where does flight (number 432) arrive/depart?
Ndege (namba mia nne thelathini na mbili) itafika/ itaondoka wapi? — n·*day*·gay (*nam*·ba *mee*·a *n*·nay thay·la·*thee*·nee na m·*bee*·lee) ee·ta·*fee*·ka/ ee·ta·ohn·*doh*·ka *wa*·pee

I'd like to charter a plane to …
Nataka kukodisha ndege kwenda … — na·*ta*·ka koo·koh·*dee*·sha n·*day*·gay *kwayn*·da …

Where's (the) …?	*… iko wapi?*	… *ee*·koh *wa*·pee
airport shuttle	*Basi ya uwanja wa ndege*	*ba*·see ya oo·*wan*·ja wa n·*day*·gay
arrivals hall	*Wanaofika*	wa·na·oh·*fee*·ka
departures hall	*Wanaoondoka*	wa·na·oh·ohn·*doh*·ka
duty-free shop	*Duty-free*	doo·tee·*free*
gate (3)	*Mlango (tatu)*	m·*lan*·goh (*ta*·too)

listen for...

mizigo inayozidi	mee·*zee*·goh ee·na·yoh·*zee*·dee	**excess baggage**
mizigo ya kubebea	mee·*zee*·goh ya koo·bay·*bay*·a	**carry-on baggage**
pasipoti	pa·see·*poh*·tee	**passport**
pasi ya kuingilia	*pa*·see ya koo·een·gee·*lee*·a	**boarding pass**
wanaohamisha	wa·na·oh·ha·*mee*·sha	**transfer passengers**
wanaopita	wa·na·oh·*pee*·ta	**transit passengers**

bus & coach

mabasi

Can you recommend a reliable/safe bus company?
Kampuni gani ina mabasi yenye uaminifu/usalama? kam·*poo*·nee *ga*·nee *ee*·na ma·*ba*·see *yay*·nyay oo·a·mee·*nee*·foo/oo·sa·*la*·ma

How often do buses come?
Mabasi hufika muda gani? ma·*ba*·see hoo·*fee*·ka *moo*·da *ga*·nee

What time is this bus leaving?
Basi hili litaondoka saa ngapi? *ba*·see *hee*·lee lee·ta·ohn·*doh*·ka sa n·*ga*·pee

Does it stop at (Tanga)?
Linasimama (Tanga)? lee·na·see·*ma*·ma (*tan*·ga)

What's the next stop?
Kipi ni kituo kijacho? *kee*·pee nee kee·*too*·oh kee·*ja*·choh

I'd like to get off at (Bagamoyo).
Nataka kushusha (Bagamoyo). — na·*ta*·ka koo·*shoo*·sha (ba·ga·*moh*·yoh)

Drop me off here!
Nishushe hapa! — nee·*shoo*·shay *ha*·pa

city bus	*daladala/ matatu* Tan/Ken	da·la·*da*·la/ ma·*ta*·too
express bus	*basi ya moja kwa moja*	*ba*·see ya *moh*·ja kwa *moh*·ja
intercity	*baini ya miji*	ba·*ee*·nee ya *mee*·jee
local bus	*basi linalosimama katika kila kituo*	*ba*·see lee·na·loh·see·*ma*·ma ka·*tee*·ka *kee*·la kee·*too*·oh

train

treni

What station is this?
Hiki ni stesheni gani? — *hee*·kee nee stay·*shay*·nee *ga*·nee

What's the next station?
Stesheni ijayo itakuwa mji gani? — stay·*shay*·nee ee·*ja*·yoh ee·ta·*koo*·wa *m*·jee *ga*·nee

Does it stop at (Dodoma)?
Itasimama (Dodoma)? — ee·ta·see·*ma*·ma (doh·*doh*·ma)

Do I need to change?
Itabidi nibadilishe? — ee·ta·*bee*·dee nee·ba·dee·*lee*·shay

Is it ...?	*Ni ...?*	nee ...
direct	*treni hii kwa safari nzima*	*tray*·nee hee kwa sa·*fa*·ree n·*zee*·ma
express	*moja kwa moja kwa haraka*	*moh*·ja kwa *moh*·ja kwa ha·*ra*·ka

Which carriage is (for) ...?	*Behewa gani ni (kwa) ...?*	bay·*hay*·wa *ga*·nee nee (kwa) ...
1st class	*daraja la kwanza*	da·*ra*·ja la *kwan*·za
dining	*kula*	*koo*·la
Tabora	*Tabora*	ta·*boh*·ra

express train	*treni ya moja kwa moja kwa haraka*	*tray*·nee ya *moh*·ja kwa *moh*·ja kwa ha·*ra*·ka
ordinary train	*treni ya kawaida*	*tray*·nee ya ka·wa·*ee*·da

boat

boti

What's the sea like today?
Bahari ikoje leo? ba·*ha*·ree ee·*koh*·jay *lay*·oh

Are there life jackets?
Kuna jaketi la kuokolea? *koo*·na ja·*kay*·tee la koo·oh·koh·*lay*·a

Which island is this?
Hiki ni kisiwa gani? *hee*·kee nee kee·*see*·wa *ga*·nee

Which beach is this?
Huu ni ufukwe gani? hoo nee oo·*fook*·way *ga*·nee

I feel seasick.
Nahitaji kutapika. na·hee·*ta*·jee koo·ta·*pee*·ka

boat	*boti*	*boh*·tee
cabin	*kibini*	kee·*bee*·nee
car deck	*sitaha ya magari*	see·*ta*·ha ya ma·*ga*·ree
deck	*sitaha*	see·*ta*·ha
ferry n	*kivuko*	kee·*voo*·koh
lifeboat	*mashua ya kuokolea*	ma·*shoo*·a ya koo·oh·koh·*lay*·a
life jacket	*jaketi la kuokolea*	ja·*kay*·tee la koo·oh·koh·*lay*·a
row boat	*mtumbwi*	m·*toom*·bwee
ship n	*meli*	*may*·lee
small wooden boat	*mashua*	ma·*shoo*·a
traditional sailing boat	*dhau*	*dha*·oo
yacht	*mashua ya anasa*	ma·*shoo*·a ya a·*na*·sa

taxi

teksi

The majority of taxis in East Africa have no signs. As taxis can be scarce, it's not unusual to share a taxi with strangers, and each person usually agrees on a price individually. Another option is to hire a *bodaboda/teksi ya baisikeli* **Ken/Tan** boh·da·*boh*·da/ *tayk*·see ya ba·ee·see·*kay*·lee – a short-haul bicycle taxi.

I'd like a taxi …	*Nataka teksi …*	na·*ta*·ka *tayk*·see …
at (9am)	*saa (tatu asubuhi)*	sa (*ta*·too a·soo·*boo*·hee)
now	*sasa*	*sa*·sa
tomorrow	*kesho*	*kay*·shoh
for the whole day	*kwa siku nzima*	kwa *see*·koo n·*zee*·ma
for (three) hours	*kwa masaa (matatu)*	kwa ma·*sa* (ma·*ta*·too)
to run various errands	*kufanya shughuli mbalimbali*	koo·*fa*·nya shoo·*goo*·lee m·*ba*·lee·m·*ba*·lee
to the airport	*kwenda kwenye uwanja wa ndege*	*kwayn*·da *kway*·nyay oo·*wan*·ja wa n·*day*·gay
to the harbor	*kwenda bandarini*	*kwayn*·da ban·da·*ree*·nee

Where's the taxi rank?	
Stendi ya teksi iko wapi?	*stayn*·dee ya *tayk*·see ee·koh *wa*·pee
Is this taxi free?	
Teksi hii inapatikana?	*tayk*·see hee ee·na·pa·tee·*ka*·na

PRACTICAL

Please take me to (this address).
Tafadhali niendeshe mpaka (anwani hii). — ta·fa·*dha*·lee nee·ayn·*day*·shay m·*pa*·ka (an·*wa*·nee hee)

Please put the meter on.
Tumia mita ya kupima nauli. — too·*mee*·a *mee*·ta ya koo·*pee*·ma na·*oo*·lee

How much should I expect to pay to ...?
Nitarajie kulipa shilingi ngapi kwenda ...? — nee·ta·ra·*jee*·ay koo·*lee*·pa shee·*leen*·gee n·*ga*·pee *kwayn*·da ...

How much is it to ...?
Ni bei gani kwenda ...? — nee bay *ga*·nee *kwayn*·da ...

How much is it?
Ni shilingi ngapi? — nee shee·*leen*·gee n·*ga*·pee

That's too expensive!
Ni ghali mno! — nee *ga*·lee *m*·noh

Please lower the price.
Punguza bei, tafadhali. — poon·*goo*·za bay ta·fa·*dha*·lee

Would you like to share a taxi to ...?
Ungependa kugawa teksi kwenda ...? — oon·gay·*payn*·da koo·*ga*·wa *tayk*·see *kwayn*·da ...

Can we share a taxi?
Tugawe teksi? — too·*ga*·way *tayk*·see

Please ...	*Tafadhali ...*	ta·fa·*dha*·lee ...
slow down	*endesha polepole*	ayn·*day*·sha poh·lay·*poh*·lay
stop here	*simama hapa*	see·*ma*·ma *ha*·pa
wait here	*subiri hapa*	soo·*bee*·ree *ha*·pa

car & motorbike

gari na pikipiki

car & motorbike hire

Are you willing to hire out …?	*Unaweza kunikodisha …?*	oo·na·*way*·za koo·nee·koh·*dee*·sha …
your car	*gari lako*	*ga*·ree *la*·koh
your motorbike	*pikipiki yako*	pee·kee·*pee*·kee *ya*·koh
I'd like to hire a/an …	*Nataka kukodi …*	na·*ta*·ka koo·*koh*·dee …
4WD	*forbaifor*	*fohr*·ba·ee·fohr
automatic	*otomatiki*	oh·toh·*ma*·tee·kee
car	*gari*	*ga*·ree
manual	*kwa mkono*	kwa m·*koh*·noh
motorbike	*pikipiki*	pee·kee·*pee*·kee
With …	*Kwenye …*	*kway*·nyay …
air conditioning	*a/c*	ay·*see*
a driver	*dereva*	day·*ray*·va
How much for … hire?	*Ni bei gani kukodi kwa …?*	nee bay *ga*·nee koo·*koh*·dee kwa …
daily	*siku*	*see*·koo
hourly	*saa*	sa
weekly	*wiki*	*wee*·kee

Does that include insurance/mileage?
Bei inazingitia bima/umbali? — bay ee·na·zeen·gee·*tee*·a *bee*·ma/oo·m·*ba*·lee

Do you have a guide to the road rules in English?
Mna mwongozo wa sheria za barabara kwa Kiingereza? — m·na mwohn·*goh*·zoh wa shay·*ree*·a za ba·ra·*ba*·ra kwa kee·een·gay·*ray*·za

Do you have a road map?
Mna ramani? — m·na ra·*ma*·nee

on the road

What's the speed limit?
Mwendo gani unaruhusiwa? — *mwayn*·doh *ga*·nee oo·na·roo·hoo·*see*·wa

Is this the road to (Embu)?
Hii ni barabara kwenda (Embu)? — hee nee ba·ra·*ba*·ra *kwayn*·da (*aym*·boo)

Where's a petrol station?
Kituo cha mafuta kiko wapi? — kee·*too*·oh cha ma·*foo*·ta *kee*·ko *wa*·pee

Please fill it up.
Jaza tangi/tanki. — *ja*·za *tan*·gee/*tan*·kee

I'd like … litres.
Nataka lita … — na·*ta*·ka *lee*·ta …

diesel	*dizeli*	dee·*zay*·lee
leaded	*na risasi*	na ree·*sa*·see
regular	*kawaida*	ka·wa·*ee*·da
premium unleaded	*super*	*soo*·payr
unleaded	*isiyo na risasi*	ee·*see*·yoh na ree·*sa*·see

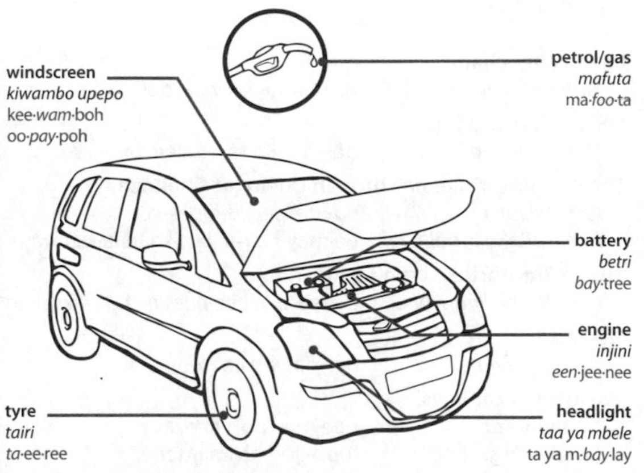

transport

Can you check the ...?	*Angalia ...?*	an·ga·*lee*·a ...
oil	*mafuta*	ma·*foo*·ta
tyre pressure	*upepo*	oo·*pay*·poh
water	*maji*	*ma*·jee

(How long) Can I park here?
Naweza kuegesha hapa (kwa muda gani)? — na·*way*·za koo·ay·*gay*·sha ha·pa (kwa *moo*·da *ga*·ni)

Do I have to pay?
Ni lazima nilipe? — nee *la*·zee·ma nee·*lee*·pay

listen for ...

bure	*boo*·ray	**free**
kilomita	kee·loh·*mee*·ta	**kilometres**
laiseni	la·ee·*say*·nee	**drivers licence**

problems

I need a mechanic.
Nahitaji fundi. — na·hee·*ta*·jee *foon*·dee

I've had an accident.
Nimepata ajali. — nee·me·*pa*·ta a·*ja*·lee

The car/motorbike has broken down (at Chalinze).
Gari/Pikipiki imeharibika (Chalinze). — *ga*·ree/pee·kee·*pee*·kee ee·may·ha·ree·*bee*·ka (cha·*leen*·zay)

The car/motorbike won't start.
Gari/Pikipiki haiwaki. — *ga*·ree/pee·kee·*pee*·kee ha·ee·*wa*·kee

I have a flat tyre.
Nina pancha. — *nee*·na *pan*·cha

I've lost my car keys.
Nimepoteza funguo za gari. — nee·may·poh·*tay*·za foon·*goo*·oh za *ga*·ree

I've locked the keys inside.
Nimefunga funguo ndani. — nee·may·*foon*·ga foon·*goo*·oh n·*da*·ni

I've run out of petrol.
Mafuta yamekwisha. — ma·*foo*·ta ya·may·*kwee*·sha

Can you fix it (today)?
Utaweza kuitengeneza (leo)? — oo·ta·*way*·za koo·ee·tayn·gay·*nay*·za (*lay*·oh)

How long will it take?
Itachukua muda gani? — ee·ta·choo·*koo*·a *moo*·da *ga*·nee

bicycle

baisikeli

I'd like …	*Nataka …*	na·*ta*·ka …
my bicycle repaired	*kutengeneza baisikeli yangu*	koo·tayn·gay·*nay*·za ba·ee·see·*kay*·lee *yan*·goo
to buy a bicycle	*kununua baisikeli*	koo·noo·*noo*·a ba·ee·see·*kay*·lee
to hire a bicycle	*kukodisha baisikeli*	koo·koh·*dee*·sha ba·ee·see·*kay*·lee

I'd like a … bike.	*Nataka baisikeli …*	na·*ta*·ka ba·ee·see·*kay*·lee …
mountain	*yenye gia kupanda milima*	*yay*·nyay *gee*·a koo·*pan*·da mee·*lee*·ma
racing	*yenye gia kukimbia mbio*	*yay*·nyay *gee*·a koo·keem·*bee*·a m·*bee*·oh
second-hand	*isiyo mpya*	ee·*see*·yoh *m*·pya

How much is it per …?	*Ni bei gani kwa …?*	nee bay *ga*·nee kwa …
day	*siku*	*see*·kuu
hour	*saa*	sa

Do I need a helmet?

Ni lazima nivai helmeti?	nee *la*·zee·ma nee·*va*·ee hayl·*may*·tee

Is there a bicycle-path map?

Kuna ramani ya njia za baisikeli?	*koo*·na ra·*ma*·nee ya n·*jee*·a za ba·ee·see·*kay*·lee

I have a puncture.

Nina pancha.	*nee*·na *pan*·cha

local transport

usafiri wa mtaani

Can I pay for a ride in your truck?

Naweza kulipa kwa lifti katika lori lako?	na·*way*·za koo·*lee*·pa kwa *leef*·tee ka·*tee*·ka *loh*·ree *la*·koh

How much to …?

Ni bei gani kwenda …?	nee bay *ga*·nee *kwayn*·da …

Are you waiting for more people?

Unangojea watu wengine?	oo·na·n·goh·*jay*·a *wa*·too wayn·*gee*·nay

How many people can ride on this?

Watu wangapi wanaweza kusafirishwa kwa hili?	*wa*·too wan·*ga*·pee wa·na·*way*·za koo·sa·fee·*ree*·shwa kwa *hee*·lee

Could I ride in the front?

Naomba kukaa mbele.	na·*ohm*·ba koo·*ka* m·*bay*·lay

I don't want to ride on top.

Sitaki kukaa juu.	see·*ta*·kee koo·*ka* joo

Could I contribute to the petrol cost?

Naweza kuchangia sehemu ya bei ya mafuta?	na·*way*·za koo·chan·*gee*·a say·*hay*·moo ya bay ya ma·*foo*·ta

Thanks for the ride.

Asante kwa lifti.	a·*san*·tay kwa *leef*·tee

border crossing

kuvuka mpaka

I'm …	*Mimi ni …*	*mee*·mee nee …
in transit	*safarini*	sa·fa·*ree*·nee
on business	*kwa biashara*	kwa bee·a·*sha*·ra
on holiday	*kwa likizo*	kwa lee·*kee*·zoh
I'm here for …	*Nipo kwa …*	*nee*·poh kwa …
(three) days	*siku (tatu)*	*see*·koo (*ta*·too)
(four) months	*miezi (minne)*	mee·*ay*·zee (mee·*n*·nay)
(two) weeks	*wiki (mbili)*	*wee*·kee (m·*bee*·lee)
Do I require a/an …?	*Ni lazima niwe na …?*	nee *la*·zee·ma *nee*·way na …
I have a/an …	*Nina …*	*nee*·na …
entry permit	*hati ya kuingia*	*ha*·tee ya koo·een·*gee*·a
customs form	*fomu ya forodha*	*foh*·moo ya foh·*roh*·dha
health certificate	*cheti cha afya*	*chay*·tee cha *af*·ya
pass/permit	*cheti*	*chay*·tee
police report	*ripoti ya polisi*	ree·*poh*·tee ya poh·*lee*·see

listen for …

familia	fa·mee·*lee*·a	**family**
kundi	*koon*·dee	**group**
pasipoti	pa·see·*poh*·tee	**passport**
peke yake	*pay*·kay *ya*·kay	**alone**
visa	*vee*·sa	**visa**

I'm going to (Malindi).
Naenda (Malindi). na·*ayn*·da (ma·*leen*·dee)

I'm staying at (the Pendo Inn).
Nakaa (Pendo Inn). na·*ka* (*payn*·doh een)

The children are on this passport.
Watoto wanasafiri kwenye pasipoti. wa·*toh*·toh wa·na·sa·*fee*·ree *kway*·nyay pa·see·*poh*·tee hee

at customs

forodhani

I have nothing to declare.
Sina ya kutaja. *see*·na ya koo·*ta*·ja

I have something to declare.
Ninacho kitu cha kutaja. nee·*na*·cho *kee*·too cha koo·*ta*·ja

Do I have to declare this?
Ni lazima nitaje hiki? nee *la*·zee·ma nee·*ta*·jay *hee*·kee

That's (not) mine.
Hiki ni (si) changu. *hee*·kee nee (see) *chan*·goo

I didn't know I had to declare it.
Sikujua ilibidi kuitaja. see·koo·*joo*·a ee·lee·*bee*·dee koo·ee·*ta*·ja

I didn't know I couldn't take this out of the country.
Sikujua kwamba hairuhusiwi kuchukua kitu hiki nje ya nchi. see·koo·*joo*·a *kwam*·ba ha·ee·roo·hoo·*see*·wee koo·choo·*koo*·a *kee*·too *hee*·kee *n*·jay ya *n*·chee

signs

Duty-Free	doo·tee·*free*	**Duty-free**
Forodha	foh·*roh*·dha	**Customs**
Karantini	ka·ran·*tee*·nee	**Quarantine**
Udhibiti wa Pasipoti	oo·dhee·*bee*·tee wa pa·see·*poh*·tee	**Passport Control**
Uhamiaji	oo·ha·mee·*a*·jee	**Immigration**

Where's (the market)?
(Soko) iko wapi? — (*soh*·koh) *ee*·koh *wa*·pee

What's the address?
Anwani ni nini? — an·*wa*·nee nee *nee*·nee

How do I get there?
Nifikaje? — nee·fee·*ka*·jay

How far is it?
Ni umbali gani? — nee oom·*ba*·lee *ga*·nee

Can you show me (on the map)?
Unaweza kunionyesha (katika ramani)? — oo·na·*way*·za koo·nee·oh·*nyay*·sha (ka·*tee*·ka ra·*ma*·nee)

It's …	*Iko …*	*ee*·koh …
behind …	*nyuma ya …*	*nyoo*·ma ya …
close	*karibu*	ka·*ree*·boo
here	*hapa*	*ha*·pa
in front of …	*mbele ya …*	m·*bay*·lay ya …
near …	*karibu na …*	ka·*ree*·boo na …
next to …	*jirani ya …*	jee·*ra*·nee ya …
on the corner	*pembeni*	paym·*bay*·nee
opposite …	*ng'ambo ya …*	ng·*am*·boh ya …
straight ahead	*moja kwa moja*	*moh*·ja kwa *moh*·ja
there	*hapo*	*ha*·poh

Turn …	*Geuza …*	gay·*oo*·za …
at the corner	*kwenye kona*	*kway*·nyay *koh*·na
at the traffic lights	*kwenye taa za barabarani*	*kway*·nyay ta za ba·ra·ba·*ra*·nee
left	*kushoto*	koo·*shoh*·toh
right	*kulia*	koo·*lee*·a

listen for …		
… *dakika*	… da·*kee*·ka	**… minutes**
… *kilomita*	… kee·loh·*mee*·ta	**… kilometres**
… *mita*	… *mee*·ta	**… metres**

north	*kaskazini*	kas·ka·*zee*·nee
south	*kusini*	koo·*see*·nee
east	*mashariki*	ma·sha·*ree*·kee
west	*magharibi*	ma·ga·*ree*·bee
by …	*kwa …*	kwa …
bus	*basi*	*ba*·see
foot	*miguu*	mee·*goo*
taxi	*teksi*	*tayk*·see
train	*treni*	*tray*·nee
What … is this?	*Hapa ni … gani?*	*ha*·pa nee … *ga*·nee
neighbourhood	*mtaa*	m·*ta*
street	*njia*	n·*jee*·a
village	*kijiji*	kee·*jee*·jee

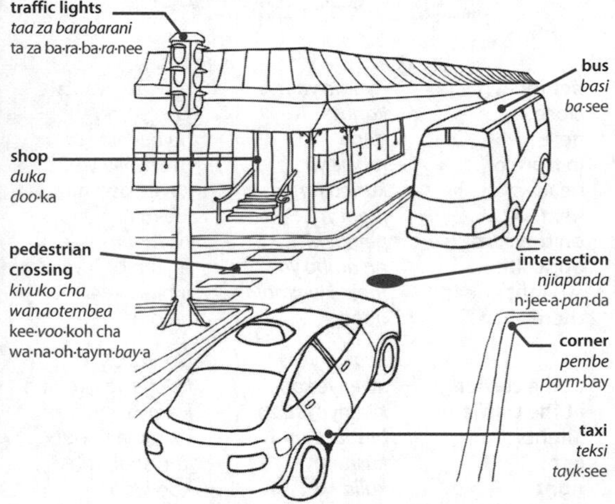

finding accommodation

kugundua malazi

Where's a …?	… *iko wapi?*	… *ee*·koh *wa*·pee
camping ground	*Uwanja wa kambi*	oo·*wan*·ja wa *kam*·bee
guesthouse	*Gesti*	*gay*·stee
hotel	*Hoteli*	hoh·*tay*·lee
restaurant	*Hoteli*	hoh·*tay*·lee
youth hostel	*Hosteli ya vijana*	hoh·*stay*·lee ya vee·*ja*·na

Can you recommend somewhere …?	*Unaweza kunipendekeze a malazi …?*	oo·na·*way*·za koo·nee·payn·*day*·kay *zay*·a ma·*la*·zee …
cheap	*rahisi*	ra·*hee*·see
good	*nzuri*	n·*zoo*·ree
luxurious	*ya anasa*	ya a·*na*·sa
nearby	*hapo karibuni*	*ha*·poh ka·ree·*boo*·nee
romantic	*kwa wapenzi*	kwa wa·*payn*·zee

What's the address?
Anwani ni nini? — an·*wa*·nee nee *nee*·nee

For responses, see **directions**, page 65.

local talk

dive	*mahali pabaya*	ma·*ha*·lee pa·*ba*·ya
rat-infested	*yenye panya*	*yay*·nyay *pa*·nya
top spot	*safi kabisa*	*sa*·fee ka·*bee*·sa

booking ahead & checking in

kufanya buking na kufika

I'd like to book a room, please.
Nataka kufanya buking, tafadhali. — na·*ta*·ka koo·*fa*·nya *boo*·keeng ta·fa·*dha*·lee

I have a reservation.
Nina buking. — *nee*·na *boo*·keeng

My name's …
Jina langu ni … — *jee*·na *lan*·goo nee …

For (three) nights/weeks.
Kwa siku/wiki (tatu). — kwa *see*·koo/*wee*·kee (*ta*·too)

From (June 30) to (July 6).
Kutoka tarehe (thelathini mwezi wa sita) mpaka tarehe (sita mwezi wa saba). — koo·*toh*·ka ta·*ray*·hay (thay·la·*thee*·nee *mway*·zee wa *see*·ta) m·*pa*·ka ta·*ray*·hay (*see*·ta *mway*·zee wa *sa*·ba)

Do you have a … room?	*Kuna chumba kwa …?*	*koo*·na *choom*·ba kwa …
double (one bed)	*watu wawili, kitanda kimoja*	*wa*·too wa·*wee*·lee kee·*tan*·da kee·*moh*·ja
single	*mtu mmoja*	*m*·too m·*moh*·ja
twin (two beds)	*watu wawili, vitanda viwili*	*wa*·too wa·*wee*·lee vee·*tan*·da vee·*wee*·lee

Do you have a suite?
Kuna chumba chenye sebule? — *koo*·na *choom*·ba *chay*·nyay say·*boo*·lay

Can I see the room?
Naomba nione chumba. — na·*ohm*·ba nee·*oh*·nay *choom*·ba

listen for ...		
Imejaa.	ee·may·*ja*	**It's full.**
mapokezi	ma·poh·*kay*·zee	**reception**
pasipoti	pa·see·*poh*·tee	**passport**
Siku ngapi?	*see*·koo n·*ga*·pee	**How many nights?**
ufunguo	oo·foon·*goo*·oh	**key**

How much is it per ...?	*Ni bei gani kwa ...?*	nee bay *ga*·ne kwa ...
day	*siku*	*see*·koo
person	*mtu*	*m*·too
week	*wiki*	*wee*·kee

That's too expensive.
Ni ghali mno. nee *ga*·lee *m*·noh

Can you lower the price?
Naomba upunguze bei? na·*ohm*·ba oo·poon·*goo*·zay bay

I'll take it.
Nataka. na·*ta*·ka

Do I need to pay upfront?
Ni lazima nilipe kwanza? nee *la*·zee·ma nee·*lee*·pay *kwan*·za

Can I pay by ...?	*Naweza kulipa kwenye ...?*	na·*way*·za koo·*lee*·pa *kway*·nyay ...
credit card	*kadi ya benki*	*ka*·dee ya *bayn*·kee
travellers cheque	*hundi ya msafiri*	*hoon*·dee ya m·sa·*fee*·ree

For other methods of payment, see **shopping**, page 77, and **money**, page 45.

signs		
Hakuna Nafasi	ha·*koo*·na na·*fa*·see	**no vacancy**
Nafasi Ipo	na·*fa*·see *ee*·po	**vacancy**

requests & queries

maombi na maswali

When/Where is breakfast served?
Chai ya asubuhi inapatikana lini/wapi? — *cha*·ee ya a·soo·*boo*·hee ee·na·pa·tee·*ka*·na *lee*·nee/*wa*·pee

Please wake me at (seven).
Tafadhali niamshe saa (moja). — ta·fa·*dha*·lee nee·*am*·shay sa (*moh*·ja)

Do you arrange tours here?
Mnapanga safari hapa? — m·na·*pan*·ga sa·*fa*·ree *ha*·pa

Do you change money here?
Mnabadilisha hela hapa? — m·na·ba·dee·*lee*·sha *hay*·la *ha*·pa

Can I use the ...?	*Je, naweza kutumia ...?*	jay na·*way*·za koo·too·*mee*·a ...
kitchen	*jiko*	*jee*·ko
laundry	*udobi*	oo·*doh*·bee
telephone	*simu*	*see*·mu

Do you have a/an ...?	*Kuna ...?*	*koo*·na ...
elevator	*lifti*	*leef*·tee
laundry service	*dobi*	*doh*·bee
message board	*kibao cha ujumbe*	kee·*ba*·oh cha oo·*joom*·bay
safe	*kasha la fedha*	*ka*·sha la *fay*·dha
swimming pool	*bwawa la kuogelea*	*bwa*·wa la koo·oh·gay·*lay*·a

a knock at the door ...

Who is it?	*Ni nani?*	nee *na*·nee
Just a moment.	*Subiri kidogo.*	soo·*bee*·ree kee·*doh*·goh
Come in.	*Ingia.*	een·*gee*·a
Come back later, please.	*Rudi baadaye, tafadhali.*	*roo*·dee ba·a·*da*·yay ta·fa·*dha*·lee

Could I have …, please?	*Naomba …, afadhali.*	na·*ohm*·ba … ta·fa·*dha*·li
a mosquito net	*chandarua*	chan·da·*roo*·a
a receipt	*risiti*	ree·*see*·tee
an extra blankt	*blanketi nyingine*	blan·*kay*·tee nyeen·*gee*·nay
my key	*ufunguo wangu*	oo·foon·*goo*·oh *wan*·goo
toilet paper	*karatasi ya choo*	ka·ra·*ta*·see ya choh

Can you wash these clothes?
Mnaweza kufua nguo hizi? — m·na·*way*·za koo·*foo*·a n·*goo*·oh *hee*·zee

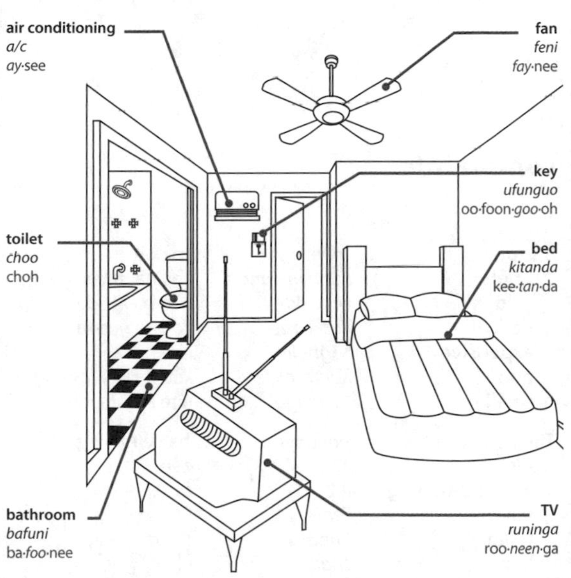

washerman/ -woman	*dobi*	*doh*·bee
wash clothes	*fua nguo*	*foo*·a n·*goo*·oh
with starch	*weka stachi*	*way*·ka *sta*·chee
without starch	*usiweke stachi*	oo·see·*way*·kay *sta*·chee

Is there a message for me?
Kuna ujumbe wangu? — *koo*·na oo·*joom*·bay *wan*·goo

Can I leave a message for someone?
Naweza kumwachia mtu ujumbe? — na·*way*·za koom·wa·*chee*·a m·too oo·*joom*·bay

I'm locked out of my room.
Nimefungwa nje ya chumba changu. — nee·may·*foon*·gwa *n*·jay ya *choom*·ba *chan*·goo

complaints

malalimiko

It's too …	*… mno.*	*… m*·noh
bright	*Kuna mwanga*	*koo*·na *mwan*·ga
cold	*Ni baridi*	nee ba·*ree*·dee
dark	*Kuna giza*	*koo*·na *gee*·za
expensive	*Ni ghali*	nee *ga*·lee
noisy	*Kuna kelele*	*koo*·na kay·*lay*·lay
small	*Ni ndogo*	nee n·*doh*·goh
The … doesn't work.	*… haifanyi kazi.*	… ha·ee·*fa*·nyee *ka*·zee
air conditioning	*A/c*	ay·*see*
fan	*Feni*	*fay*·nee
toilet	*Choo*	choh
light	*Taa*	ta

Can I get another (blanket)?
Inawezekana nipate (blanketi) nyingine? — ee·na·way·zay·*ka*·na nee·*pa*·tay (blan·*kay*·tee) nyeen·*gee*·nay

Can you clean the room?
Inawezekana kusafisha chumba? — ee·na·way·zay·*ka*·na koo·sa·*fee*·sha *choom*·ba

This (pillow) isn't clean.
(Mto) huu si safi. — (*m*·toh) hoo see *sa*·fee

There's no …	*Hakuna …*	ha·*koo*·na …
electricity	*umeme*	oo·*may*·may
hot water	*maji ya moto*	*ma*·jee ya *moh*·toh

checking out

kuachia chumba

What time is checkout?
Muda wa kuachia chumba ni saa ngapi? — *moo*·da wa koo·ach·*ee*·a *choom*·ba nee sa n·*ga*·pee

Can I have a late checkout?
Naweza kuchelewa kuachia chumba? — na·*way*·za koo·chay·*lay*·wa koo·ach·*ee*·a *choom*·ba

Can you call a taxi for me (for 11 o'clock)?
Naomba teksi kwa saa (tano). — na·*ohm*·ba *tayk*·si kwa sa (*ta*·noh)

I'm leaving now.
Naondoka sasa. — na·ohn·*doh*·ka *sa*·sa

Can I leave my bags here?
Naweza kuacha mizigo yangu hapa? — na·*way*·za koo·*ach*·a mee·*zee*·goh *yan*·goo *ha*·pa

There's a mistake in the bill.
Mmekosa kwenye bili yangu. — m·may·*koh*·sa *kway*·nyay *bee*·lee *yan*·goo

Can I have my …?	*Naomba …yangu.*	na·*ohm*·ba …*yan*·goo
deposit	*maweko*	ma·*way*·koh
passport	*pasipoti*	pa·see·*poh*·tee
valuables	*vitu vya thamani*	*vee*·too vya *tha*·ma·nee

I'll be back …	*Nitarudi …*	nee·ta·*roo*·dee …
in (three) days	*baada ya siku (tatu)*	ba·*a*·da ya *see*·koo (*ta*·too)
on (Tuesday)	*(Jumanne)*	(joo·ma·*n*·nay)

I've been very happy here, thank you.
Nimefurahi sana hapa, asante. — nee·may·foo·*ra*·hee *sa*·na *ha*·pa a·*san*·tay

I'll recommend it to my friends.
Nitawapendekezea rafiki zangu. — nee·ta·wa·payn·day·kay·*zay*·a ra·*fee*·kee *zan*·goo

camping

kupiga kambi

Do you have …?	*Kuna …?*	*koo*·na …
a laundry	*udobi*	oo·*doh*·bee
a tent site	*nafasi kupiga hema*	na·*fa*·see koo·*pee*·ga *hay*·ma
a car site	*nafasi kuegesha gari*	na·*fa*·see koo·ay·*gay*·sha *ga*·ree
electricity	*umeme*	oo·*may*·may
hot water	*maji ya moto*	*ma*·jee ya *moh*·toh
shower facilities	*bafuni*	ba·*foo*·nee
tents for hire	*hema kukodisha*	*hay*·ma koo·koh·*dee*·sha

How much is it per …?	*Ni bei gani kila …?*	nee bay *ga*·nee *kee*·la …
caravan	*lori*	*loh*·ree
person	*mtu*	*m*·too
tent	*hema*	*hay*·ma
vehicle	*gari*	*ga*·ree

Can I …?	*Naweza …?*	na·*way*·za …
camp here	*kuwa hapa kwa usiku*	koo·wa *ha*·pa kwa oo·*see*·koo
park next to my tent	*kuegesha gari jirani ya hema*	koo·ay·*gay*·sha *ga*·ree jee·*ra*·nee ya *hay*·ma

Is the water drinkable?
Je, maji ni safi kunywa? — jay *ma*·jee nee *sa*·fee *koony*·wa

Who do I ask to stay here?
Niongee na nani nikitaka kukaa hapa? — nee·ohn·*gay*·ay na *na*·nee nee·kee·*ta*·ka koo·*ka* *ha*·pa

Could I borrow …?
Naomba niazimie … — na·*ohm*·ba nee·a·zee·*mee*·ay …

renting

kukodisha

I'm here about the … for rent.	*Nimekuja kuhusu kukodisha …*	nee·may·*koo*·ja koo·*hoo*·soo koo·koh·*dee*·sha …
Do you have a/an … for rent?	*Kuna … kukodisha?*	*koo*·na … koo·koh·*dee*·sha
apartment	*fleti*	*flay*·tee
cabin	*kibanda*	kee·*ban*·da
house	*nyumba*	*nyoom*·ba
room	*chumba*	*choom*·ba
furnished	*kwenye fenicha zote*	*kway*·nyay *fay*·nee·cha *zoh*·tay
partly furnished	*kwenye fenicha kadhaa*	*kway*·nyay *fay*·nee·cha ka·*dha*
unfurnished	*bila fenicha*	*bee*·la *fay*·nee·cha

staying with locals

kukaa na wenyeji

Can I stay at your place?
Naweza kukaa nyumbani kwako? — na·*way*·za koo·*ka* nyoom·*ba*·nee *kwa*·koh

Is there anything I can do to help?
Nisaidie namna gani? — nee·sa·ee·*dee*·ay *nam*·na *ga*·nee

I have my own ...	*Nina ...*	*nee*·na ...
mattress	*godolo langu*	goh·*doh*·loh *lan*·goo
sleeping bag	*mfuko wa kulalia wangu*	m·*foo*·koh wa koo·la·*lee*·a *wan*·goo

Can I ...?	*Naweza ...?*	na·*way*·za ...
bring anything for the meal	*kuchangia lisho*	koo·chan·*gee*·a *lee*·shoh
do the dishes	*safisha vyombo*	sa·*fee*·sha *vyohm*·boh
set/clear the table	*kutayarisha/ kuondoa meza*	koo·ta·ya·*ree*·sha/ koo·ohn·*doh*·a *may*·za
take out the rubbish	*kufuta takataka*	koo·*foo*·ta ta·ka·*ta*·ka

Thanks for your hospitality.
Asante sana kwa wema wako. — a·*san*·tay *sa*·na kwa *way*·ma *wa*·koh

For dining-related expressions, see **food**, page 153.

address: unknown

Other than downtown in some cities, exact street addresses – or even street names – are not common. The best way to find a specific person or place is often to go to the centre of a neighbourhood, eg the local bus stop, and ask for a particular landmark or a person who can lead you to your destination.

What's the address?	*Ni anwani gani?*	nee an·*wa*·nee *ga*·nee
road	*barabara*	ba·ra·*ba*·ra
street	*njia*	n·*jee*·a

looking for ...

kutafutia

Where's a ...?	*... iko wapi?*	... *ee*·koh *wa*·pee
department store	*Duka lenye vitu vingi*	*doo*·ka *lay*·nyay *vee*·too *veen*·gee
general store	*Duka lenye vitu mbalimbali*	*doo*·ka *lay*·nyay *vee*·too m·ba·lee·m·*ba*·lee
market	*Soko*	*soh*·koh

Where can I buy (a padlock)?
Naweza kununua (kufuli) wapi? — na·*way*·za koo·noo·*noo*·a (koo·*foo*·lee) *wa*·pee

For phrases on directions, see **directions**, page 65.
For more on shops and services, see the **dictionary**.

making a purchase

wakati wa kununua

I'm just looking.
Naangalia tu. — na·an·ga·*lee*·a too

I'd like to buy (an adaptor plug).
Nataka kununua (adapta ya umeme). — na·*ta*·ka koo·noo·*noo*·a (a·*dap*·ta ya oo·*may*·may)

How much is it?
Ni bei gani? — ni bay *ga*·nee

it's not what you say, it's how you say it

Swahili speakers tend to reserve *tafadhali* ta·fa·*dha*·lee (please) for fairly formal situations, and generally don't use it in ordinary encounters such as shopping. Instead of saying 'could you' or 'I'd like' or 'please show me', a simple request such as *Nipe …* *nee*·pay … (give me …), *Naomba …* na·*ohm*·ba … (I request …) or *Nataka …* na·*ta*·ka … (I want …), when spoken with a pleasant tone of voice, will usually convey all the necessary politeness of casual interactions.

Can you write down the price?
Andika bei. an·*dee*·ka bay

Do you have any others?
Kuna nyingine? *koo*·na nyeen·*gee*·nay

Can I look at it?
Naomba nione. na·*ohm*·ba nee·*oh*·nay

I don't like it.
Sipendi. see·*payn*·dee

I'll take it.
Nataka. na·*ta*·ka

Could I have it wrapped?
Funga, tafadhali. *foon*·ga ta·fa·*dha*·lee

Does it have a guarantee?
Kuna dhamana? *koo*·na dha·*ma*·na

Can I have it sent overseas?
Naweza kuipostia kwenye nchi za nje? na·*way*·za koo·ee·poh·*stee*·a *kway*·nyay *n*·chee za *n*·jay

Can you order it for me?
Unaweza kuniagizia? oo·na·*way*·za koo·nee·a·gee·*zee*·a

Can I pick it up later?
Naweza kuichukua baadaye? na·*way*·za koo·ee·choo·*koo*·a ba·a·*da*·yay

It's faulty.
Haifanyi kazi. ha·ee·*fa*·nyee *ka*·zee

local talk		
bargain	*bei nafuu*	bay na·*foo*
bottom price	*bei ya mwisho*	bay ya m·*wee*·shoh
cheap	*rahisi*	ra·*hee*·see
rip-off	*feki*	*fay*·kee
sale	*seli*	*say*·lee
specials	*maalum*	*ma*·loom

Do you accept …?	*Mnakubali …*	m·na·koo·*ba*·lee …
credit cards	*kadi ya benki*	*ka*·dee ya *bayn*·kee
travellers cheques	*hundi ya msafiri*	*hoon*·dee ya m·sa·*fee*·ree
I'd like …, please.	*Nataka …, tafadhali.*	na·*ta*·ka … ta·fa·*dha*·lee
my change	*chenji yangu*	*chayn*·jee *yan*·goo
a refund	*unirudishie hela*	oo·nee·roo·dee·*shee*·ay *hay*·la
to return this	*kurudisha kitu hiki*	koo·roo·*dee*·sha *kee*·too *hee*·kee
Could I have a …, please?	*Naomba …*	na·*ohm*·ba …
bag	*mfuko*	m·*foo*·koh
receipt	*risiti*	ree·*see*·tee

bargaining

kubishana bei

How much is it?
Ni bei gani? — ni bay *ga*·nee

That's too expensive.
Ni ghali mno. — nee *ga*·lee *m*·noh

Please lower the price.
Punguza bei. — poon·*goo*·za bay

It's not a fair price.
Siyo bei nafuu. — *see*·yoh bay na·*foo*

Do you have something cheaper?
Kuna rahisi zaidi? koo·na ra·*hee*·see za·*ee*·dee

I'll give you (500 shillings).
Nitakupa (shilingi mia tano). nee·ta·*koo*·pa (shee·*leen*·gee *mee*·a *ta*·noh)

clothes

nguo

My size is …	*Saizi yangu ni …*	*sa*·ee·zee *yan*·goo nee …
(40)	*(arobaini)*	(a·roh·ba·*ee*·nee)
small	*ndogo*	n·*doh*·goh
medium	*wastani*	*wa*·sta·nee
large	*kubwa*	*koob*·wa

Can I try it on?
Je, naweza kujaribu kuvaa? jay na·*way*·za koo·ja·*ree*·boo koo·*va*

It doesn't fit.
Haifai. ha·ee·*fa*·ee

Can you recommend a seamstress/tailor?
Unaweza kupendekeza mshonaji? oo·na·*way*·za koo·payn·day·*kay*·za m·shoh·*na*·jee

Could you alter/mend this?
Unaweza kubadilisha/ kushona hii? oo·na·*way*·za koo·ba·dee·*lee*·sha/ koo·*sho*·na hee

Could you make me a (dress)?
Unaweza kunishonea (gauni)? oo·na·*way*·za koo·nee·shoh·*nay*·a (ga·*oo*·nee)

For clothing items, see the **dictionary**.

PRACTICAL

kanga writings

Throughout East Africa you'll come across women wearing *kanga kan*·ga – brightly coloured lengths of cotton cloth with Swahili sayings printed along the edge. Many of the sayings are social commentaries or messages often indirectly worded, or containing puns and double meanings. Others are simply a local form of advertising, such as those bearing the logo of political parties.

Here are some common Swahili proverbs that might appear on a *kanga*. It's easy to pair them with their English equivalents but the choice of words is typical for the East African culture:

Not all that glitters is gold.

Si kila mwenye	see *kee*·la *mway*·nyay
makucha huwa simba.	ma·*koo*·cha *hoo*·wa *seem*·ba

(lit: not all those that have claws are lions)

Strike the iron while it's hot.

Ngozi ivute	n·*goh*·zee *ee*·voo·tay
ili maji.	*ee*·lee *ma*·jee

(lit: stretch the hide while it's wet)

repairs

matengenezo

Can I have my … repaired here?	*Mnaweza kutengeneza … yangu hapa?*	m·na·*way*·za koo·tayn·gay·*nay*·za … *yan*·goo *ha*·pa
When will my … be ready?	*… yangu itakuwa tayari lini?*	… *yan*·goo ee·ta·*koo*·wa ta·*ya*·ree *lee*·nee
backpack	*shanta*	*shan*·ta
camera	*kemra*	*kaym*·ra
(sun)glasses	*miwani (ya jua)*	mee·*wa*·nee (ya *joo*·a)
shoes	*viatu*	vee·*a*·too

hairdressing

nywele

I'd like (a) …	*Nataka …*	na·*ta*·ka …
colour	*kuweka rangi*	koo·*way*·ka *ran*·gee
haircut	*kukata nywele*	koo·*ka*·ta *nyway*·lay
my hair braided	*kusuka nywele*	koo·*soo*·ka *nyway*·lay
my hair washed	*kuosha nywele*	koo·*oh*·sha *nyway*·lay
shave	*kunyoa ndevu*	koo·*nyoh*·a n·*day*·voo
trim	*kupunguza nywele kidogo*	koo·poon·*goo*·za *nyway*·lay kee·*doh*·goh

Don't cut it too short.
Usipunguze mno. — oo·see·poon·*goo*·zay *m*·noh

Please use a new blade.
Tumia wembe mpya. — too·*mee*·a *waym*·bay *m*·pya

Please use hot water.
Tumia maji ya moto. — too·*mee*·a *ma*·jee ya *moh*·toh

Shave it all off!
Nyoa zote! — *nyoh*·a *zoh*·tay

I should never have let you near me!
Nilikosa hata uliponikaribia! — nee·lee·*koh*·sa *ha*·ta oo·lee·poh·nee·ka·ree·*bee*·a

barber	*kinyozi*	kee·*nyoh*·zee
hairdresser for braiding	*msusi*	m·*soo*·see
hairdresser for cutting	*mtengenezaji wa nywele*	m·tayn·gay·nay·*za*·jee wa *nyway*·lay

For colours, see the **dictionary**.

books & reading

vitabu na kusoma

Do you have a book by (Ngugi wa Thiong'o)?

Kuna kitabu kuandikwa na (Ngugi wa Thiong'o)?	*koo*·na kee·*ta*·boo koo·an·*deek*·wa na (n·*goo*·gee wa thee·*ohng*·oh)

Is there an English-language bookshop?

Kuna duka la vitabu vya Kiingereza?	*koo*·na *doo*·ka la vee·*ta*·boo vya kee·een·gay·*ray*·za

Can you recommend a book for me?

Unaweza kunipendekezea kitabu?	oo·na·*way*·za koo·nee·payn·day·kay·*zay*·a kee·*ta*·boo

Do you have Lonely Planet guidebooks?

Mna vitabu vya Lonely Planet?	*m*·na vee·*ta*·boo vya *lohn*·lee *pla*·nayt

I'd like a …	*Nataka …*	na·*ta*·ka …
dictionary	*kamusi*	ka·*moo*·see
newspaper (in English)	*gazeti (kwa Kiingereza)*	ga·*zay*·tee (kwa kee·een·gay·*ray*·za)
notepad	*daftari*	daf·*ta*·ree

electronic goods

bidhaa za umeme

Where can I buy duty-free electronic goods?

Duty-free kununua bidhaa za umeme iko wapi?	doo·tee·*free* koo·noo·*noo*·a bee·*dha* za oo·*may*·may *ee*·koh *wa*·pee

Will this work on any DVD player?

Itafanya kazi katika DVD zote?	ee·ta·*fa*·nya *ka*·zee ka·*tee*·ka dee·vee·*dee zoh*·tay

Is this a (PAL/NTSC) system?

Ni mfumo wa (PAL/NTSC)?	nee m·*foo*·moh wa (pal/ayn·tee·*ays*·see)

Is this the latest model?

Ni aina mpya kabisa?	nee a·*ee*·na *m*·pya ka·*bee*·sa

Is this (240) volts?

Ni volti (mia mbili arobaini)?	nee *vol*·tee (*mee*·a m·*bee*·lee a·roh·ba·*ee*·nee)

music

muziki

I'd like a ...	*Nataka ...*	na·*ta*·ka ...
blank tape	*kanda tupo*	*kan*·da *too*·poh
CD	*CD*	see·*dee*
drum	*ngoma*	n·*goh*·ma
xylophone	*marimba*	ma·*reem*·ba

I'm looking for something by (Remi Ongala).

Natafuta muziki ya (Remi Ongala).	na·ta·*foo*·ta moo·*zee*·kee ya (*ray*·mee ohn·*ga*·la)

What's their best recording?

Kanda gani yao inazidi?	*kan*·da *ga*·nee *ya*·oh ee·na·*zee*·dee

Can I listen to this?

Naomba tusikilize.	na·*ohm*·ba too·see·kee·*lee*·zay

listen for ...

Unataka msaada? oo·na·*ta*·ka m·*sa*·da	**Do you want help?**
Nyingine? nyeen·*gee*·nay	**Anything else?**
Hamna/Hakuna. *ham*·na/ha·*koo*·na	**No, we don't have any.**

photography

kupiga picha

I need ... film for this camera.	*Nahitaji filamu ... kwa kemra hii.*	na·hee·*ta*·jee fee·*la*·moo ... kwa *kaym*·ra hee
APS	*APS*	a·pee·*ays*
B&W	*nyeusi na nyeupe*	nya·*oo*·see na nyay·*oo*·pay
colour	*ya rangi*	ya *ran*·gee
slide	*ya slaidi*	ya *sla*·ee·dee
(400) speed	*ya spidi (mia nne)*	ya *spee*·dee (*mee*·a *n*·nay)

Can you ...?	*Mnaweza ...?*	m·na·*way*·za ...
develop this film	*kusafisha mkanda huu*	koo·sa·*fee*·sha m·*kan*·da hoo
develop digital photos	*kusafisha picha za tarakimu*	koo·sa·*fee*·sha *pee*·cha za ta·ra·*kee*·moo
load my film	*kuweka mkanda katika kemra*	koo·*way*·ka m·*kan*·da ka·*tee*·ka *kaym*·ra
recharge the battery for my digital camera	*kuchajisha betri kwa kemra yangu ya tarakimu*	koo·cha·*jee*·sha *bay*·tree kwa *kaym*·ra *yan*·goo ya ta·ra·*kee*·moo
transfer photos from my camera to CD	*kuhamisha picha kutoka kemra kwenye CD*	koo·ha·*mee*·sha *pee*·cha koo·*toh*·ka *kaym*·ra *kway*·nyay see·*dee*

Please don't use a red tint.

Usitumie rangi nyekundu nyekundu.	oo·see·too·*mee*·ay *ran*·gee nyay·*koon*·doo nyay·*koon*·doo

When will it be ready?

Itakuwa tayari lini?	ee·ta·*koo*·wa ta·*ya*·ree *lee*·nee

How much is it?

Ni bei gani?	ni bay *ga*·nee

I need a passport photo taken.

Nahitaji picha ya pasipoti.	na·hee·*ta*·jee *pee*·cha ya pa·see·*poh*·tee

I'm not happy with these photos.

Sifurahi na picha hizi.	see·foo·*ra*·hee na *pee*·cha *hee*·zee

souvenirs		
basket	*kikapu*	kee·*ka*·poo
batik	*batiki*	ba·*tee*·kee
bowl	*bakuli*	ba·*koo*·lee
candlestick holder	*mshumaa*	m·shoo·*ma*
ceramic pot	*chungu*	*choo*·ngoo
copper tray	*sinia ya shaba*	see·*nee*·a ya *sha*·ba
(folding safari) chair	*kiti*	*kee*·tee
jewellery	*vipuli*	vee·*poo*·lee
leather shield	*ngao ya ngazi*	n·*ga*·oh ya n·*ga*·zee
mask	*kinyago*	kee·*nya*·goh
plaited mat	*mkeka*	m·*kay*·ka
spear	*mkuki*	m·*koo*·kee
textiles	*vitambaa*	vee·tam·*ba*
three-legged stool	*kigoda*	kee·*goh*·da
woodcarving	*uchongaji*	oo·chohn·*ga*·jee

post office

posta

I want to send a/an ...	*Nataka kupeleka ...*	na·*ta*·ka koo·pay·*lay*·ka ...
fax	*faksi*	*fak*·see
letter	*barua*	ba·*roo*·a
parcel	*kifurushi*	kee·foo·*roo*·shee
postcard	*postkadi*	pohst·*ka*·dee
trunk (tea chest)	*sanduku*	san·*doo*·koo
I want to buy a/an ...	*Nataka kununua ...*	na·*ta*·ka koo·noo·*noo*·a ...
aerogram	*aerogramu*	a·ay·roh·*gra*·moo
envelope	*bahasha*	ba·*ha*·sha
stamp	*stempu*	*staym*·poo
customs declaration	*azimio la forodha*	a·zee·*mee*·oh la foh·*roh*·dha
domestic	*ndani ya nchi*	n·*da*·nee ya *n*·chee
fragile	*dhaifu*	dha·*ee*·foo
international	*nje ya nchi*	*n*·jay ya *n*·chee
mail	*barua*	ba·*roo*·a
mailbox	*sanduku la posta*	san·*doo*·koo la *poh*·sta
PO Box	*Sanduku la Posta*	san·*doo*·koo la *poh*·sta
postcode	*simbo ya posta*	*seem*·boh ya *poh*·sta

snail mail

air	*kwa ndege*	kwa n·*day*·gay
express	*ekspres*	ayk·*sprays*
registered	*barua ya rejesta*	ba·*roo*·a ya ray·*jay*·sta
sea	*kwa meli*	kwa *may*·lee
surface (land)	*kwa lori*	kwa *loh*·ree

Please send it by air/surface mail to (Australia).

Peleka kwa ndege/ meli kwenda (Australia).	pay·*lay*·ka kwa n·*day*·gay/ *may*·lee *kwayn*·da (a·oo·*stra*·lee·a)

It contains (souvenirs).

Kuna (kumbukumbu) ndani.	*koo*·na (koom·boo·*koom*·boo) n·*da*·nee

Where's the poste restante section?

Posta restante iko wapi?	*poh*·sta ray·*stan*·tay *ee*·koh *wa*·pee

Is there any mail for me?

Kuna barua zozote zangu?	*koo*·na ba·*roo*·a zoh·*zoh*·tay *zan*·goo

phone

simu

What's your phone number?

Nipe simu yako?	*nee*·pay *see*·moo *ya*·koh

Where's the nearest public phone?

Kuna simu ya kadi wapi jirani?	*koo*·na *see*·moo ya *ka*·dee *wa*·pee jee·*ra*·nee

Where's the nearest telecom centre?

Telekom iko wapi?	tay·lay·*kohm ee*·ko *wa*·pee

Can I look at a phone book?

Nionyeshe kitabu cha namba za simu?	nee·oh·*nyay*·shay kee·*ta*·boo cha *nam*·ba za *see*·moo

The number is …

Namba ni …	*nam*·ba ni …

What's the area/country code for (New Zealand)?

Namba ya miito/ kimataifa kwa (New Zealand) ni nini?	*nam*·ba ya mee·*ee*·toh/ kee·ma·ta·*ee*·fa kwa (noo *zee*·land) nee *nee*·nee

I want to ...	*Nataka ...*	na·*ta*·ka ...
buy a phonecard	*kununua kadi ya simu*	koo·noo·*noo*·a *ka*·dee ya *see*·moo
call (Singapore)	*kupiga simu kwa (Singapore)*	koo·*pee*·ga *see*·moo kwa (seen·ga·*pohr*)
make a (local) call	*kupiga simu (jirani)*	koo·*pee*·ga *see*·moo (jee·*ra*·nee)
reverse the charges	*kugeuza gharama*	koo·gay·*oo*·za ga·*ra*·ma
speak for (three) minutes	*kuongea kwa dakika (tatu)*	koo·ohn·*gay*·a kwa da·*kee*·ka (*ta*·too)
How much for ...?	*... ni bei gani?*	... nee bay *ga*·nee
a (three)-minute call	*Kupiga simu kwa dakika (tatu)*	koo·*pee*·ga *see*·moo kwa da·*kee*·ka (*ta*·too)
each extra minute	*Kila dakika nyingine*	*kee*·la da·*kee*·ka nyeen·*gee*·nay

listen for ...

Umekosa namba. oo·may·*koh*·sa *nam*·ba	**Wrong number.**
Ni nani? nee *na*·nee	**Who's calling?**
Unataka (kuongea na) nani? oo·na·*ta*·ka (koo·ohn·*gay*·a na) *na*·nee	**Who do you want (to speak to)?**
Dakika moja. da·*kee*·ka *moh*·ja	**One moment.**
Hayupo. ha·*yoo*·poh	**He/She is not here.**

It's engaged.
Inatumika. ee·na·too·*mee*·ka

I've been cut off.
Imekatika. ee·may·ka·*tee*·ka

The connection's bad.
Kiungo ni kibaya. kee·*oon*·goh nee kee·*ba*·ya

Hello.
Halo. ha·*loh*

It's …
Ni … nee …

Is … there?
… yuko? … *yoo*·koh

Can I speak to …?
Nataka kuongea na … na·*ta*·ka koo·ohn·*gay*·a na …

Who am I speaking to?
Naongea na nani? na·ohn·*gay*·a na *na*·nee

Please tell him/her I called.
Mwambie nilipiga simu. m·wam·*bee*·ay nee·lee·*pee*·ga *see*·moo

Can I leave a message?
Naomba niache ujumbe? na·*ohm*·ba nee·*a*·chay oo·*joom*·bay

My number is …
Simu yangu ni … *see*·moo *yan*·goo nee …

I don't have a contact number.
Sina simu. *see*·na *see*·moo

I'll call back later.
Nitajaribu tena baadaye. nee·ta·ja·*ree*·boo *tay*·na ba·a·*da*·yay

just hang up

Swahili speakers often don't make a ceremony of saying 'goodbye' at the end of a phone call. Instead, phone conversations often end with *haya/sawa* ha·ya/*sa*·wa (OK), after which both parties hang up.

mobile/cell phone

simu ya mkononi

I'd like a …	*Nataka …*	na·*ta*·ka …
charger for my phone	*chaja kwa simu yangu*	*cha*·ja kwa *see*·moo *yan*·goo
mobile/cell phone for hire	*kukodisha simu ya mkononi*	koo·koh·*dee*·sha *see*·moo ya m·koh·*noh*·nee
prepaid mobile/ cell phone	*kadi ya simu ya mkononi*	*ka*·dee ya *see*·moo ya m·koh·*noh*·nee
SIM card	*kadi ya sim*	*ka*·dee ya seem

What are the rates?
Ni bei gani? nee bay *ga*·nee

(500 shillings) per (30) seconds.
(Shilingi mia tano) kwa sekundi (thelathini). (shee·*leen*·gee *mee*·a *ta*·noh) kwa say·*koon*·dee (thay·la·*thee*·nee)

the internet

intaneti

Where's the local Internet cafe?
Intanet Kafe iko wapi? een·*ta*·nayt ka·*fay ee*·koh *wa*·pee

I'd like to …	*Nataka …*	na·*ta*·ka …
check my email	*kusoma barua pepe yangu*	koo·*soh*·ma ba·*roo*·a *pay*·pay *yan*·goo
get Internet access	*kutumia intaneti*	koo·too·*mee*·a een·ta·*nay*·tee
use a printer	*kutumia printa*	koo·too·*mee*·a *preen*·ta
use a scanner	*kutumia skana*	koo·too·*mee*·a *ska*·na

communications

Do you have …?	*Kuna …?*	*koo*·na …
Macs	*Mac*	mak
PCs	*PC*	pee·*see*
a Zip drive	*draivu ya zip*	*dra*·ee·voo ya zeep
How much per …?	*Ni bei gani kwa …?*	nee bay *ga*·nee kwa …
hour	*saa*	sa
(five) minutes	*dakika (tano)*	da·*kee*·ka (*ta*·noh)
page	*ukurasa*	oo·koo·*ra*·sa

How do I log on?
Nianziaje? nee·an·zee·*a*·jay

Please change it to the English-language setting.
Tafadhali badilisha kutumia Kiingereza. ta·fa·*dha*·lee ba·dee·*lee*·sha koo·too·*mee*·a kee·een·gay·*ray*·za

The connection is too slow.
Kiungo ni polepole mno. kee·*oon*·goh nee poh·lay·*poh*·lay *m*·noh

It's crashed.
Imekwama. ee·may·*kwa*·ma

I've finished.
Nimemaliza. nee·may·ma·*lee*·za

PRACTICAL

banking
kwenda benki

In major urban areas you'll be able to use your overseas ATM card, make purchases at upscale locations with your credit card, and change cash or travellers cheques in foreign exchange offices.

Where's ...?	*... iko wapi?*	... *ee*·koh *wa*·pee
an automated teller machine	*Mashine ya kutolea pesa*	ma·*shee*·nay ya koo·toh·*lay*·a *pay*·sa
a foreign exchange office	*Foreks*	*foh*·rayks

What time does the bank open?
Benki inafungua saa ngapi? — *bayn*·kee ee·na·foon·*goo*·a sa n·*ga*·pee

Can I use my credit card to withdraw money?
Naweza kutumia kadi ya benki kuondoa hela? — na·*way*·za koo·too·*mee*·a *ka*·dee ya *bayn*·kee koo·ohn·*doh*·a *hay*·la

listen for ...

kitambulisho	kee·tam·boo·*lee*·shoh	**identification**
pasipoti	pa·see·*poh*·tee	**passport**

Hatuwezi.
ha·too·*way*·zee — **We can't do that.**

Kiungo kimekwisha.
kee·*oon*·goh kee·may·*kwee*·sha — **The connection's down.**

Kuna shida.
koo·na *shee*·da — **There's a problem.**

Pesa zako zimekwisha.
pay·sa *za*·koh zee·may·*kwee*·sha — **You have no funds left.**

Saini hapa.
sa·*ee*·nee *ha*·pa — **Sign here.**

I'd like to ...	*Nataka ...*	na·*ta*·ka ...
cash a cheque	*kulipwa fedha kutokana na hundi*	koo·*leep*·wa *fay*·dha koo·toh·*ka*·na na *hoon*·dee
change a travellers cheque	*kubadilisha hundi ya msafiri*	koo·ba·dee·*lee*·sha *hoon*·dee ya m·sa·*fee*·ree
change money	*kubadilisha hela*	koo·ba·dee·*lee*·sha *hay*·la
get a cash advance	*kupata hela ya awali*	koo·*pa*·ta *hay*·la ya *a*·wa·lee
withdraw money	*kuondoa hela*	koo·ohn·*doh*·a *hay*·la

What's the ...?	*... ni nini?*	... nee *nee*·nee
charge for that	*Gharama yake*	ga·*ra*·ma *ya*·kay
exchange rate	*Kiwango cha kubadilisha hela*	kee·*wan*·goh cha koo·ba·dee·*lee*·sha *hay*·la
large bill exchange rate	*Kiwango cha kubadilisha noti kubwa*	kee·*wan*·goh cha koo·ba·dee·*lee*·sha *noh*·tee *koob*·wa
small bill exchange rate	*Kiwango cha kubadilisha noti ndogo*	kee·*wan*·goh cha koo·ba·dee·*lee*·sha *noh*·tee n·*doh*·goh

The automated teller machine took my card.
Mashine ya kutolea pesa ilichukua kadi yangu. — ma·*shee*·nay ya koo·toh·*lay*·a *pay*·sa ee·lee·choo·*koo*·a *ka*·dee *yan*·goo

I've forgotten my PIN.
Nimesahau pin namba siri. — nee·may·sa·*ha*·oo peen *nam*·ba *see*·ree

Has my money arrived yet?
Je, hela yangu imeshafika? — jay *hay*·la *yan*·goo ee·may·sha·*fee*·ka

How long will it take to arrive?
Je, itachukua muda gani kufika? — jay ee·ta·choo·*koo*·a *moo*·da *ga*·nee koo·*fee*·ka

sightseeing

matembezi ya kuangalia mandhari

I'd like a …	*Nataka …*	na·*ta*·ka …
guide	*kiongozi*	kee·ohn·*goh*·zee
guidebook in English	*kitabu cha kuongoza kwa Kiingereza*	kee·*ta*·boo cha koo·ohn·*goh*·za kwa kee·een·gay·*ray*·za
(local) map	*ramani (ya eneo hili)*	ra·*ma*·nee (ya ay·*nay*·oh *hee*·lee)

Do you have information on … sights?	*Mna maarifa kuhusu sehemu za …?*	*m*·na ma·*ree*·fa koo·*hoo*·soo say·*hay*·moo za …
cultural	*utamaduni*	oo·ta·ma·*doo*·nee
historical	*historia*	hee·stoh·*ree*·a
religious	*dini*	*dee*·nee
wildlife	*wanyama pori*	wa·*nya*·ma *poh*·ree

I'd like to see …
Nataka kuona … — na·*ta*·ka koo·*oh*·na …

What's that?
Hiyo ni nini? — *hee*·yoh nee *nee*·nee

Who made it?
Ilitengenezwa na nani? — ee·lee·tayn·gay·*nayz*·wa na *na*·nee

How old is it?
Ina umri gani? — *ee*·na *oom*·ree *ga*·nee

Can I take a photograph (of you)?
Ni sawa nikipiga picha (ya wewe)? — nee *sa*·wa nee·kee·*pee*·ga *pee*·cha (ya *way*·way)

to the point

Polite requests, which in English have the form of questions, are usually statements in Swahili. If you'd ask 'Can you take my picture?' the answer in Swahili is likely to be a factual 'yes' (I know how to use a camera) or 'no' (I'm not a photographer). If you actually want your picture taken, a request, such as, 'I ask that you take my picture', is more likely to yield the answer 'Sure, I'll do it', or 'Sorry, I can't'.

I ask that you take my picture.
Naomba upige picha yangu. — na·*ohm*·ba oo·*pee*·gay *pee*·cha *yan*·goo

I'll send you the photograph.
Nitakutumia picha hii. — nee·ta·koo·too·*mee*·a *pee*·cha hee

Can you write down your address so I can send you the picture?
Andika anwani ili nikutumie picha. — an·*dee*·ka an·*wa*·nee *ee*·lee nee·koo·too·*mee*·ay *pee*·cha

I didn't realise I'd have to pay you.
Sikuelewa inabidi nikulipe. — see·koo·ay·*lay*·wa ee·na·*bee*·dee nee·koo·*lee*·pay

getting in

kuingia

What time does it open/close?
Inafungua/Inafunga saa ngapi? — ee·na·foon·*goo*·a/ee·na·*foon*·ga sa n·*ga*·pee

What's the admission charge?
Ni bei gani kuingia? — nee bay *ga*·nee koo·een·*gee*·a

Can I enter this building?
Inaruhusiwa kuingia jengo hili? — ee·na·roo·hoo·*see*·wa koo·een·*gee*·a *jayn*·goh *hee*·lee

Are women allowed in this mosque?

Wanawake huruhusiwa kuingia msikiti huu?	wa·na·*wa*·kay hoo·roo·hoo·*see*·wa koo·een·*gee*·a m·see·*kee*·tee hoo

Is there a discount for ...?	*Kuna upungufu wa bei kwa ...?*	*koo*·na oo·poon·*goo*·foo wa bay kwa ...
children	*watoto*	wa·*toh*·toh
families	*familia*	fa·mee·*lee*·a
groups	*vikundi*	vee·*koon*·dee
older people	*wazee*	wa·*zay*
students	*wanafunzi*	wa·na·*foon*·zee

tours/safaris

safari

Safari is the Swahili word for 'trip'. It has come into English to mean 'wildlife spotting' or 'adventure travel', and is of course used so along the African safari circuit. However, it also retains its original meaning in Swahili – so don't be surprised if people use it to refer to any sort of travel, no matter how mundane.

Can you recommend a ...?	*Unajua ... nzuri?*	oo·na·*joo*·a ... n·*zoo*·ree
boat trip	*safari ya boti*	sa·*fa*·ree ya *boh*·tee
camel safari	*safari ya ngamia*	sa·*fa*·ree ya n·ga·*mee*·a
day trip	*safari ya siku moja*	sa·*fa*·ree ya *see*·koo *moh*·ja
safari/tour	*safari*	sa·*fa*·ree
walking safari	*safari ya kutembea*	sa·*fa*·ree ya koo·taym·*bay*·a

When's the next (safari)?

(Safari) ijayo itakuwa lini?	(sa·*fa*·ree) ee·*ja*·yoh ee·ta·*koo*·wa *lee*·nee

What time should we be back?

Turudi saa ngapi?	too·*roo*·dee sa n·*ga*·pee

Is/Are … included?	*Inazingatia …?*	ee·na·zeen·ga·*tee*·a …
accommodation (before/after)	*malazi (kabla/ baadaye)*	ma·*la*·zee (*ka*·bla/ ba·a·*da*·yay)
airport transfers	*usafiri kwenda na kutoka uwanja wa ndege*	oo·sa·*fee*·ree *kwayn*·da na koo·*toh*·ka oo·*wan*·ja wa n·*day*·gay
equipment rental	*kukodisha vifaa*	koo·koh·*dee*·sha vee·*fa*
fuel	*mafuta*	ma·*foo*·ta
food	*chakula*	cha·*koo*·la
park entrance fees	*ada za hifadhi*	*a*·da za hee·*fa*·dhee
tent rental	*kukodisha hema*	koo·koh·*dee*·sha *hay*·ma
transport	*usafiri*	oo·sa·*fee*·ree

The guide has paid.
Kiongozi amelipa. kee·ohn·*goh*·zee a·may·*lee*·pa

How large a tip should I pay?
Nilipe bakshishi kiasi gani? nee·*lee*·pay bak·*shee*·shee kee·*a*·see *ga*·nee

How long is the tour?
Safari itachukua muda gani? sa·*fa*·ree ee·ta·choo·*koo*·a *moo*·da *ga*·nee

How many people will be in the group?
Kundi itakuwa na watu wangapi? *koon*·dee ee·ta·*koo*·wa na *wa*·too wan·*ga*·pee

What animals are we likely to see?
Tutegemee kuona wanyama gani? too·tay·gay·*may* koo·*oh*·na wa·*nya*·ma *ga*·nee

We're very keen to see (elephants).
Tunataka sana kuona (tembo). too·na·*ta*·ka *sa*·na koo·*oh*·na (*taym*·bo)

I've lost my group.
Nimepotea kundi yangu. nee·may·poh·*tay*·a *koon*·dee *yan*·goo

For information on responsible travel and safaris in East Africa, see **sustainable travel – safari**, page 195.

business
biashara

I'm attending a …	*Nahudhuria …*	na·hoo·dhoo·*ree*·a …
conference	*mikutano*	mee·koo·*ta*·noh
course	*mafunzo*	ma·*foon*·zoh
meeting	*mkutano*	m·koo·*ta*·noh
trade fair	*maonyesho ya biashara*	ma·oh·*nyay*·shoh ya bee·a·*sha*·ra

I'm with …	*Nipo na …*	*nee*·poh na …
(Tanzania Breweries)	*(Tanzania Breweries)*	(tan·za·*nee*·a *broo*·ay·rees)
my colleague	*mwenzi*	*mwayn*·zee
my colleagues	*wenzi wangu*	*wayn*·zee *wan*·goo
(two) others	*(wawili) wengine*	(wa·*wee*·lee) wayn·*gee*·nay

I'm alone.
Nipo peke yangu. — *nee*·poh *pay*·kay *yan*·goo

I have an appointment with …
Nina mkutano na … — *nee*·na m·koo·*ta*·noh na …

I'm staying at …, room …
Ninakaa …, chumba … — nee·na·*ka* … *choom*·ba …

I'm here for (two) days/weeks.
Nipo kwa siku/ wiki (mbili). — *nee*·poh kwa *see*·koo/ *wee*·kee (m·*bee*·lee)

What's your …?	*… yako ni nini?*	… *ya*·koh nee *nee*·nee
(email) address	*Anwani (ya barua pepe)*	an·*wa*·nee (ya ba·*roo*·a *pay*·pay)
fax number	*Namba ya faksi*	*nam*·ba ya *fak*·see
mobile number	*Simu ya mkononi*	*see*·moo ya m·koh·*noh*·ni
pager number	*Namba ya bipa*	*nam*·ba ya *bee*·pa
work number	*Simu ya kazi*	*see*·moo ya *ka*·zee

Here's my …	*Hii ni … yangu.*	hee nee … *yan*·goo
business card	*kadi ya biashara*	*ka*·dee ya bee·a·*sha*·ra
(email) address	*anwani (ya barua pepe)*	an·*wa*·nee (ya ba·*roo*·a *pay*·pay)
fax number	*namba ya faksi*	*nam*·ba ya *fak*·see
mobile number	*simu ya mkononi*	*see*·moo ya m·koh·*noh*·ni
pager number	*namba ya bipa*	*nam*·ba ya *bee*·pa
work number	*simu ya kazi*	*see*·moo ya *ka*·zee

Where's the …?	*… iko wapi?*	… *ee*·koh *wa*·pee
business centre (eg in hotel)	*Kituo ya biashara*	kee·*too*·oh ya bee·a·*sha*·ra
conference	*Mikutano*	mee·koo·*ta*·noh
meeting	*Mkutano*	m·koo·*ta*·noh

I need …	*Nahitaji …*	na·hee·*ta*·jee …
a computer	*kompyuta*	kohm·*pyoo*·ta
the Internet	*intaneti*	een·ta·*nay*·tee
an interpreter	*mkalimani*	m·ka·lee·*ma*·nee
more business cards	*kadi zaidi za biashara*	*ka*·dee za·*ee*·dee za bee·a·*sha*·ra
some space to set up	*mahali pa kuandaa*	ma·*ha*·lee pa koo·an·*da*
to send a fax	*kupeleka faksi*	koo·pay·*lay*·ka *fak*·see

That went very well.
Ilikwenda vizuri. ee·lee·*kwayn*·da vee·*zoo*·ree

Thank you for your time.
Asante kwa muda wako. a·*san*·tay kwa *moo*·da *wa*·koh

Thank you all for your time.
Asanteni kwa muda wenu. a·san·*tay*·nee kwa *moo*·da *way*·noo

Shall we go for a drink/meal?
Twende kwa vinywaji/chakula? *twayn*·day kwa vee·*nywa*·jee/cha·*koo*·la

It's on me.
Ofa yangu. *oh*·fa *yan*·goo

senior & disabled travellers
watalii wazee na wasioweza

In East Africa you're very unlikely to encounter special facilities such as modified toilets or bathroom rails, accessible parking spaces, or special taxis.

I have a disability.
Nina ulemavu. — *nee*·na oo·lay·*ma*·voo

I need assistance.
Nahitaji msaada. — na·hee·*ta*·jee m·*sa*·da

What services do you have for people with a disability?
Kuna huduma gani kwa watu wenye ulemavu? — *koo*·na hoo·*doo*·ma *ga*·nee kwa *wa*·too *way*·nyay oo·lay·*ma*·voo

Is there wheelchair access?
Kuna njia ya kuingia kwa kiti cha magurudumu? — *koo*·na n·*jee*·a ya koo·een·*gee*·a kwa *kee*·tee cha ma·goo·roo·*doo*·moo

How wide is the entrance?
Mlango ni upana gani? — m·*lan*·goh nee oo·*pa*·na *ga*·nee

How many steps are there?
Kuna ngazi ngapi? — *koo*·na n·*ga*·zee n·*ga*·pee

Is there a lift?
Kuna lifti? — *koo*·na *leef*·tee

I'm deaf.
Mimi ni kiziwi. — *mee*·mee nee kee·*zee*·wee

I have a hearing aid.
Nina chombo cha kusaidia kusikia. — *nee*·na *chohm*·boh cha koo·sa·ee·*dee*·a koo·see·*kee*·a

Where can I buy a hearing aid battery?
Naweza kununua wapi kibetri cha chombo cha kusaidia kusikia? — na·*way*·za koo·noo·*noo*·a *wa*·pee kee·*bay*·tree cha *chohm*·boh cha koo·sa·ee·*dee*·a koo·see·*kee*·a

I can't see well.
Siwezi kuona vizuri. — see·*way*·zee koo·*oh*·na vee·*zoo*·ree

I'm blind.
Mimi ni kipofu. — *mee*·mee nee kee·*poh*·foo

Are guide dogs permitted?
Mbwa wa kuongoza kipofu huruhusiwa hapa? — m·bwa wa koo·ohn·*goh*·za kee·*poh*·foo hoo·roo·hoo·*see*·wa *ha*·pa

Could you help me cross the street safely?
Naomba unisaidie kuvuka barabara kwa usalama. — na·*ohm*·ba oo·nee·sa·ee·*dee*·ay koo·*voo*·ka ba·ra·*ba*·ra kwa oo·sa·*la*·ma

Is there somewhere I can sit down?
Kuna kiti? — *koo*·na *kee*·tee

guide dog	*mbwa wa kuongoza*	m·bwa wa koo·ohn·*goh*·za
older person	*mzee*	m·*zay*
person with a disability	*mtu mwenye ulemavu*	m·too *mway*·nyay oo·lay·*ma*·voo
ramp	*mbao wa kushukia*	m·*ba*·oh wa ku·shoo·*kee*·a
walking frame	*magongo ya kutembelea*	ma·*gohn*·goh ya koo·taym·bay·*lay*·a
walking stick	*fimbo*	*feem*·boh
wheelchair	*kiti cha magurudumu*	*kee*·tee cha ma·goo·roo·*doo*·moo

children
watoto

travelling with children

kusafiri na watoto

Is there a …?	*Kuna …?*	koo·na …
baby change room	*chumba cha kuvalia mtoto*	*choom*·ba cha koo·va·*lee*·a m·*toh*·toh
child-minding service	*anayeweza kumlea mtoto*	a·na·yay·*way*·za koom·*lay*·a m·*toh*·toh
child-sized portion	*kiasi kwa mtoto*	kee·*a*·see kwa m·*toh*·toh
children's menu	*menyu kwa watoto*	*may*·nyoo kwa wa·*toh*·toh
crèche	*wanapolea watoto wadogo*	wa·na·poh·*lay*·a wa·*toh*·toh wa·*doh*·goh
discount for children	*punguzo la bei kwa watoto*	poon·*goo*·zoh la bay kwa wa·*toh*·toh
family ticket	*tiketi kwa familia*	tee·*kay*·tee kwa fa·mee·*lee*·a
Do you sell …?	*Mnauza …?*	m·na·*oo*·za …
baby wipes	*vitambaa kupangusa watoto*	vee·tam·*ba* koo·pan·*goo*·sa wa·*toh*·toh
disposable nappies/diapers	*nepi*	*nay*·pee
painkillers for infants	*dawa la kutuliza maumivu kwa watoto*	*da*·wa la koo·too·*lee*·za ma·oo·*mee*·voo kwa wa·*toh*·toh

I need a/an …	*Nahitaji …*	na·hee·*ta*·jee …
baby seat	*kiti cha kitoto*	*kee*·tee cha kee·*toh*·toh
(English-speaking) babysitter	*yaya (anayesema Kiingereza)*	*ya*·ya (a·na·yay·*say*·ma kee·een·gay·*ray*·za)
booster seat	*kiti kumpandisha mtoto juu*	*kee*·tee koom·pan·*dee*·sha m·*toh*·toh joo
cot/crib	*kitanda cha mtoto mchanga*	kee·*tan*·da cha m·*toh*·toh m·*chan*·ga
highchair	*kiti juu cha mtoto*	*kee*·tee juu cha m·*toh*·toh
plastic bag	*mfuko wa plastiki*	m·*foo*·koh wa pla·*stee*·kee
potty	*choo cha mtoto*	choh cha m·*toh*·toh
pram/stroller	*kigari cha mtoto*	kee·*ga*·ree cha m·*toh*·toh

Do you hire prams/strollers?
Mnakodisha vigari vya watoto? — m·na·koh·*dee*·sha vee·*ga*·ree vya wa·*toh*·toh

Where can I change a nappy?
Nibadilishe nepi wapi? — nee·ba·dee·*lee*·shay *nay*·pee *wa*·pee

Where's a water tap?
Kuna bomba la maji wapi? — *koo*·na *bohm*·ba la *ma*·jee *wa*·pee

Are there any good places to take children around here?
Kuna mahali pazuri kwa watoto hapa eneo hili? — *koo*·na ma·*ha*·lee pa·*zoo*·ree kwa wa·*toh*·toh *ha*·pa ay·*nay*·oh *hee*·lee

Are children under (12) allowed?
Watoto chini ya miaka (kumi na miwili) huruhusiwa? — wa·*toh*·toh *chee*·nee ya mee·*a*·ka (*koo*·mee na mee·*wee*·lee) hoo·roo·hoo·*see*·wa

Is this suitable for (three)-year old children?
Inafaa kwa watoto wa miaka (mitatu)? — ee·na·*fa* kwa wa·*toh*·toh wa mee·*a*·ka (mee·*ta*·too)

Do you know a doctor who is good with children?

Unajua daktari ambaye watoto wanapenda?	oo·na·*joo*·a dak·*ta*·ree am·*ba*·yay wa·*toh*·toh wa·na·*payn*·da

If your child is sick, see **health**, page 183.

talking with children

kuongea na watoto

What's your name?

Jina lako nani?	*jee*·na *la*·koh *na*·nee

How old are you?

Una miaka mingapi?	*oo*·na mee·*a*·ka meen·*ga*·pee

When's your birthday?

Siku yako ya kuzaliwa ni lini?	*see*·koo *ya*·koh ya koo·za·*lee*·wa nee *lee*·nee

Do you go to school?

Unahudhuria shule?	oo·na·hoo·dhoo·*ree*·a *shoo*·lay?

What grade are you in?

Unasoma darasa gani?	oo·na·*soh*·ma da·*ra*·sa *ga*·nee

Do you learn English?

Unajifunza Kiingereza?	oo·na·jee·*foon*·za kee·een·gay·*ray*·za

Do you like sport?

Unapenda michezo?	oo·na·*payn*·da mee·*chay*·zoh

kids' talk

Children will often greet adult strangers by calling out *shikamoo* shee·ka·*moh* (lit: respectful greetings), and will be delighted if you reply with a warm *marahaba* ma·ra·*ha*·ba (lit: thank you for your respectful greetings). In many areas they'll run towards you with both hands raised above their heads. You can kneel or squat for them to place their hands on your forehead while they greet you. After this initial respectful greeting you'll usually continue by exchanging one or many of the standard greetings (see page 107).

talking about children

kuongea kuhusu watoto

Is this your first child?
Huyu ni mtoto wako wa kwanza? — *hoo*·yoo nee m·*toh*·toh *wa*·koh wa *kwan*·za

How many children do you have?
Una watoto wangapi? — *oo*·na wa·*toh*·toh wan·*ga*·pee

What a beautiful child!
Kumbe, huyu ni mtoto anayependeza! — *koom*·bay *hoo*·yoo nee m·*toh*·toh a·na·yay·payn·*day*·za

Is it a boy or a girl?
Je, huyu ni mvulana au msichana? — jay *hoo*·yoo nee m·voo·*la*·na *a*·oo m·see·*cha*·na

How old is he/she?
Ana umri gani? — *a*·na *oom*·ree *ga*·nee

What's his/her name?
Anaitwa nani? — a·na·*eet*·wa *na*·nee

He/She looks like you.
Anakufanana. — a·na·koo·fa·*na*·na

Does he/she go to school?
Anahudhuria shule? — a·na·hoo·dhoo·*ree*·a *shoo*·lay

Is he/she well behaved?
Ana tabia nzuri? — *a*·na ta·*bee*·a n·*zoo*·ree

baby talk

Attitude towards pregnancy and motherhood in East Africa can be surprising for a Western visitor. For example, breast-feeding in public is always acceptable and a permission would never be asked for in Swahili.

On the other hand, two questions you shouldn't ask expectant mothers are: 'When's the baby due?' and 'What are you going to call the baby?' With events like childbirth, many Swahili speakers prefer not to count their chickens before they hatch.

basics

misingi

Yes.	*Ndiyo.*	n·*dee*·yoh
No.	*Hapana.*	ha·*pa*·na
Please.	*Tafadhali.*	ta·fa·*dha*·lee
Thank you (very much).	*Asante (sana).*	a·*san*·tay (*sa*·na)
Thank you all (very much).	*Asanteni (sana).*	a·san·*tay*·nee (*sa*·na)
You're welcome.	*Karibu.*	ka·*ree*·boo
You're all welcome.	*Karibuni.*	ka·ree·*boo*·nee
Excuse me.	*Samahani.*	sa·ma·*ha*·nee
Forgive me.	*Nisamele.*	nee·sa·*may*·lay
Sorry.	*Pole.*	*poh*·lay

greetings & goodbyes

kusalimiana na kuaga

You can never spend too long exchanging greetings in East Africa. They vary depending on whether you're speaking to one person or several, or to an older or younger person. People often spend a few minutes with hands clasped, catching up on all the latest news.

You may notice many gestures that accompany greetings – respectful curtsies, grasped upper forearms, hand kisses or cool handshakes. Expect to shake hands often in East Africa. If your right hand is full or dirty, offer your wrist instead.

hi there

The most common greeting is *habari* ha·*ba*·ree (lit: news). The variations on this greeting are many. Common ones include *salama* sa·*la*·ma (lit: safe) instead of *habari*, which may be dropped from the greeting altogether: *(Habari) Za leo?* (ha·*ba*·ree) za *lay*·oh (lit: news of today). You can use *salama* to greet anybody you pass or to reply to any greeting.

Hello./How are you?
Habari? ha·*ba*·ree

What's the news?
Habari gani? ha·*ba*·ree *ga*·nee

How are you all?
Habari zenu? ha·*ba*·ree *zay*·noo

How's everyone at home?
Habari za nyumbani? ha·*ba*·ree za nyoom·*ba*·nee

How's work?
Habari za kazi? ha·*ba*·ree za *ka*·zee

Good …	*Habari za …?*	ha·*ba*·ree za …
day	*leo*	*lay*·oh
morning	*asubuhi*	a·soo·*boo*·hee
afternoon	*mchana*	m·*cha*·na
evening	*jioni*	jee·*oh*·nee

You can reply to almost any *habari* greeting using *nzuri* n·*zoo*·ree, *salama* sa·*la*·ma or *safi* *sa*·fee (fine). If things are just OK, add *tu* too (only) after any of these replies. Even if things are really bad, most people will reply to greetings with *nzuri tu* (lit: only fine), rather than *mbaya* m·*ba*·ya (bad). If things are really good, you can add *sana* *sa*·na (very), or *kabisa* ka·*bee*·sa (totally) instead of *tu*.

What's your name?
Jina lako nani? *jee*·na *la*·koh *na*·nee

My name is …
Jina langu ni … *jee*·na *lan*·goo nee …

I'd like to introduce you to …
Huyu ni … *hoo*·yoo nee …

This is my ...	*Huyu ni ...*	*hoo*·yoo nee ...
child	*mtoto wangu*	m·*toh*·toh *wan*·goo
colleague	*mwenzi wangu*	*mwayn*·zee *wan*·goo
friend	*rafiki yangu*	ra·*fee*·kee *yan*·goo
husband	*mume wangu*	*moo*·may *wan*·goo
partner (intimate)	*mpenzi wangu*	m·*payn*·zee *wan*·goo
wife	*mke wangu*	*m*·kay *wan*·goo

For more kinship terms, see also **family**, page 115 and the **dictionary**.

I'm pleased to meet you.	*Nafurahi kukufahamu.*	na·foo·*ra*·hee koo·koo·fa·*ha*·moo
See you later.	*Baadaye.*	ba·a·*da*·yay
Goodbye.	*Tutaonana.*	too·ta·oh·*na*·na
Bye.	*Kwa heri.*	kwa *hay*·ree
Good night.	*Usiku mwema.*	oo·*see*·koo *mway*·ma
Bon voyage!	*Safari njema!*	sa·*fa*·ree n·*jay*·ma

addressing people

vyeo vya watu

There are two forms of addressing women, different in the level of formality. The word *bibi bee*·bee is more informal than *bi* bee, and can be used by anyone to refer to their grandmother, and by a husband to refer to his wife. The general term *bwana bwa*·na is used for addressing men both in formal and informal situations.

Mr/Sir	*Bwana*	*bwa*·na
Mrs/Madam	*Bi*	bee
Ms/Miss	*Bibi*	*bee*·bee

When addressing an older person or an authority figure, the usual exchange of greetings is:

Respectful greetings.
Shikamoo. shee·ka·*moh*

Thank you for your respectful greetings. (an older person to a younger person)
Marahaba. ma·ra·*ha*·ba

Thank you for your respectful greetings. (a younger person to an older person)
Asante. a·*san*·tay

It's common to address people by their likely position within a family. You can call an elder man 'grandfather', a middle-aged man 'father', and a youthful man 'brother'. In addition, parents are often addressed as the mother or father of one of their children (not necessarily the first born), rather than using the parent's own name, eg *mama Amina ma*·ma a·*mee*·na (Amina's mother), *baba Flora ba*·ba *floh*·ra (Flora's father).

auntie (any elder woman)	*shangazi*	shan·*ga*·zee
brother	*kaka*	*ka*·ka
father	*baba*	*ba*·ba
grandmother	*bibi*	*bee*·bee
grandfather	*babu*	*ba*·boo
mother	*mama*	*ma*·ma
respected elder	*mzee*	m·*zay*
sister	*dada*	*da*·da
sibling/friend	*ndugu*	n·*doo*·goo
uncle (any elder man)	*mjomba*	m·*johm*·ba

For information on addressing children, see **talking with children**, page 105.

hello stranger

The usual greeting for tourists who are presumed not to understand the language is *jambo* **jam**-boh (hello). There are two possible responses – both mean 'hello' too, but while *jambo* indicates that the speaker would rather use English, *sijambo* see-**jam**-boh means that he or she is willing to try a little Swahili.

How are you? (to one person)	*Hujambo?*	hoo·*jam*·boh
How are all of you?	*Hamjambo?*	ham·*jam*·boh
I'm fine.	*Sijambo.*	si·*jam*·boh
We're fine.	*Hatujambo.*	ha·too·*jam*·boh

making conversation

kuzungumza

What a beautiful day!	
Ni siku nzuri sana!	nee *see*·koo n·*zoo*·ree *sa*·na
Nice/Awful weather, isn't it?	
Hali ya hewa ni nzuri/mbaya, sivyo?	*ha*·lee ya *hay*·wa nee n·*zoo*·ree/m·*ba*·ya *seev*·yoh
Do you live here?	
Unakaa hapa?	oo·na·*ka* *ha*·pa
Where are you going?	
Unaenda wapi?	oo·na·*ayn*·da *wa*·pee
What are you doing?	
Unafanya nini?	oo·na·*fa*·nya *nee*·nee
Do you like it here?	
Unapapenda hapa?	oo·na·pa·*payn*·da *ha*·pa
I love it here.	
Napapenda hapa.	na·pa·*payn*·da *ha*·pa
What's this called?	
Hii inaitwa nini?	hee ee·na·*eet*·wa *nee*·nee
That's beautiful, isn't it?	
Inapendeza sana, sivyo?	ee·na·payn·*day*·za *sa*·na *seev*·yo

Where are you coming from?	*Umetoka wapi?*	oo·may·*toh*·ka *wa*·pee
I'm coming from …	*Nimetoka …*	nee·may·*toh*·ka …
home	*nyumbani*	nyoom·*ba*·nee
the market	*sokoni*	soh·*koh*·nee
town	*mjini*	m·*jee*·nee
Are you here on holiday?	*Uko hapa kwa likizo?*	*oo*·koh *ha*·pa kwa lee·*kee*·zoh
I'm here …	*Nipo kwa …*	*nee*·poh kwa …
for a holiday	*likizo*	lee·*kee*·zoh
on business	*biashara*	bee·a·*sha*·ra
to study	*masomo*	ma·*soh*·moh

How long are you here for?

Upo kwa muda gani? — *oo*·poh kwa *moo*·da *ga*·nee

I'm here for (four) weeks/days.

Nipo kwa wiki/ siku (nne). — *nee*·poh kwa *wee*·kee/ *see*·koo (*n*·nay)

local talk

Cool.	*Poa.*	*poh*·a
Great!	*Safi!*	*sa*·fee
Hey!	*We!*	way
How are things?	*Mambo?*	*mam*·boh
It's OK.	*Ni sawa.*	nee *sa*·wa
Just a minute.	*Subiri kidogo.*	soo·*bee*·ree kee·*doh*·goh
Just joking.	*Natania tu.*	na·ta·*nee*·a too
Maybe.	*Labda.*	*lab*·da
No problem.	*Hamna shida.*	*ham*·na *shee*·da
No way!	*Haiwezekani!*	ha·ee·way·zee·*ka*·nee
Sure.	*Sawa.*	*sa*·wa
What's the news?	*Lete habari.*	*lay*·tay ha·*ba*·ree
What's up?	*Vipi?*	*vee*·pee

mind your manners

The following tips on East African etiquette should help you wherever you travel in the region.

- Men and women maintain a formal distance in many social situations. Public displays of affection between sexes don't happen, but friends of the same sex often hold hands when walking around town. Feel honoured if someone of your gender makes such a display of friendship.
- It's fine to wear shorts in tourist areas. However, long pants or skirts, as well as tops with sleeves, are essential when visiting government offices or people's homes, and are preferable at most other times, especially along the Muslim-dominated coast and in rural areas.
- If you accept a gift or treat from someone, they'll often anticipate some reciprocal gesture of friendship, often a meal or gift of equivalent value. Spoken thanks are not so common In East Africa, so don't be surprised if the appreciation isn't expressed verbally.

nationalities

uraia

Where are you from?
Unatoka wapi? oo·na·*toh*·ka *wa*·pee

I'm from ...	*Natoka ...*	na·*toh*·ka ...
America	*Marekani*	ma·ray·*ka*·nee
Australia	*Australia*	a·oo·*stra*·lee·a
Canada	*Kanada*	*ka*·na·da
England	*Uingereza*	oo·een·gay·*ray*·za

age

umri

How old are you?
Una miaka mingapi? oo·na mee·*a*·ka meen·*ga*·pee

How old is your child?
Mtoto wako ana miaka mingapi? m·*toh*·toh *wa*·koh *a*·na mee·*a*·ka meen·*ga*·pee

I'm … years old.
Nina miaka … *nee*·na mee·*a*·ka …

He/She is … years old.
Ana miaka … *a*·na mee·*a*·ka …

Too old!
Mzee mno! m·*zay* *m*·noh

For your age, see **numbers & amounts**, page 37.

occupations & studies

kazi na masomo

What's your occupation?
Unafanya kazi gani? oo·na·*fa*·nya *ka*·zee *ga*·nee

I'm a …	*Mimi ni …*	*mee*·mee nee …
business person	*mfanyabiashara*	m·fa·nya·bee·a·*sha*·ra
chef	*mpishi*	m·*pee*·shee
driver	*dereva*	day·*ray*·va
farmer	*mkulima*	m·koo·*lee*·ma
fisher	*mvuvi*	m·*voo*·vee
journalist	*ripota*	ree·*poh*·ta
soldier	*askari*	as·*ka*·ree
teacher	*mwalimu*	mwa·*lee*·moo

I work in …	*Nafanya kazi kwenye …*	na·*fa*·nya *ka*·zee *kway*·nyay …
administration	*usimamizi*	oo·see·ma·*mee*·zee
health	*afya*	*af*·ya
sales & marketing	*uuzaji*	oo·oo·*za*·jee

I'm …		
retired	*Nimestaafu.*	nee·may·*sta*·foo
self-employed	*Najiajiri.*	na·jee·a·*jee*·ree
unemployed	*Sina kazi sasa.*	*see*·na *ka*·zee *sa*·sa
What are you studying?	*Unasoma masomo gani?*	oo·na·*soh*·ma ma·*soh*·mo *ga*·nee
I'm studying …	*Nasoma …*	na·*soh*·ma …
African music/ dance	*densi/muziki ya kiafrika*	*dayn*·see/moo·*zee*·kee ya kee·af·*ree*·ka
humanities	*sayansi za jamii*	sa·*yan*·see za ja·*mee*
Swahili	*Kiswahili*	kee·swa·*hee*·lee
science	*sayansi*	sa·*yan*·see

family

familia

Do you have a …?	*Una …?*	*oo*·na …
I have/don't have a …	*Nina/Sina …*	*nee*·na/*see*·na …
boyfriend	*mpenzi*	m·*payn*·zee
brother	*kaka*	*ka*·ka
daughter	*binti*	*been*·tee
girlfriend	*mpenzi*	m·*payn*·zee
grandchild	*mjukuu*	m·joo·*koo*
husband	*mume*	*moo*·may
partner/fiancé(e)	*mchumba*	m·*choom*·ba
sister	*dada*	*da*·da
son	*mwana*	*mwa*·na
wife	*mke*	*m*·kay

For more kinship terms, see the **dictionary**.

family tree

Swahili kinship connections through your father's brothers and your mother's sisters are regarded very highly. Rather than being 'uncles' and 'aunts', they're considered your parents too. If they're older than your birth parents they're *mkubwa* m·*koob*·wa ('big'), if they're younger they're *mdogo* m·*doh*·goh ('little'). However, mother's brothers and father's sisters don't get distinguished by age. Many families in East Africa consist of one husband and two or more wives. Children of co-wives generally consider themselves brothers and sisters.

aunt *shangazi* shan·*ga*·zee
(father's sister)

aunt *mama mkubwa* *ma*·ma m·*koob*·wa
(mother's older sister)

aunt *mama mdogo* *ma*·ma m·*doh*·goh
(mother's younger sister)

uncle *mjomba* m·*johm*·ba
(mother's brother)

uncle *baba mkubwa* *ba*·ba m·*koob*·wa
(father's older brother)

uncle *baba mdogo* *ba*·ba m·*doh*·goh
(father's younger brother)

big mother *mama mkubwa* *ma*·ma m·*koob*·wa
(father's wife senior to your mother – the one he married before)

little mother *mama mdogo* *ma*·ma m·*doh*·goh
(father's wife junior to your mother – the one he married after)

Do you have children?
Una watoto? *oo*·na wa·*toh*·toh

How many children do you have?
Una watoto wangapi? *oo*·na wa·*toh*·toh wan·*ga*·pee

Are you married?
Umeoa?/Umeolewa? m/f oo·may·*oh*·a/oo·may·oh·*lay*·wa

I live with someone.
Naishi na mchumba. na·*ee*·shee na m·*choom*·ba

I'm …

divorced	*Tumeachana.*	too·may·a·*cha*·na
married	*Nimeoa/ Nimeolewa.* m/f	nee·may·*oh*·a/ nee·may·oh·*lay*·wa
not married yet	*Sijaoa/ Sijaolewa bado.* m/f	see·ja·*oh*·a/ see·ja·oh·*lay*·wa *ba*·doh
separated	*Tumetengana.*	too·may·tayn·*ga*·na
single	*Mimi sina mpenzi.*	*mee*·mee *see*·na m·*payn*·zee

farewells

kuagana

In contrast to the amount of time East Africans spend greeting each other, they put relatively little energy into saying goodbye. Often farewells simply involve confirming when you'll next meet, then walking away with a simple *haya ha*·ya (OK). Saying goodbyes before a long trip is more involved: hands clasped, the traveller is wished well and told to greet everybody at their destination.

Tomorrow is my last day here.
Kesho ni siku yangu ya mwisho hapa. — *kay*·shoh nee *see*·koo *yan*·goo ya *mwee*·shoh *ha*·pa

It's been great meeting you.
Nimefurahi kukufahamu. — nee·may·foo·*ra*·hee koo·koo·fa·*ha*·moo

well-wishing

Bless you!	*Heri zote!*	*hay*·ree *zoh*·tay
Bon voyage!	*Safari njema!*	sa·*fa*·ree n·*jay*·ma
Congratulations!	*Hongera!*	hohn·*gay*·ra
Good luck!	*Bahati njema!*	ba·*ha*·tee n·*jay*·ma
Happy birthday!	*Heri za siku kuu ya kuzaliwa!*	*hay*·ree za *see*·koo koo ya koo·za·*lee*·wa
Merry Christmas!	*Heri za Krismasi!*	*hay*·ree za krees·*ma*·see

If you come to (Scotland) you can stay with me.

Ukija (Skotland), karibu sana kukaa kwetu.	oo·*kee*·ja (*skoht*·land) ka·*ree*·boo *sa*·na koo·*ka kway*·too

Keep in touch!

Niwasiliane!	nee·wa·see·lee·*a*·nay

Here's my ...	*Hii ni ... yangu.*	hee nee ... *yan*·goo
address	*anwani*	an·*wa*·nee
email address	*anwani ya barua pepe*	an·*wa*·nee ya ba·*roo*·a *pay*·pay
phone number	*simu*	*see*·moo

What's your ...?	*... yako ni nini?*	... *ya*·koh nee *nee*·nee
address	*Anwani*	an·*wa*·nee
email address	*Anwani ya barua pepe*	an·*wa*·nee ya ba·*roo*·a *pay*·pay

common interests

shauku za pamoja

What do you do in your spare time?
Unafanya nini kwa starehe? — oo·na·*fa*·nya *nee*·nee kwa sta·*ray*·hay

Do you like ...?	*Unapenda ...?*	oo·na·*payn*·da ...
I like ...	*Ninapenda ...*	nee·na·*payn*·da ...
I don't like ...	*Sipendi ...*	see·*payn*·dee ...
***bao* (board game)**	*bao*	*ba*·oh
cooking	*kupika*	koo·*pee*·ka
dancing	*kucheza densi*	koo·*chay*·za *dayn*·see
films	*filamu*	fee·*la*·moo
gardening	*kulima bustani*	koo·*lee*·ma boo·*sta*·nee
hiking	*kutembea porini*	koo·taym·*bay*·a poh·*ree*·nee
music	*muziki*	moo·*zee*·kee
painting	*sanaa*	sa·*na*
photography	*kupiga picha*	koo·*pee*·ga *pee*·cha
reading	*kusoma*	koo·*soh*·ma
shopping	*ununuzi*	oo·noo·*noo*·zee
socialising	*kuchanganyika na wengine*	koo·chan·ga·*nyee*·ka na wayn·*gee*·nay
sport	*michezo*	mee·*chay*·zoh
surfing the Internet	*kutumia intaneti*	koo·too·*mee*·a een·ta·*nay*·tee
travelling	*kusafiri*	koo·sa·*fee*·ree
watching TV	*kutazama televisheni*	koo·ta·*za*·ma tay·lay·vee·*shay*·nee

For sporting activities, see **sport**, page 141.

music

muziki

Do you ...?	*Wewe ...?*	*way*·way ...
dance	*hucheza densi*	hoo·*chay*·za *dayn*·see
go to concerts	*huenda kuona muziki*	hoo·*ayn*·da koo·*oh*·na moo·*zee*·kee
listen to music	*husikiliza muziki*	hoo·see·kee·*lee*·za moo·*zee*·kee
play an instrument	*hucheza ala ya muziki*	hoo·*chay*·za *a*·la ya moo·*zee*·kee
sing	*huimba*	hoo·*eem*·ba

Which ... do you like?	*Unapenda ... gani?*	oo·na·*payn*·da ... *ga*·nee
bands	*vikundi*	vee·*koon*·dee
music	*muziki*	moo·*zee*·kee
singers	*waimbaji*	wa·eem·*ba*·jee

Which African music videos do you like?
Unapenda video gani za muziki ya kiafrika? — oo·na·*payn*·da vee·*day*·oh *ga*·nee za moo·*zee*·kee ya kee·af·*ree*·ka

Where can I see music videos by local bands?
Niende wapi kuona video za muziki za vikundi vya hapa? — nee·*ayn*·day *wa*·pee koo·*oh*·na vee·*day*·oh za moo·*zee*·kee za vee·*koon*·dee vya *ha*·pa

drums	*ngoma*	n·*goh*·ma
horns	*siwa*	*see*·wa
shakers	*kayamba*	ka·*yam*·ba
tambourine	*dufu*	*doo*·foo
xylophone	*marimba*	ma·*reem*·ba

blues	*muziki ya Marekani ya kusikitisha*	moo·*zee*·kee ya ma·ray·*ka*·nee ya koo·see·kee·*tee*·sha
brass music	*muziki ya ngoma*	moo·*zee*·kee ya n·*goh*·ma
classical music	*muziki ya Ulaya ya zamani*	moo·*zee*·kee ya oo·*la*·ya ya za·*ma*·nee
electronic music	*muziki ya Ulaya ya kilabuni*	moo·*zee*·kee ya oo·*la*·ya ya kee·la·*boo*·nee
jazz	*jazi*	*ja*·zee
Kenyan dance music	*benga*	*bayn*·ga
pop	*muziki ya kisasa*	moo·*zee*·kee ya kee·*sa*·sa
rock	*roki*	*roh*·kee
popular music of Zanzibar	*taarab*	*ta*·rab
traditional music	*muziki ya mila na desturi*	moo·*zee*·kee ya *mee*·la na day·*stoo*·ree
world music	*muziki ya sehemu mbalimbali za dunia*	moo·*zee*·kee ya say·*hay*·moo m·ba·lee·m·*ba*·lee za doo·*nee*·a
Zairean jazz	*sukosi*	soo·*koh*·see

Off to a concert? See **tickets**, page 49 and **going out**, page 127.

cinema & theatre

sinema na tamthilia

I feel like going to a …	*Nataka kwenda …*	na·*ta*·ka *kwayn*·da …
Did you like the …?	*Ulipenda …?*	oo·lee·*payn*·da …
ballet	*densi*	*dayn*·see
film	*filamu*	fee·*la*·moo
play	*tamthilia*	tam·thee·*lee*·a

What's showing at the cinema/theatre tonight?
Kuna filamu/tamthilia gani leo? — *koo*·na fee·*la*·moo/tam·thee·*lee*·a *ga*·nee *lay*·oh

Is it in English?
Ni kwa Kiingereza? — nee kwa kee·een·gay·*ray*·za

Does it have (English) subtitles?
kuna maandishi (ya Kiingereza) chini? — *koo*·na man·*dee*·shee (ya kee·een·gay·*ray*·za) *chee*·nee

Have you seen …?
Umeona …? — oo·may·*oh*·na …

Who's in it?
Kuna waigizaji gani? — *koo*·na wa·ee·gee·*za*·jee *ga*·nee

It stars …
Mwigizaji mkuu ni … — mwee·gee·*za*·jee m·*koo* nee …

I like …	*Napenda …*	na·*payn*·da …
I don't like …	*Sipendi …*	see·*payn*·dee …
action movies	*filamu zenye misisimko*	fee·*la*·moo *zay*·nyay mee·see·*seem*·koh
African cinema	*filamu za kiafrika*	fee·*la*·moo za kee·af·*ree*·ka
animated films	*katuni hai*	ka·*too*·nee *ha*·ee
comedies	*filamu za kuchekesha*	fee·*la*·moo za koo·chay·*kay*·sha
documentaries	*filamu za hali halisi*	fee·*la*·moo za *ha*·lee ha·*lee*·see
drama	*hadithi kama riwaya*	ha·*dee*·thee *ka*·ma ree·*wa*·ya
Hindi cinema	*filamu za kihindi*	fee·*la*·moo za kee·*heen*·dee
horror movies	*filamu za kutisha*	fee·*la*·moo za koo·*tee*·sha
sci-fi	*hadithi za kubuni za kisayansi*	ha·*d ee*·thee za koo·*boo*·nee za kee·sa·*yan*·see
short films	*filamu fupi*	fee·*la*·moo *foo*·pee
war movies	*filamu kuhusu vita*	fee·*la*·moo koo·*hoo*·soo *vee*·ta

feelings

hisia

Do you feel ...?	*Unasikia ...?*	oo·na·see·*kee*·a ...
I feel ...	*Nasikia ...*	na·see·*kee*·a ...
I don't feel ...	*Sisikii ...*	see·see·*kee* ...
cold	*baridi*	ba·*ree*·dee
happy	*furaha*	foo·*ra*·ha
hot	*joto*	*joh*·toh
hungry	*njaa*	n·*ja*
sad	*masikitiko*	ma·see·kee·*tee*·koh
thirsty	*kiu*	*kee*·oo

If feeling unwell, see **health**, page 183.

mixed feelings		
a little	*kidogo*	kee·*doh*·goh
I'm a little sad.	*Nasikitika kidogo.*	na·see·kee·*tee*·ka kee·*doh*·goh
extremely/very	*sana*	*sa*·na
I'm very happy.	*Nafurahi sana.*	na·foo·*ra*·hee *sa*·na
somewhat	*tu*	too
I feel just OK.	*Nasikia nzuri tu.*	na·see·*kee*·a n·*zoo*·ree too

opinions

maoni

Do you like it?
Unaipenda? oo·na·ee·*payn*·da

What do you think of it?
Unaionaje? oo·na·ee·oh·*na*·jay

I thought it was …	*Nilifikiri ilikuwa …*	nee·lee·fee·*kee*·ree ee·lee·*koo*·wa …
It's …	*Ni …*	nee …
awful	*mbaya sana*	m·*ba*·ya *sa*·na
boring	*ya kuchosha*	ya koo·*choh*·sha
great	*nzuri kabisa*	n·*zoo*·ree ka·*bee*·sa
interesting	*ya kuvutia*	ya koo·voo·*tee*·a
OK	*sawa tu*	*sa*·wa too
strange	*siyo kawaida*	*see*·yoh ka·wa·*ee*·da

politics & social issues

siasa na mada za jamii

Conversing and debating with friends is an important part of daily life in East Africa. People express strong opinions about sport, politics and the latest local gossip.

Which party do you vote for?
Unapiga kura kwa chama gani? oo·na·*pee*·ga *koo*·ra kwa *cha*·ma *ga*·nee

I support the … party.	*Mimi napendelea chama cha …*	*mee*·mee na·payn·day·*lay*·a *cha*·ma cha …
communist	*kikomunisti*	kee·koh·moo·*nee*·stee
democratic	*demokrasia*	day·moh·kra·*see*·a
green	*kijani*	kee·*ja*·nee
socialist	*soshalisti*	soh·sha·*lee*·stee

Did you hear about …?
Ulisikia kuhusu …? oo·lee·see·*kee*·a koo·*hoo*·soo …

I agree/don't agree with …
Nakubali/Sikubali na … na·koo·*ba*·lee/see·koo·*ba*·lee na …

How do people feel about …?
Watu wana maoni gani kuhusu …? *wa*·too *wa*·na ma·*oh*·nee *ga*·nee koo·*hoo*·soo …

abortion	*kutoa mimba*	koo·*toh*·a *meem*·ba
AIDS	*ukimwi*	oo·*keem*·wee
animal rights	*haki za wanyama*	*ha*·kee za wa·*nya*·ma
crime	*uhalifu*	oo·ha·*lee*·foo
drugs	*madawa ya kulevya*	ma·*da*·wa ya koo·*lay*·vya
the economy	*uchumi*	oo·*choo*·mee
education	*elimu*	ay·*lee*·moo
euthanasia	*eutanasia*	ay·oo·ta·na·*see*·a
Christian missionaries	*mamishionari wakristo*	ma·mee·shee·oh·*na*·ree wa·*kree*·stoh
globalisation	*utandawazi*	oo·tan·da·*wa*·zee
human rights	*haki za binadamu*	*ha*·kee za bee·na·*da*·moo
indigenous issues	*mada za wenyeji*	*ma*·da za way·*nyay*·jee
religious fundamentalism	*imani kali ya kidini*	ee·*ma*·nee *ka*·lee ya kee·*dee*·nee
racism	*ubaguzi wa rangi*	oo·ba·*goo*·zee wa *ran*·gee
sexism	*ubaguzi wa kijinsia*	oo·ba·*goo*·zee wa kee·jeen·*see*·a
terrorism	*ugaidi*	oo·ga·*ee*·dee
unemployment	*ukosefu wa kazi*	oo·koh·*say*·foo wa *ka*·zee
the war in …	*vita katika …*	*vee*·ta ka·*tee*·ka …

the environment

mazingira

Is there a … problem here?
Kuna shida ya … hapa? koo·na *shee*·da ya … *ha*·pa

What should be done about …?
Ni afadhali kufanya nini kuhusu …? nee·a·fa·*dha*·lee koo·*fa*·nya *nee*·nee koo·*hoo*·soo …

drought	*ukame*	oo·*ka*·may
endangered species	*spishi zilizo hatarini*	*spee*·shee zee·*lee*·zoh ha·ta·*ree*·nee
genetically modified food	*chakula chenye jini iliyoumbwa*	cha·*koo*·la *chay*·nyay *jee*·nee ee·lee·yoh·*oom*·bwa
hunting	*uwindaji*	oo·ween·*da*·jee
nuclear testing	*majaribio ya nyuklia*	ma·ja·ree·*bee*·oh ya *nyook*·lee·a
ozone layer	*tabaka la hewa ya ozoni*	ta·*ba*·ka la *hay*·wa ya oh·*zoh*·nee
pesticides	*viuavisumbufu*	vee·oo·a·vee·soom·*boo*·foo
petroleum resource exploitation	*utumiaji ovyo wa maliasili ya mafuta*	oo·too·mee·*a*·jee *oh*·vyoh wa ma·lee·a·*see*·lee ya ma·*foo*·ta
poaching	*uwindaji kinyume na sheria*	oo·ween·*da*·jee kee·*nyoo*·may na shay·*ree*·a
pollution	*uchafuzi*	oo·cha·*foo*·zee
recycling programme	*mradi wa urejelezaji*	m·*ra*·dee wa oo·ray·jay·lay·*za*·jee
toxic waste	*taka za sumu*	*ta*·ka za *soo*·moo
water supply	*upatikanaji wa maji*	oo·pa·tee·ka·*na*·jee wa *ma*·jee

Is it a protected …? *… inahifadhiwa?* ee·na·hee·fa·*dhee*·wa …

park	*Mbuga*	m·*boo*·ga
species	*Spishi*	*spee*·shee

where to go

kuenda wapi

What's there to do in the evenings?
Kuna nini kufanya saa za jioni? — koo·na *nee*·nee koo·*fa*·nya sa za jee·*oh*·nee

What's on ...?	*Nini inatokea ...?*	*nee*·nee ee·na·toh·*kay*·a ...
this weekend	*wikendi hii*	wee·*kayn*·dee hee
tonight	*usiku huu*	oo·*see*·koo hoo

I feel like going to a ...	*Nataka kwenda kwenye ...*	na·*ta*·ka *kwayn*·da *kway*·nyay ...
bar	*baa*	ba
beer club	*kilabu*	kee·*la*·boo
café	*mgahawa*	m·ga·*ha*·wa
casino	*kasino*	ka·*see*·noh
coffee house	*mgahawa*	m·ga·*ha*·wa
dance and drumming performance	*ngoma*	n·*goh*·ma
concert	*kusikiliza muziki*	koo·see·kee·*lee*·za moo·*zee*·kee
film	*filamu*	fee·*la*·moo
karaoke bar	*karaoke*	ka·ra·*oh*·kay
nightclub	*klabu ya usiku*	*kla*·boo ya oo·*see*·koo
party	*sherehe*	shay·*ray*·hay
pub	*baa*	ba
restaurant	*hoteli kula*	hoh·*tay*·lee *koo*·la

Are gay people bothered here?
Wasenge huteswa hapa? — wa·*sayn*·gay hoo·*tays*·wa *ha*·pa

Is there a local … guide?	*Kuna mwongozo wa mji kuhusu …?*	koo·na mwohn·*goh*·zoh wa *m*·jee koo·*hoo*·soo …
entertainment	*burudani*	boo·roo·*da*·nee
film	*filamu*	fee·*la*·moo
gay	*wasenge*	wa·*sayn*·gay
music	*muziki*	moo·*zee*·kee

Where can I find …?	*… iko wapi?*	… *ee*·koh *wa*·pee
clubs	*Kilabu/Vilabu*	kee·*la*·boo/vee·*la*·boo
gay venues	*Mahali pa wasenge*	ma·*ha*·lee pa wa·*sayn*·gay
places to eat	*Hoteli kula*	hoh·*tay*·lee *koo*·la
pubs	*Baa*	ba

For more on bars and drinks, see **eating out**, page 153.

invitations

mialiko

What are you doing …?	*Unafanya nini …?*	oo·na·*fa*·nya *nee*·nee …
this weekend	*wikendi hii*	wee·*kayn*·dee hee
tonight	*usiku huu*	oo·*see*·koo hoo

Would you like to go (for a) …?	*Unataka kwenda (kwa) …?*	oo·na·*ta*·ka *kwayn*·da (kwa) …
dancing	*kucheza densi*	koo·*chay*·za *dayn*·see
drink	*kunywa vinywaji*	*koo*·nywa vee·*nywa*·jee
meal	*chakula*	cha·*koo*·la
walk	*kutembea*	koo·taym·*bay*·a

My round.
Ofa yangu. — *oh*·fa *yan*·goo

Do you know a good restaurant?
Unajua hoteli nzuri kula? — oo·na·*joo*·a hoh·*tay*·lee n·*zoo*·ree *koo*·la

We're having a party.
Tutakuwa na sherehe. too·ta·*koo*·wa na shay·*ray*·hay

You should come.
Uje. *oo*·jay

responding to invitations

kuitika mialiko

Sure!
Sawa! *sa*·wa

Yes, I'd love to.
Sawa, nitafurahi. *sa*·wa nee·ta·foo·*ra*·hee

It's very kind of you to invite me.
Wewe ni mwema kunialika. *way*·way nee *mway*·ma koo·nee·a·*lee*·ka

Where shall we go?
Twende wapi? *twayn*·day *wa*·pee

No, I'm afraid I can't.
Asante, lakini siwezi. a·*san*·tay la·*kee*·nee see·*way*·zee

What about tomorrow?
Kesho, je? *kay*·shoh jay

arranging to meet

kupanga kukutana

What time will we meet?
Tukutane saa ngapi? too·koo·*ta*·nay sa n·*ga*·pee

Where will we meet?
Tukutane wapi? too·koo·*ta*·nay *wa*·pee

Let's meet at …	*Tukutane …*	too·koo·*ta*·nay …
(eight) o'clock	*saa (mbili)*	sa (m·*bee*·lee)
the entrance	*mlango wa kuingia*	m·*lan*·goh wa koo·een·*gee*·a

I'll pick you up.
Nitakuja kukuchukua. nee·ta·*koo*·ja koo·koo·choo·*koo*·a

Are you ready?
Tayari? ta·*ya*·ree

I'm ready.
Mimi ni tayari. *mee*·mee nee ta·*ya*·ree

I'll be coming later.
Nitakuja baadaye. nee·ta·*koo*·ja ba·a·*da*·yay

See you later/tomorrow.
Tutaonana baadaye/ kesho. too·ta·oh·*na*·na ba·a·*da*·yay/ *kay*·sho

I'm looking forward to it.
Natarejea sana. na·ta·ray·*jay*·a *sa*·na

Sorry I'm late.
Samahani kwa kuchelewa. sa·ma·*ha*·ni kwa koo·chay·*lay*·wa

Never mind.
Usijali. oo·see·*ja*·lee

For the Swahili time system, go to **time & dates**, page 39.

drugs

madawa ya kulevya

I don't take drugs.
Situmii madawa ya kulevya. see·too·*mee* ma·*da*·wa ya koo·*lay*·vya

I take (*miraa*) occasionally.
Natumia (miraa) mara kwa mara. na·too·*mee*·a (mee·*ra*) *ma*·ra kwa *ma*·ra

Do you want to have a smoke?
Unataka kuvuta? oo·na·*ta*·ka koo·*voo*·ta

Do you have a light?
Una kibiriti? *oo*·na kee·bee·*ree*·tee

I'm high.
Nimelewa. nee·may·*lay*·wa

asking someone out

kuomba miadi

Where would you like to go (tonight)?
Unataka kwenda wapi (jioni hii)? — oo·na·*ta*·ka *kwayn*·da *wa*·pee (jee·*oh*·nee hee)

Would you like to do something (tomorrow)?
Unataka kupanga pamoja (kwa kesho)? — oo·na·*ta*·ka koo·*pan*·ga pa·*moh*·ja (kwa *kay*·shoh)

Yes, I'd love to.
Asante, ndiyo. — a·*san*·tay n·*dee*·yoh

Sorry, I can't.
Asante, siwezi. — a·*san*·tay see·*way*·zee

local talk

He/She is a babe.
Huyu ni mrembo. — *hoo*·yoo nee m·*raym*·boh

He/She is hot.
Huyu amependeza sana sana. — *hoo*·yoo a·may·payn·*day*·za *sa*·na *sa*·na

He's a bastard.
Yeye ni mshenzi. — *yay*·yay nee m·*shayn*·zee

She's a bitch.
Yeye ni jahili. — *yay*·yay nee ja·*hee*·lee

He/She gets around.
Yeye ni jamvi la wageni. — *yay*·yay nee *jam*·vee la wa·*gay*·nee

pick-up lines

kuokota

Would you like a drink?
Unywe kinywaji? — *oony*·way keeny·*wa*·jee

You look like someone I know.
Unafanana mtu ninayejua. — oo·na·fa·*na*·na *m*·too nee·na·yay·*joo*·a

You're a fantastic dancer.
Wewe ni mchezadensi mzuri sana. — *way*·way nee m·chay·za·*dayn*·se m·*zoo*·ree *sa*·na

Can I dance with you?
Tucheze densi? — too·*chay*·zay *dayn*·see

Can I sit here?
Naomba nikae hapa? — na·*ohm*·ba nee·*ka*·ay *ha*·pa

Can I accompany you to your home?
Nikusindikize kwako? — nee·koo·seen·dee·*kee*·zay *kwa*·koh

Can I take you to my place?
Twende kwangu? — *twayn*·day *kwan*·goo

rejections

kukataa

No, thank you.
Hapana, asante. — ha·*pa*·na a·*san*·tay

I'd rather not.
Nisingependa, asante. — nee·seen·gay·*payn*·da a·*san*·tay

I'm here with my girlfriend/boyfriend.
Nipo na mpenzi wangu. — *nee*·poh na m·*payn*·zee *wan*·goo

Excuse me, I have to go now.
Samahani, lazima niondoke sasa. — sa·ma·*ha*·nee *la*·zee·ma nee·ohn·*doh*·kay *sa*·sa

Leave me alone (now)!
Niache (sasa)! — nee·*a*·chay (*sa*·sa)

Piss off!
Toka! — *toh*·ka

getting closer

kukaribisha

I like you very much.
Nakupenda sana. — na·koo·*payn*·da *sa*·na

You're great.
Wewe ni mzuri sana. — *way*·way nee m·*zoo*·ree *sa*·na

Can I kiss you?
Nikubusu? — nee·koo·*boo*·soo

Do you want to come inside for a while?
Unataka kuingia ndani kidogo? — oo·na·*ta*·ka koo·een·*gee*·a n·*da*·nee kee·*doh*·goh

Do you want a massage?
Unataka kuchuliwa? — oo·na·*ta*·ka koo·choo·*lee*·wa

Can I stay over?
Nikae usiku huu? — nee·*ka*·ay oo·*see*·koo hoo

sex

kufanya mapenzi

Kiss me.
Nibusu. — nee·*boo*·soo

I want you.
Nakutaka. — na·koo·*ta*·ka

Let's go to bed.
Twende kitandani. — *twayn*·day kee·tan·*dan*·ee

Touch me here.
Niguse hapa. — nee·*goo*·say *ha*·pa

Do you like this?
Unapenda hii? — oo·na·*payn*·da hee

I like that.
Napenda hiyo. na·*payn*·da *hee*·yoh

I don't like that.
Sipendi hiyo. see·*payn*·dee *hee*·yoh

I think we should stop now.
Tusimame sasa. too·see·*ma*·may *sa*·sa

Do you have a condom?
Una kondom? *oo*·na *kohn*·dom

I have a condom.
Nina kondom. *nee*·na *kohn*·dom

Let's use a condom.
Tutumie kondom. too·too·*mee*·ay *kohn*·dom

I won't do it without protection.
Sitafanya bila kinga. see·ta·*fa*·nya *bee*·la *keen*·ga

It's my first time.
Ni mara yangu ya kwanza. nee *ma*·ra *yan*·goo ya *kwan*·za

Don't worry, I'll do it myself.
Usiwe na wasiwasi, nitafanya mwenyewe. oo·*see*·way na wa·see·*wa*·see nee·ta·*fa*·nya mway·*nyay*·way

It helps to have a sense of humour.
Husaidia kuweza kucheka. hoo·sa·ee·*dee*·a koo·*way*·za koo·*chay*·ka

Oh my God!
Mwenyezi Mungu! mway·*nyay*·zee *moon*·goo

That's great.
Safi sana. *sa*·fee *sa*·na

Easy, lion!
Tulia, simba! too·*lee*·a *seem*·ba

faster	*kwa mwendo*	kwa *mwayn*·doh
harder	*kwa nguvu*	kwa n·*goo*·voo
slower	*pole pole*	*poh*·lay *poh*·lay
softer	*punguza nguvu*	poon·*goo*·za n·*goo*·voo

That was …	*Ilikuwa …*	ee·lee·*koo*·wa …
amazing	*barabara*	ba·*ra*·ba·ra
animalistic	*kama wanyama*	*ka*·ma wa·*nya*·ma
like a dream	*kama ndoto*	*ka*·ma n·*doh*·toh

love

upenzi

Will you go out with me?
Utakuwa mpenzi wangu? oo·ta·*koo*·wa m·*payn*·zee *wan*·goo

Will you meet my parents?
Utakutana na wazazi wangu? oo·ta·koo·*ta*·na na wa·*za*·zee *wan*·goo

I think we're good together.
Nafikiri tunafaa pamoja. na·fee·*kee*·ree too·na·*fa* pa·*moh*·ja

I love you.
Nakupenda. na·koo·*payn*·da

Will you marry me? (man asking woman)
Niolewe. nee·oh·*lay*·way

Will you marry me? (woman asking man)
Nioe. nee·*oh*·ay

is it a he or a she?

Swahili doesn't distinguish between 'he' and 'she' – the language treats all people the same, regardless of gender. The only exceptions are verbs like 'to marry' (a woman is married, while a man marries), and certain sexual terms.

problems

matatizo

Are you seeing someone else?
Umekuwa unatembea na mwengine? — oo·may·*koo*·wa oo·na·taym·*bay*·a na mwayn·*gee*·nay

He/She is just a friend.
Yeye ni rafiki tu. — *yay*·yay nee ra·*fee*·kee too

You're just using me for sex.
Unanitumia kwa mapenzi tu. — oo·na·nee·too·*mee*·a kwa ma·*payn*·zee too

I never want to see you again.
Sitaki kukuona tena daima. — see·*ta*·kee koo·koo·*oh*·na *tay*·na da·*ee*·ma

I don't think it's working out.
Sidhani inafaa. — see·*dha*·nee ee·na·*fa*

We'll work it out.
Itafanikiwa. — ee·ta·fa·nee·*kee*·wa

leaving

kuondoka

I have to leave (tomorrow).
Inabidi niondoke (kesho). — ee·na·*bee*·dee nee·ohn·*doh*·kay (*kay*·sho)

I'll keep in touch.
Nitakuwasiliana. — nee·ta·koo·wa·see·lee·*a*·na

I'll miss you.
Nitakukosa. — nee·ta·koo·*koh*·sa

I'll visit you.
Nitakutembelea. — nee·ta·koo·taym·bay·*lay*·a

religion

imani

What's your religion?
Wewe ni dini gani? — *way*·way nee *dee*·nee *ga*·nee

I'm not religious.
Sina dini. — see·na *dee*·nee

I'm …	*Mimi ni …*	*mee*·mee nee …
agnostic	*agnostiki*	ag·noh·*stee*·kee
Buddhist	*Mbudisti*	m·boo·*dee*·stee
Catholic	*Mkatoliki*	m·ka·toh·*lee*·kee
Christian	*Mkristo*	m·*kree*·stoh
Hindu	*Mhindu*	m·*heen*·doo
Jewish	*Myahudi*	m·ya·*hoo*·dee
Lutheran	*Mluteri*	m·loo·*tay*·ree
Muslim	*Mwislamu*	mwee·*sla*·moo
Protestant	*Mprotestanti*	m·proh·tay·*stan*·tee
Sikh	*Msiik*	m·*seek*

I believe/don't believe in …	*Naamini/ Siamini mambo ya …*	na·a·*mee*·nee/ see·a·*mee*·nee *mam*·boh ya …
fate	*majaliwa*	ma·ja·*lee*·wa
God	*Mungu*	*moon*·goo

Where can I …?	*Naweza … wapi?*	na·*way*·za … *wa*·pee
attend mass	*kuhudhuria misa*	koo·hoo·dhoo·*ree*·a *mee*·sa
attend a service	*kuhudhuria ibada*	koo·hoo·dhoo·*ree*·a ee·*ba*·da
pray	*kusali*	koo·*sa*·lee
worship	*kutoa huduma*	koo·*toh*·a hoo·*doo*·ma

Could I visit the mosque?

Naweza kutembelea msikiti?	na·*way*·za koo·taym·bay·*lay*·a m·see·*kee*·tee

Have you been on a Haj?

Umekwenda kwenye Haji?	oo·may·*kwayn*·da *kway*·nyay *ha*·jee

Are you planning to do a Haj?

Unategemea kwenda kwenye Haji?	oo·na·tay·gay·*may*·a *kwayn*·da *kway*·nyay *ha*·jee

cultural differences

tofauti za utamaduni

Is this a local or national custom?

Je, ni mila ya watu wa hapa, au ni mila ya taifa nzima?	jay nee *mee*·la ya *wa*·too wa *ha*·pa *a*·oo nee *mee*·la ya ta·*ee*·fa n·*zee*·ma

I don't want to offend you.

Sitaki kukusafihi.	see·*ta*·kee koo·koo·sa·*fee*·hee

I'm not used to this.

Sijazoea kufanya hivyo.	see·ja·zoh·*ay*·a koo·*fa*·nya *heev*·yoh

I'd rather not join in.

Napendelea kutoshiriki.	na·payn·day·*lay*·a koo·toh·shee·*ree*·kee

I'll try it.

Nitajaribu.	nee·ta·ja·*ree*·boo

This is different.

Ni tofauti.	nee toh·fa·*oo*·tee

This is interesting.

Ni ya kuvutia.	nee ya koo·voo·*tee*·a

It's against my beliefs.

Inavuka imani zangu.	ee·na·*voo*·ka ee·*ma*·nee *zan*·goo

I didn't mean to do/say anything wrong.

Sikukusudia kufanya/ kusema vibaya.	see·koo·koo·soo·*dee*·a koo·*fa*·nya/ koo·*say*·ma vee·*ba*·ya

When's the gallery/museum open?
Nyumba ya sanaa/ makumbusho hufungua saa ngapi? — nyoom·ba ya sa·*na*/ ma·koom·*boo*·shoh hoo·foon·*goo*·a sa n·*ga*·pee

What kind of art are you interested in?
Unapenda sanaa ya aina gani? — oo·na·*payn*·da sa·*na* ya a·*ee*·na *ga*·nee

What's in the collection?
Kuna sanaa gani hapa? — *koo*·na sa·*na ga*·nee *ha*·pa

What do you think of ...?
Unafikiriaje kuhusu ...? — oo·na·fee·kee·ree·*a*·jay koo·*hoo*·soo ...

It's an exhibition of ...
Ni onyesho la ... — nee oh·*nyay*·shoh la ...

I'm interested in ...
Napenda ... — na·*payn*·da ...

I like the works of ...
Napenda kazi ya ... — na·*payn*·da *ka*·zee ya ...

It reminds me of ...
Inanikumbusha kuhusu ... — ee·na·nee·koom·*boo*·sha koo·*hoo*·soo ...

... art	*sanaa ya ...*	sa·*na* ya ...
African	*kiafrika*	kee·a·*free*·ka
contemporary	*kisasa*	kee·*sa*·sa
figurative	*tamathali*	ta·ma·*tha*·lee
graphic	*grafu*	*gra*·foo
performance	*uigizaju*	oo·ee·gee·*za*·jee

architecture	*ujenzi*	oo·*jayn*·zee
artwork	*usanii*	oo·sa·*nee*
curator	*afisa mkuu wa sanaa*	a·*fee*·sa m·*koo* wa sa·*na*
design	*usanifu*	oo·sa·*nee*·foo
drawing	*mchoro*	m·*choh*·roh
etching	*uchoraji picha kwa asidi*	oo·choh·*ra*·jee *pee*·cha kwa a·*see*·dee
exhibit	*onyesho*	oh·*nyay*·shoh
exhibition hall	*chumba cha maonyesho*	*choom*·ba cha ma·oh·*nyay*·shoh
installation	*ufungaji*	oo·foon·*ga*·jee
Makonde carvings	*uchongaji wa Makonde*	oo·chohn·*ga*·jee wa ma·*kohn*·day
opening	*ufunguzi*	oo·foon·*goo*·zee
painter	*msanii wa rangi*	m·sa·*nee* wa *ran*·gee
painting (canvas)	*picha ya uchoraji*	*pee*·cha ya oo·choh·*ra*·jee
painting (the art)	*uchoraji kwa rangi*	oo·choh·*ra*·jee kwa *ran*·gee
period	*kipindi*	kee·*peen*·dee
permanent collection	*makusanyo ya kudumu*	ma·koo·*sa*·nyoh ya koo·*doo*·moo
print	*picha*	*pee*·cha
sculptor	*mchongaji*	m·chohn·*ga*·jee
sculpture	*uchongaji*	oo·chohn·*ga*·jee
statue	*sanamu*	sa·*na*·moo
studio	*chumba cha msanii*	*choom*·ba cha m·sa·*nee*
style	*mtindo*	m·*teen*·doh
technique	*mbinu*	m·*bee*·noo
Tingatinga paintings	*tingatinga*	teen·ga·*teen*·ga
wood carving	*uchongaji wa mbao*	oo·chohn·*ga*·jee wa m·*ba*·oh

sporting interests

kupenda michezo

What sport do you …?	… *mchezo gani?*	… m·*chay*·zoh *ga*·nee
play	*Unacheza*	oo·na·*chay*·za
follow	*Unafuata*	oo·na·foo·*a*·ta
I play/do …	*Nacheza …*	na·*chay*·za …
I follow …	*Nafuata …*	na·foo·*a*·ta …
athletics	*michezo ya riadha*	mee·*chay*·zo ya ree·*a*·dha
basketball	*mpira wa kikapu*	m·*pee*·ra wa kee·*ka*·poo
boxing	*ndondi*	n·*dohn*·dee
football (soccer)	*soka*	*so*·ka
karate	*kareti*	ka·*ray*·tee
netball	*netibali*	nay·tee·*ba*·lee
running	*kukimbia*	koo·keem·*bee*·a
swimming	*kuogelea*	koo·oh·gay·*lay*·a
tennis	*tenesi*	tay·*nay*·see
volleyball	*mpira wa wavu*	m·*pee*·ra wa *wa*·voo

Do you like (cricket)?
Unapenda (kriketi)? — oo·na·*payn*·da (kree·*kay*·tee)

Yes, very much.
Ndiyo, sana. — n·*dee*·yoh *sa*·na

Not really.
Siyo sana. — *see*·yo *sa*·na

I like watching it.
Napenda kutazama. — na·*payn*·da koo·ta·*za*·ma

Who's your favourite ...?	*Unapendelea ... gani?*	oo·na·payn·day·*lay*·a ... *ga*·nee
long-distance runner	*mkimbiaji*	m·keem·bee·*a*·jee
sportsperson	*mwanamichezo*	mwa·na·mee·*chay*·zoh
team	*timu*	*tee*·moo

For more sports, see the **dictionary**.

going to a game

kuangalia mchezo

Would you like to go to a game?
Unataka kwenda kwenye mchezo? — oo·na·*ta*·ka *kwayn*·da *kwa*·nyay m·*chay*·zoh

Who are you supporting?
Unapendelea nani? — oo·na·payn·day·*lay*·a *na*·nee

Who's playing/winning?
Nani wanacheza/ wanashinda? — *na*·nee wa·na·*chay*·za/ wa·na·*sheen*·da

That was a bad/great game!
Mchezo ulikuwa mbaya/safi sana! — m·*chay*·zoh oo·lee·*koo*·wa m·*ba*·ya/*sa*·fee *sa*·na

scoring

What's the score?
Nini matokeo? — *nee*·nee ma·toh·*kay*·oh

It's (a) ...	*Ni ...*	nee ...
draw/even	*sare*	*sa*·ray
love (zero)	*bila*	*bee*·la
match point	*pointi ya mechi*	poh·*een*·tee ya *may*·chee
nil (zero)	*sifuri*	see·*foo*·ree

playing sport

kucheza michezo

Do you want to play?	
Unataka kucheza?	oo·na·*ta*·ka koo·*chay*·za
Can I join in?	
Naweza kucheza?	na·*way*·za koo·*chay*·za
That would be great.	
Safi.	*sa*·fee
I can't.	
Siwezi.	see·*way*·zee
I have an injury.	
Nimejeruhiwa.	nee·may·jay·roo·*hee*·wa
Your/My point.	
Pointi yako/yangu.	poh·*een*·tee *ya*·koh/*yan*·goo
Kick/Pass it to me!	
Nitoe pasi!	nee·*toh*·ay *pa*·see
You're a good player.	
Wewe ni mchezaji mzuri.	*way*·way nee m·chay·*za*·jee m·*zoo*·ree
Thanks for the game.	
Asante kwa mchezo.	a·*san*·tay kwa m·*chay*·zoh

Where's a good place to ...?	*Wapi ni pazuri ...?*	*wa*·pee nee pa·*zoo*·ree ...
fish	*kuvua samaki*	koo·*voo*·a sa·*ma*·kee
go horse riding	*kutembea kwa farasi*	koo·taym·*bay*·a kwa fa·*ra*·see
run	*kukimbia*	koo·keem·*bee*·a

Where's a ...?	*Kuna ... wapi?*	*koo*·na ... *wa*·pee
golf course	*uwanja wa gofu*	oo·*wan*·ja wa *goh*·foo
gym	*kilabu ya mazoezi*	kee·*la*·boo ya ma·zoh·*ay*·zee
swimming pool	*bwawa la kuogelea*	*bwa*·wa la koo·oh·gay·*lay*·a
tennis court	*kiwanja cha tenesi*	kee·*wan*·ja cha tay·*nay*·see

What's the charge per ...?	*Ni bei gani kwa ...?*	nee bay *ga*·nee kwa ...
day	*siku*	*see*·koo
game	*mchezo*	m·*chay*·zoh
hour	*saa*	sa
visit	*kutembelea*	koo·taym·bay·*lay*·a

Do I have to be a member to attend?
Ni lazima kuwa mwanachama ili kuingia? — nee *la*·zee·ma *koo*·wa mwa·na·*cha*·ma *ee*·lee koo·een·*gee*·a

Is there a women-only session?
Kuna kipindi kwa wanawake tu? — *koo*·na kee·*peen*·dee kwa wa·na·*wa*·kay too

Where are the changing rooms?
Chumba cha kubadilisha nguo kiko wapi? — *choom*·ba cha koo·ba·dee·*lee*·sha n·*goo*·oh *kee*·koh *wa*·pee

Can I hire a (court)?
Naweza kukodisha (kiwanja)? — na·*way*·za koo·koh·*dee*·sha kee·*wan*·ja

sports talk

What a ...!	*... gani!*	... *ga*·nee
goal	*goli*	*goh*·lee
hit	*ushindi*	oo·*sheen*·dee
kick	*teke*	*tay*·kay
pass	*pasi*	*pa*·see
performance	*onyesho*	oh·*nyay*·shoh

football/soccer

soka

Who plays for (Yanga)?

Nani ni wachezaji wa (Yanga)?	*na*·nee nee wa·chay·*za*·jee wa (*yan*·ga)

He's a great (player).

Yeye ni (mchezaji) mzuri sana.	*yay*·yay nee (m·chay·*za*·jee) m·*zoo*·ree *sa*·na

Which team is at the top of the league?

Timu gani ni juu ya ligi?	*tee*·moo *ga*·nee nee joo ya *lee*·gee

What a great/terrible team!

Timu hiyo ni safi/ mbaya sana!	*tee*·moo *hee*·yoh nee *sa*·fee/ m·*ba*·ya sa·na

ball	*mpira*	m·*pee*·ra
fan	*mshabiki*	m·sha·*bee*·kee
goal	*mlango*	m·*lan*·goh
player	*mchezaji wa mpira*	m·chay·*za*·jee wa m·*pee*·ra
red card	*kadi nyekundu*	*ka*·dee nyay·*koon*·doo
referee	*rifa/refa*	*ree*·fa/*ray*·fa

water sports

michezo ya maji

Where's a good diving site?

Wapi ni pazuri kuzamia?	*wa*·pee nee pa·*zoo*·ree koo·za·*mee*·a

Can I book a lesson?

Naweza kupanga mafunzo?	na·*way*·za koo·*pan*·ga ma·*foon*·zoh

Is the equipment regularly maintained?

Vifaa huthibitishwa vizuri?	vee·*fa* hoo·thee·bee·*tee*·shwa vee·*zoo*·ree

Can I hire (a) …?	*Nataka kukodisha …*	na·*ta*·ka koo·koh·*dee*·sha …
boat	*boti*	*boh*·tee
canoe	*mtumbwi*	m·*toom*·bwee
diving gear	*vifaa vya kuzamia*	vee·*fa* vya koo·za·*mee*·a
kayak	*kayaki*	ka·*ya*·kee
life jacket	*jaketi la kuokolea*	ja·*kay*·tee la ku·oh·koh·*lay*·a
water-skis	*skii za maji*	skee za *ma*·jee
wetsuit	*vazi la kuzamia*	*va*·zee la koo·za·*mee*·a

Are there any …?	*Kuna …?*	*koo*·na …
currents	*mikondo*	mee·*kohn*·doh
reefs	*miamba*	mee·*am*·ba
rips	*mikondo*	mee·*kohn*·doh
sharks	*papa*	*pa*·pa
water hazards	*hatari katika maji*	ha·*ta*·ree ka·*tee*·ka *ma*·jee
whales	*nyangumi*	nyan·*goo*·mee

cave	*pango*	*pan*·goh
coral formations	*mwamba wa tumbawe*	*mwam*·ba wa toom·*ba*·way
diving boat	*boti ya safari za kuzamia*	*boh*·tee ya sa·*fa*·ree za koo·za·*mee*·a
guide	*kiongozi*	kee·ohn·*goh*·zee
motorboat	*motaboti*	moh·ta·*boh*·tee
night dive	*kuzamia wakati wa usiku*	koo·za·*mee*·a wa·*ka*·tee wa oo·*see*·koo
sailing boat	*chombo chenye tanga*	*chohm*·boh *chay*·nyay *tan*·ga
surfboard	*ubao wa kutelezea*	oo·*ba*·oh wa koo·tay·lay·*zay*·a
wall dive	*kuzamia kwenye ukuta*	koo·za·*mee*·a *kway*·nyay oo·*koo*·ta
(wind)surfing	*kuteleza (na tanga)*	koo·tay·*lay*·za (na *tan*·ga)
wreck	*msambaratiko*	m·sam·ba·ra·*tee*·koh

hiking

kutembea porini

Where can I ...?	*Naweza ... wapi?*	na·*way*·za ... *wa*·pee
buy supplies	*kununua mahitaji*	koo·noo·*noo*·a ma·hee·*ta*·jee
find someone who knows this area	*kumkuta mtu anayejua eneo hili*	koom·*koo*·ta *m*·too a·na·yay·*joo*·a ay·*nay*·oh *hee*·lee
get a map	*kununua ramani*	koo·noo·*noo*·a ra·*ma*·nee
hire hiking gear	*kukodisha vifaa vya kutembea porini*	koo·koh·*dee*·sha vee·*fa* vya koo·taym·*bay*·a poh·*ree*·nee

Do we need to take ...?	*Inabidi tuchukue ...?*	ee·na·*bee*·dee too·choo·*koo*·ay ...
food	*chakula*	cha·*koo*·la
a sheet and cover	*shuka na tandiko*	*shoo*·ka na tan·*dee*·koh
water	*maji*	*ma*·jee

We'd like to go wildlife spotting.
Tunataka kwenda kutafuta wanyama pori. — too·na·*ta*·ka *kwayn*·da koo·ta·*foo*·ta wa·*nya*·ma *poh*·ree

Can you recommend a trekking company?
Unaweza kupendekeza kampuni ya safari kwa miguu? — oo·na·*way*·za koo·payn·day·*kay*·za kam·*poo*·nee ya sa·*fa*·ree kwa mee·*goo*

Do we need a guide?
Inabidi tuwe na kiongozi? — ee·na·*bee*·dee *too*·way na kee·ohn·*goh*·zee

Are there guided treks?
Kuna safari kwa miguu kwenye viongozi? — koo·na sa·*fa*·ree kwa mee·*goo* *kway*·nyay vee·ohn·*goh*·zee

Are park fees included?
Ada za hifadhi zinazingatiwa? — *a*·da za hee·*fa*·dhee zee·na·zeen·ga·*tee*·wa

Will we be staying in huts?
Tutakaa kibandani? — too·ta·*ka* kee·ban·*dan*·ee

Will we be camping?
Tutapiga hema? — too·ta·*pee*·ga *hay*·ma

I'd like to hire a porter.
Nataka kuajiri mchukuzi. — na·*ta*·ka koo·a·*jee*·ree m·choo·*koo*·zee

Can I see your permit?
Naomba kuona kibali chako. — na·*ohm*·ba koo·*ohn*·a kee·*ba*·lee *cha*·koh

Which route would you recommend?
Unapendekeza njia gani? — oo·na·payn·day·*kay*·za n·*jee*·a *ga*·nee

How high is the climb?
Ni mita ngapi juu? — nee *mee*·ta n·*ga*·pee joo

How long is the trail?
Njia ni urefu gani? — n·*jee*·a nee oo·*ray*·foo *ga*·nee

Is it safe?
Ni salama? — nee sa·*la*·ma

Which is the … route?	*Njia gani … zaidi?*	n·*jee*·a *ga*·nee … za·*ee*·dee
easiest	*ni rahisi*	nee ra·*hee*·see
shortest	*ni fupi*	nee *foo*·pee

Is the track …?	*Njia …?*	n·*jee*·a …
icy	*yenye barafu*	*yay*·nyay ba·*ra*·foo
(well-)marked	*iliotiwa alama (nzuri)*	ee·lee·oh·*tee*·wa a·*la*·ma (n·*zoo*·ree)
very steep	*huongezeka ghafla*	hoo·ohn·gay·*zay*·ka *ga*·fla

Does this path go to …?
Njia hii inaenda …? n·*jee*·a hee ee·na·*ayn*·da …

Is the water OK to drink?
Maji yananywika? *ma*·jee ya·nany·*wee*·ka

I think I'm suffering from altitude sickness.
Nadhani nimeugua kwa sababu ya kimo. na·*dha*·nee nee·may·oo·*goo*·a kwa sa·*ba*·boo ya *kee*·moh

I need to descend immediately.
Ni lazima nitelemke sasa hivi. nee *la*·zee·ma nee·tay·*laym*·kay *sa*·sa *hee*·vee

Thanks for running a great trek.
Asante kwa kuongoza safari nzuri sana. a·*san*·tay kwa koo·ohn·*goh*·za sa·*fa*·ree n·*zoo*·ree *sa*·na

Thanks for carrying our bags.
Asante kwa kubeba mizigo yetu. a·*san*·tay kwa koo·*bay*·ba mee·*zee*·goh *yay*·too

Where can I find the …?	*… iko wapi?*	… *ee*·koh *wa*·pee
camping ground	*Uwanja wa kupiga kambi*	oo·*wan*·ja wa koo·*pee*·ga *kam*·bee
nearest village	*Kijiji jirani*	kee·*jee*·jee jee·*ra*·nee
showers	*Bafuni*	ba·*foo*·nee
toilet	*Choo*	cho

active volcano	*volkeno hai*	vol·*kay*·noh *ha*·ee
forest	*msitu*	m·*see*·too
glacier	*uwanja wa barafu*	oo·*wan*·ja wa ba·*ra*·foo
grassland	*ukanda wa mbuga*	oo·*kan*·da wa m·*boo*·ga
mountain peak	*kilele cha mlima*	kee·*lay*·lay cha m·*lee*·ma
national park	*hifadhi ya taifa*	hee·*fa*·dhee ya ta·*ee*·fa
summit	*kilele*	kee·*lay*·lay
wildlife reserve	*hifadhi ya wanyama*	hee·*fa*·dhee ya wa·*nya*·ma

beach

ufukwe

Where's the … beach?	*Ufukwe … uko wapi?*	oo·*fook*·way … oo·koh wa·pee
nearest	*karibu zaidi*	ka·*ree*·boo za·*ee*·dee
nudist	*kwa watu uchi*	kwa *wa*·too *oo*·chee
public	*kwa hadhara*	kwa *ha*·dha·ra

How much for a/an …?	*Ni bei gani kwa …?*	nee bay *ga*·nee kwa …
chair	*kiti*	*kee*·tee
hut	*kibanda*	kee·*ban*·da
umbrella	*mwamvuli*	mwam·*voo*·lee

Where can I find the …?	*… iko wapi?*	… *ee*·koh *wa*·pee
showers	*Bafuni*	ba·*foo*·nee
toilets	*Choo*	cho

Do we have to pay?
Ni lazima kulipa? — nee *la*·zee·ma koo·*lee*·pa

Is it safe to dive/swim here?
Ni salama kuzamia/kuogelea hapa? — nee sa·*la*·ma koo·za·*mee*·a/koo·oh·gay·*lay*·a *ha*·pa

What time is high/low tide?
Maji kujaa/kupwa ni saa ngapi? — *ma*·jee koo·*ja*/*koop*·wa nee sa n·*ga*·pee

signs

Usipige Mbizi	oo·see·*pee*·gay m·*bee*·zee	**No Diving**
Usiogelee	oo·see·oh·gay·*lay*	**No Swimming**

weather

hali ya hewa

What's the weather like?
Hali ya hewa ikoje? — *ha*·lee ya *hay*·wa ee·*koh*·jay

It's ...		
cold	*Ni baridi.*	nee ba·*ree*·dee
hot	*Ni joto.*	nee *joh*·toh
raining	*Inanyesha mvua.*	ee·na·*nyay*·sha m·*voo*·a
snowing	*Theluji inaanguka.*	thay·*loo*·jee ee·na·an·*goo*·ka
sunny	*Kuna jua.*	*koo*·na *joo*·a
windy	*Kuna upepo.*	*koo*·na oo·*pay*·poh

... season	*kipindi cha ...*	kee·*peen*·dee cha ...
cold	*baridi*	ba·*ree*·dee
dry	*kiangazi*	kee·an·*ga*·zee
harvest	*kuvuna*	koo·*voo*·na
hot	*joto*	*joh*·toh
rainy	*mvua*	m·*voo*·a

Where can I buy ...?	*Ninunue ... wapi?*	nee·noo·*noo*·ay ... *wa*·pee
a rain jacket	*koti la mvua*	*koh*·tee la m·*voo*·a
an umbrella	*mwamvuli*	mwam·*voo*·lee

flora & fauna

mimea na wanyama

What ... is that?	*Ni ... gani?*	nee ... *ga*·nee
animal	*mnyama*	m·*nya*·ma
plant	*mmea*	m·*may*·a

Is it ...?	*Ni ...?*	nee ...
dangerous	*yenye hatari*	*yay*·nyay ha·*ta*·ree
endangered	*spishi zilizo hatarini*	*spee*·shee zee·*lee*·zoh ha·ta·*ree*·nee
poisonous	*yenye sumu*	*yay*·nyay *soo*·moo
protected	*hifadhiwa*	hee·fa·*dhee*·wa

What's it used for?
Ina matumizi gani? — *ee*·na ma·too·*mee*·zee *ga*·nee

Can you eat the fruit?
Tunda linalika? — *toon*·da lee·na·*lee*·ka

We're very keen to see (elephants).
Tunataka sana kuona (tembo). — too·na·*ta*·ka *sa*·na koo·*oh*·na (*taym*·boh)

Yesterday we saw (impala).
Jana tuliona (swala). — *ja*·na too·lee·*oh*·na (*swa*·la)

local plants & animals

baobab	*mbuyu*	m·*boo*·yoo
coconut palm	*mnazi*	m·*na*·zee
mangrove	*mkoko*	m·*koh*·koh
***miombo* woodland**	*msitu wa miombo*	m·*see*·too wa mee·*ohm*·boh
rainforest	*msitu wa mvua*	m·*see*·too wa m·*voo*·a
savanna	*mbuga*	m·*boo*·ga
camel	*ngamia*	nga·*mee*·a
crocodile	*mamba*	*mam*·ba
gazelle	*swala/swara*	*swa*·la/*swa*·ra
giraffe	*twiga*	*twee*·ga
hippopotamus	*kiboko*	kee·*boh*·koh
monkey	*tumbili*	toom·*bee*·lee
python	*chatu*	*cha*·too
sable antelope	*pala hala*	*pa*·la *ha*·la
spitting cobra	*swila*	*swee*·la
zebra	*punda milia*	*poon*·da mee·*lee*·a

For the Big Five animals, see the box on page 197.

basics

misingi

breakfast	*chai ya asubuhi*	*cha*·ee ya a·soo·*boo*·hee
lunch	*chakula cha mchana*	cha·*koo*·la cha m·*cha*·na
dinner	*chakula cha jioni*	cha·*koo*·la cha jee·*oh*·nee
snack	*kumbwe*	*koom*·bway
eat v	*kula*	*koo*·la
drink v	*kunywa*	*koony*·wa

Is there food?
Kuna chakula? — *koo*·na cha·*koo*·la

Can you cook for us?
Unaweza kutupikia chakula? — oo·na·*way*·za koo·too·pee·*kee*·a cha·*koo*·la

I'd like …
Nataka … — na·*ta*·ka …

I'm starving!
Nina njaa kali! — *nee*·na n·*ja ka*·lee

finding a place to eat

kutafuta mahali kula

Can you recommend a …?	*Unaweza kupendekeza …?*	oo·na·*way*·za koo·payn·day·*kay*·za …
bar	*baa*	ba
café/coffee house	*mgahawa*	m·ga·*ha*·wa
restaurant	*hoteli kula*	hoh·*tay*·lee *koo*·la

Where would you go for …?	*Unapenda kwenda wapi kwa …?*	oo·na·*payn*·da *kwayn*·da *wa*·pee kwa …
a celebration	*sherehe*	shay·*ray*·hay
a cheap meal	*chakula rahisi*	cha·*koo*·la ra·*hee*·see
Chinese food	*chakula cha kichina*	cha·*koo*·la cha kee·*chee*·na
European food	*chakula cha kiulaya*	cha·*koo*·la cha kee·oo·*la*·ya
Indian food	*chakula cha kihindi*	cha·*koo*·la cha kee·*heen*·dee
local specialities	*chakula cha kienyeji*	cha·*koo*·la cha kee·ay·*nyay*·jee

I'd like to reserve a table for …	*Nataka kuhifadhi meza kwa …*	na·*ta*·ka koo·hee·*fa*·dhee *may*·za kwa …
(two) people	*watu (wawili)*	*wa*·too (wa·*wee*·lee)
(eight) o'clock	*saa (mbili)*	sa (m·*bee*·lee)

I'd like …, please.	*Naomba …*	na·*ohm*·ba …
a children's menu	*menyu kwa watoto*	*may*·nyoo kwa wa·*toh*·toh
the drink list	*orodha ya vinywaji*	oh·*roh*·dha ya veeny·*wa*·jee
a half portion	*nusu*	*noo*·soo
a menu (in English)	*menyu (kwa Kiingereza)*	*may*·nyoo (kwa kee·een·gay·*ray*·za)
a table for (five)	*meza kwa (watano)*	*may*·za kwa (wa·*ta*·noh)
the nonsmoking section	*eneo ambalo hakuna sigara*	ay·*nay*·oh am·*ba*·loh ha·*koo*·na see·*ga*·ra
the smoking section	*eneo kwa kuvuta sigara*	ay·*nay*·oh kwa koo·*voo*·ta see·*ga*·ra

listen for ...	
Tumefunga. too·may·*foon*·ga	**We're closed.**
Tumejaa. too·may·*ja*	**We're full.**
Dakika moja. da·*kee*·ka *moh*·ja	**One moment.**
Unataka kukaa wapi? oo·na·*ta*·ka koo·*ka* *wa*·pee	**Where would you like to sit?**
Nikusaidiaje? nee·koo·sa·ee·dee·*a*·jay	**What can I get for you?**
Karibu. ka·*ree*·boo	**Here you go.**
Karibu chakula. ka·*ree*·boo cha·*koo*·la	**Enjoy your meal.**

Are you still serving food?
Kuna chakula bado? — *koo*·na cha·*koo*·la *ba*·doh

How long is the wait?
Inabidi kusubiri kwa muda gani? — ee·na·*bee*·dee koo·soo·*bee*·ree kwa *moo*·da *ga*·nee

restaurant

hoteli

What would you recommend?
Chakula gani ni kizuri? — cha·*koo*·la *ga*·nee nee kee·*zoo*·ree

What's in that dish?
Chakula hicho kinapikwaje? — cha·*koo*·la *hee*·choh kee·na·peek·*wa*·jay

I'll have that.
Nataka hicho. — na·*ta*·ka *hee*·choh

Does it take long to prepare?

Inachukua muda mrefu kuandaa?	ee·na·choo·*koo*·a *moo*·da m·*ray*·foo koo·an·*da*

Are the meals freshly cooked?

Milo hupikwa sasa hivi au zamani kidogo?	*mee*·loh hoo·*peek*·wa *sa*·sa *hee*·vee *a*·oo za·*ma*·ni kee·*doh*·goh

Is it self-serve?

Ni lazima kujihuduma?	nee *la*·zee·ma koo·jee·hoo·*doo*·ma

Is there a cover charge?

Kuna bei ya kuingia?	*koo*·na bay ya koo·een·*gee*·a

Is service included in the bill?

Bili inazingatia huduma?	*bee*·lee ee·na·zeen·*ga*·tee·a hoo·*doo*·ma

Are these complimentary?

Hizi ni bure?	*hee*·zee nee *boo*·ray

look for ...

Kiamsha Hamu	kee·*am*·sha *ha*·moo	Appetisers
Supu	*soo*·poo	Soups
Chakula Kikuu	cha·*koo*·la kee·*koo*	Main Courses
Saladi	sa·*la*·dee	Salads
Vinginevyo	veen·gee·*nay*·vyo	Side Dishes
Kitindamlo	kee·teen·da·*m*·loh	Desserts
Vinywaji	veeny·*wa*·jee	Drinks
Soda	*soh*·da	Soft Drinks
Pombe Kali	*pohm*·bay *ka*·lee	Spirits
Bia	*bee*·a	Beers
Mvinyo Mwenye Povu	m·*vee*·nyoh *mway*·nyay *poh*·voo	Sparkling Wines
Mvinyo Mweupe	m·*vee*·nyoh mway·*oo*·pay	White Wines
Mvinyo Mwekundu	m·*vee*·nyoh mway·*koon*·doo	Red Wines

For more words you might see on a menu, see the **culinary reader**, page 173.

I'd like …	*Nataka …*	na·*ta*·ka …
a local speciality	*chakula maalum cha kienyeji*	cha·*koo*·la *ma*·loom cha kee·ay·*nyay*·jee
a meal fit for a king	*chakula kama kingefaa kwa mfalme*	cha·*koo*·la *ka*·ma keen·gay·*fa* kwa m·*fal*·may
a sandwich	*sandwichi*	sand·*wee*·chee
that dish	*chakula hicho*	cha·*koo*·la *hee*·choh
the chicken	*kuku*	*koo*·koo

I'd like it with/ without …	*Nataka na/ bila …*	na·*ta*·ka na/ *bee*·la …
cheese	*chizi*	*chee*·zee
chilli (sauce)	*(mchuzi wa) pilipili hoho*	(m·*choo*·zee wa) pee·lee·*pee*·lee *hoh*·hoh
garlic	*kitunguu saumu*	kee·toon·*goo* sa·*oo*·moo
peanuts	*karanga*	ka·*ran*·ga
oil	*mafuta*	ma·*foo*·ta
pepper	*pilipili*	pee·lee·*pee*·lee
salad	*saladi*	sa·*la*·dee
salt	*chumvi*	*choom*·vee
vinegar	*siki*	*see*·kee
tomato sauce/ ketchup	*mchuzi wa nyanya*	m·*choo*·zee wa *nya*·nya

For additional items, see the **culinary reader**. For other specific meal requests, see **vegetarian & special meals**, page 171.

listen for …

Unapenda…? oo·na·*payn*·da …	**Do you like …?**
Napendekeza … na·payn·day·*kay*·za …	**I suggest the …**
Unapenda kipikwaje? oo·na·*payn*·da kee·peek·*wa*·jay	**How would you like that cooked?**

at the table

mezani

Please bring …	*Lete …*	*lay*·tay …
a cloth	*kitambaa kufunika meza*	kee·tam·*ba* koo·foo·*nee*·ka *may*·za
a (wine-) glass	*glasi (ya mvinyo)*	*gla*·see (ya m·*vee*·nyoh)
a serviette	*kitambaa cha mikono*	kee·tam·*ba* cha mee·*koh*·noh
the bill	*bili*	*bee*·lee

I didn't order that.
Sikuagiza hicho. — see·koo·a·*gee*·za *hee*·choh

There's a mistake in the bill.
Kuna kosa kwenye bili. — *koo*·na *koh*·sa *kwayn*·yay *bee*·lee

I'll pay!
Nitalipa! — nee·ta·*lee*·pa

I invited you, you're my guest.
Nilikukaribisha, wewe ni mgeni wangu. — nee·lee·koo·ka·ree·*bee*·sha *way*·way nee m·*gay*·nee *wan*·goo

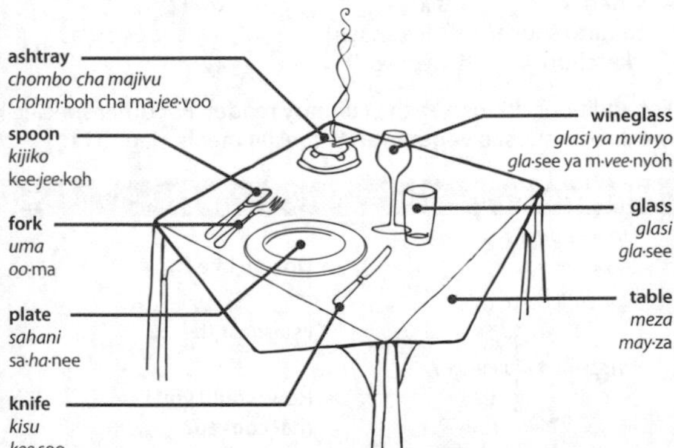

talking food

kuongea kuhusu chakula

I love this dish.
Napenda sana chakula hiki. — na·*payn*·da *sa*·na cha·*koo*·la *hee*·kee

I love the local cuisine.
Napenda sana chakula cha kienyeji. — na·*payn*·da *sa*·na cha·*koo*·la cha kee·ay·*nyay*·jee

That was delicious!
Chakula kitamu sana! — cha·*koo*·la kee·*ta*·moo *sa*·na

street food		
chapati	cha·*pa*·tee	a round bread cooked like a pancake
chipsi	*chee*·psee	deep-fried potatoes
chipsi mayai	*chee*·psee ma·*ya*·ee	omelette made with chips
chungwa	*choon*·gwa	orange (usually eaten by squeezing the juice into your mouth)
kande	*kan*·day	a stew with beans & whole kernels of maize
mahindi	ma·*heen*·dee	grilled corn on the cob
mkate wa mayai	m·*ka*·tay wa ma·*ya*·ee	a mixture of eggs, ground meat, onion & spices, fried until brown
mishkaki	meesh·*ka*·kee	meat on a skewer, grilled until crisp
samosa/ sambusa	sa·*moh*·sa/ sam·*boo*·sa	a mixture of meat, onions, vegetables & spices fried in a triangular pastry
supu	*soo*·poo	soup with a piece of meat
wali maharagwe	*wa*·lee ma·ha·*ra*·gway	cooked rice & beans

My compliments to the chef.

Mwambie mpishi chakula ni kizuri.	mwam·*bee*·ay m·*pee*·shee cha·*koo*·la nee kee·*zoo*·ree

I'm full.

Nimeshiba.	nee·may·*shee*·ba

This isn't very good.

Chakula hiki si kizuri sana.	cha·*koo*·la *hee*·kee see kee·*zoo*·ree *sa*·na

This is too spicy.

Chakula hiki ni mno chenye viungo.	cha·*koo*·la *hee*·kee nee *m*·noh *chay*·nyay vee·*oon*·goh

methods of preparation

mibinu ya kuandaa

I'd like it …	*Nataka …*	na·*ta*·ka …
I don't want it …	*Sitaki …*	si·*ta*·kee …
boiled	*ya kuchemshwa*	ya koo·*chaym*·shwa
broiled	*ya kuchomwa*	ya koo·*chohm*·wa
fried	*ya kukaangwa*	ya koo·*kan*·gwa
grilled	*ya kuchomwa*	ya koo·*chohm*·wa
mashed	*ya kuponda*	ya koo·*pohn*·da
medium	*ya kuiva wastani*	ya koo·*ee*·va *wa*·sta·nee
rare	*ya kuiva kidogo*	ya koo·*ee*·va kee·*doh*·goh
reheated	*kiwekwe moto tena*	kee·*wayk*·way *moh*·toh *tay*·na
steamed	*ya kupikwa kwa mvuke*	ya koo·*pee*·kwa kwa m·*voo*·kay
well-done	*ya kuiva sana*	ya koo·*ee*·va *sa*·na
with the dressing/sauce on the side	*kwenye mchuzi pembeni*	*kway*·nyay m·*choo*·zee paym·*bay*·nee
without …	*bila …*	*bee*·la …

in the bar

kwenye baa

Excuse me!
Samahani! — sa·ma·*ha*·nee

I'm next.
Zamu yangu ijayo. — *za*·moo *yan*·goo ee·*ja*·yoh

I'll have …
Nipe … — *nee*·pay …

Same again, please.
Hiki tena. — *hee*·kee *tay*·na

No ice, thanks.
Bila barafu, asante. — *bee*·la ba·*ra*·foo a·*san*·tay

I'll buy you a drink.
Nitakununulia kinywaji. — nee·ta·koo·noo·noo·*lee*·a keeny·*wa*·jee

What would you like?
Unataka nini? — oo·na·*ta*·ka *nee*·nee

I don't drink alcohol.
Sinywi pombe. — *seeny*·wee *pohm*·bay

It's my round.
Mzunguko wangu. — m·zoon·*goo*·koh *wan*·goo

How much is that?
Ni bei gani? — nee bay *ga*·nee

Do you serve meals here?
Kuna chakula hapa? — *koo*·na cha·*koo*·la *ha*·pa

listen for …

Unakunywa nini?
oo·na·*koony*·wa *nee*·nee — **What are you having?**

Nafikiri umekunywa ya kutosha.
na·fee·*kee*·ree oo·may·*koony*·wa ya koo·*toh*·sha — **I think you've had enough.**

Maagizo ya mwisho.
ma·a·*gee*·zoh ya *mwee*·shoh — **Last orders.**

nonalcoholic drinks

vinywaji bila kilevi

All water sold in sealed bottles in East Africa is clean, but usually flat – the only water you'll find with bubbles is soda water. If you can't find water in a bottle, make sure any water you drink has been boiled.

Has this water been boiled?
Maji haya yalichemshwa? — *ma*·jee *ha*·ya ya·lee·*chaym*·shwa

… water	*maji …*	*ma*·jee …
boiled	*yaliyochemshwa*	ya·lee·yoh·*chaym*·shwa
bottled	*kwenye chupa*	*kway*·nyay *choo*·pa
cold	*ya baridi*	ya ba·*ree*·dee
hot	*ya moto*	ya *moh*·toh
mineral	*ya madini*	ya ma·*dee*·nee
orange juice	*maji ya machungwa*	*ma*·jee ya ma·*choon*·gwa
soda water	*klub soda*	kloob *soh*·da
(cold) soft drink	*soda (ya baridi)*	*soh*·da (ya ba·*ree*·dee)
(cup of) …	*(kikombe cha) …*	(kee·*kohm*·bay cha) …
ginger tea	*chai ya tangawizi*	*cha*·ee ya tan·ga·*wee*·zee
spiced tea	*chai masala*	*cha*·ee ma·*sa*·la
tea	*chai*	*cha*·ee
(cup of) coffee …	*(kikombe cha) kahawa …*	(kee·*kohm*·bay cha) ka·*ha*·wa …
with milk	*na maziwa*	na ma·*zee*·wa
with lemon	*na limau*	na lee·*ma*·oo
with spices	*na viungo*	na vee·*oon*·goh
without (sugar)	*bila (sukari)*	*bee*·la (soo·*ka*·ree)

coffee break

East Africans drink tea and coffee at all hours, even on a hot afternoon. It's different in Central Africa, where cool drinks are the go on hot days. You might be offered a soda or a beer instead of a hot drink – but it's quite common that soft drinks or beer will be served at room temperature.

... coffee	*kahawa ...*	ka·*ha*·wa ...
black	*ya rangi*	ya *ran*·gee
decaffeinated	*bila kafini*	*bee*·la ka·*fee*·nee
iced	*baridi yenye barafu*	ba·*ree*·dee *yay*·nyay ba·*ra*·foo
strong	*yenye nguvu*	*yay*·nyay n·*goo*·voo
weak	*isiye na nguvu*	ee·*see*·yay na n·*goo*·voo
white	*ya maziwa*	ya ma·*zee*·wa

alcoholic drinks

pombe

Most East Africans drink their beer warm. When you order, you should specify whether you want your beer *baridi* ba·*ree*·dee (cold) or *ya moto* ya *moh*·toh (warm).

a ... of beer	*... ya bia*	... ya *bee*·a
glass	*glasi*	*gla*·see
half liter	*nusu lita*	*noo*·soo *lee*·ta
jug	*lita*	*lee*·ta
large bottle	*chupa kubwa*	*choo*·pa *koob*·wa
pint	*painti*	pa·*een*·tee
small bottle	*chupa ndogo*	*choo*·pa n·*doh*·goh

local drinks

There are different types of home-made brews in East Africa, depending on the region, but the most common ones are made of maize, millet or banana. Local brews are usually drunk from a shared plastic pot called *lita lee*·ta, though you can agree to pour from the pot into glasses. When joining a group of people drinking *pombe pohm*·bay (alcoholic drink) the accepted practice is to promptly order another litre which then gets added to the pot. If you're tempted to partake in drinking local brews, be aware of the health risks that are often associated with the consumption of some of them.

Can I have a glass, please?
Naomba bilauri. na·*ohm*·ba bee·la·*oo*·ree

mbege	m·*bay*·gay	banana beer
pombe	*pohm*·bay	alcoholic beverage
pombe ya kienyeji	*pohm*·bay ya kee·ay·*nyay*·jee	home-made brew
konyagi	koh·*nya*·gee	local distilled spirit

a bottle/glass of … wine	*chupa/glasi ya mvinyo …*	*choo*·pa/*gla*·see ya m·*vee*·nyoh …
dessert	*tamu*	*ta*·moo
red	*mwekundu*	mway·*koon*·doo
rosé	*pinki*	*peen*·kee
sparkling	*yenye mapovu*	*yay*·nyay ma·*poh*·voo
white	*mweupe*	mway·*oo*·pay

a shot of …	*toti ya …*	*toh*·tee ya …
gin	*gini*	*gee*·nee
rum	*rumi*	*roo*·mee
tequila	*tekila*	tay·*kee*·la
vodka	*vodka*	*vohd*·ka
whisky	*wiski*	*wee*·skee

drinking up

kunywa pombe

Cheers!
Heri! — *hay*·ree

This is hitting the spot.
Inatosheka. — ee·na·toh·*shay*·ka

I feel fantastic!
Nasikia nzuri sana! — na·see·*kee*·a n·*zoo*·ree *sa*·na

I think I've had one too many.
Nafikiri nimekunywa moja mno. — na·fee·*kee*·ree nee·may·*koony*·wa *moh*·ja *m*·noh

I'm feeling drunk.
Nimelewa. — nee·may·*lay*·wa

I feel ill.

Nasikia mgonjwa. — na·see·*kee*·a m·*gohn*·jwa

Where's the toilet?

Choo kiko wapi? — choh *kee*·koh *wa*·pee

I'm tired, I'd better go home.

Nimechoka, nirudi nyumbani. — nee·may·*choh*·ka nee·*roo*·dee nyoom·*ba*·nee

Can you call a taxi for me?

Niitie teksi. — nee·ee·*tee*·ay *tayk*·see

I don't think you should drive.

Sidhani ni salama kwa wewe kuendesha. — see·*dha*·nee nee sa·*la*·ma kwa *way*·way koo·ayn·*day*·sha

dining East African style

Being invited to share a meal with East Africans at home is a treat not to be turned down, but be prepared for some customs that are different from what you might be used to.

Before eating, a bowl and a pitcher of water are often passed around for washing hands. The usual procedure is to hold your hands over the bowl while your host pours water over them. Sometimes soap is provided, as is a towel for drying off.

The centre of the meal itself is usually *ugali* oo·*ga*·lee (a staple made from maize or cassava flour) which is normally taken with the right hand from a communal pot, rolled into a small ball with the fingers, dipped into some sort of sauce and eaten. Food is never handled or eaten with the left hand.

At the end of the meal, try to avoid being the one who takes the last handful from the communal bowl, as this may leave your hosts worrying they haven't provided enough. After the meal, the water and wash basin are brought around again so that everyone can wash their hands.

Sharing a meal with others forms the basis for social life in East Africa, but don't be surprised if conversation stops while the food is being eaten.

buying food

kununua chakula

What's the local speciality?
Chakula cha kienyeji gani ni maalum sana? — cha·*koo*·la cha kee·ay·*nyay*·jee *ga*·nee nee *ma*·loom *sa*·na

What's that?
Hicho ni nini? — *hee*·choh nee *nee*·nee

Can I taste it?
Naomba nionje. — na·*ohm*·ba nee·*ohn*·jay

How much is a kilo of (mangoes)?
Kilo ya (maembe) ni bei gani? — *kee*·loh ya (ma·*aym*·bay) nee bay *ga*·nee

Can I have a bag, please?
Nipe mfuko. — *nee*·pay m·*foo*·koh

food stuff

cooked	*kupikwa*	koo·*pee*·kwa
cured	*kutiwa na chumvi na kukaushwa*	koo·*tee*·wa na *choom*·vee na koo·ka·*oo*·shwa
dried	*kukaushwa*	koo·ka·*oo*·shwa
fresh	*mbichi*	m·*bee*·chee
frozen	*kugandishwa katika barafu*	koo·gan·*dee*·shwa ka·*tee*·ka ba·*ra*·foo
smoked	*kukaushwa na moshi*	koo·ka·*oo*·shwa na *moh*·shee
raw	*mbichi*	m·*bee*·chee

I'd like …	*Nataka …*	na·*ta*·ka …
(200) grams	*gramu (mia mbili)*	*gra*·moo (*mee*·a m·*bee*·lee)
a dozen	*kumi na mbili*	*koo*·mee na m·*bee*·lee
half a kilo	*nusu kilo*	*noo*·soo *kee*·loh
a kilo	*kilo moja*	*kee*·loh *moh*·ja
(two) kilos	*kilo (mbili)*	*kee*·loh (m·*bee*·lee)
a bottle	*chupa*	*choo*·pa
a jar	*chupa ndogo*	*choo*·pa n·*doh*·goh
a piece	*kipande*	kee·*pan*·day
(three) pieces	*vipande (vitatu)*	vee·*pan*·day (vee·*ta*·too)
(six) slices	*slaisi (sita)*	sla·*ee*·see (*see*·ta)
(just) a little	*kidogo (tu)*	kee·*doh*·goh (too)
more	*zaidi*	za·*ee*·dee
some …	*kiasi …*	kee·*a*·see …
this/that one	*hiki/hicho*	*hee*·kee/*hee*·choh

Less.	*Punguza.*	poon·*goo*·za
A bit more.	*Ongeza kidogo.*	ohn·*gay*·za kee·*doh*·goh
Enough.	*Bas.*	bas

Do you have ...?	*Kuna ...?*	*koo*·na...
anything cheaper	*rahisi zaidi*	ra·*hee*·see za·*ee*·dee
other kinds	*aina nyingine*	a·*ee*·na nyeen·*gee*·nay

Where's the ... section?	*... iko wapi?*	... *ee*·koh *wa*·pee
dairy	*Ma ziwa*	ma·*zee*·wa
fish	*Samaki*	sa·*ma*·kee
frozen goods	*Vyakula vilivyo-gandishwa katika barafu*	vya·*koo*·la vee·lee·vyo·gan·*dee*·shwa ka·*tee*·ka ba·*ra*·foo
fruit and vegetables	*Matunda na mboga*	ma·*toon*·da na m·*boh*·ga
meat	*Nyama*	*nya*·ma
poultry	*Kuku*	*koo*·koo

listen for ...

Nikusaidie? nee·koo·sa·ee·*de*·ay	**Can I help you?**
Unataka nini? oo·na·*ta*·ka *nee*·nee	**What would you like?**
Kiasi gani? kee·*a*·see *ga*·nee	**How much? (quantity)**
Kitu kingine? *kee*·too keen·*gee*·nay	**Anything else?**
Hamna/Hakuna. *ham*·na/ha·*koo*·na	**There isn't any.**

cooking utensils

vyombo vya kupikia

Could I please borrow a ...?	*Naomba kuazima ...*	na·*ohm*·ba koo·a·*zee*·ma ...
I need a ...	*Nahitaji ...*	na·hee·*ta*·jee ...
chopping board	*bao la kukatia*	*ba*·oh la koo·ka·*tee*·a
frying pan	*kikaango*	kee·ka·*an*·goh
knife	*kisu*	*kee*·soo
meat cleaver	*kisu kikubwa cha nyama*	*kee*·soo kee·*koob*·wa cha *nya*·ma
saucepan	*sufuria*	soo·foo·*ree*·a

For more cooking implements, see the **dictionary**.

ordering food

kuagiza chakula

Is there a … restaurant near here?	*Kuna hoteli ya chakula … hapa karibuni?*	*koo*·na hoh·*tay*·lee ya cha·*koo*·la … *ha*·pa ka·ree·*boo*·nee
Do you have … food?	*Mna chakula …?*	*m*·na cha·*koo*·la …
halal	*halali*	ha·*la*·lee
vegetarian	*bila nyama*	*bee*·la *nya*·ma
I don't eat …	*Sili …*	*see*·lee …
butter	*siagi*	see·*a*·gee
eggs	*mayai*	ma·*ya*·ee
fish	*samaki*	sa·*ma*·kee
fish stock	*supu ya samaki*	*soo*·poo ya sa·*ma*·kee
meat stock	*supu ya nyama*	*soo*·poo ya *nya*·ma
oil	*mafuta*	ma·*foo*·ta
pork	*nyama nguruwe*	*nya*·ma n·goo·*roo*·way
poultry	*kuku*	*koo*·koo
red meat	*nyama*	*nya*·ma
Is this …?	*Hiki …?*	*hee*·kee …
decaffeinated	*ni bila kafini*	nee *bee*·la ka·*fee*·nee
low-fat	*ni chenye mafuta machache*	nee *chay*·nyay ma·*foo*·ta ma·*cha*·chay
low in sugar	*ni chenye sukari kidogo tu*	nee *chay*·nyay soo·*ka*·ree kee·*doh*·goh too
salt-free	*bila chumvi*	*bee*·la *choom*·vee

Is it cooked in/with ...?

Kinapikwa na ...? kee·na·*pee*·kwa na ...

Could you prepare a meal without ...?

Unaweza kuandaa mlo bila ...? oo·na·*way*·za koo·an·*da* m·loh *bee*·la ...

special diets & allergies

vyakula maalum na mzio

I'm on a special diet.

Nakula vyakula maalum tu. na·*koo*·la vya·*koo*·la *ma*·loom too

I'm vegetarian.

Mimi ni mlaji wa mboga za majani tu. *mee*·mee nee m·*la*·jee wa m·*boh*·ga za ma·*ja*·nee too

I'm vegan.

Mimi ni mtu asiyetumia aina yoyote ya mazao ya mnyama. *mee*·mee nee a·see·yay·too·*mee*·a a·*ee*·na yoh·*yoh*·tay ma·*za*·oh ya m·*nya*·ma

I'm (a) ...	*Mimi ni ...*	*mee*·mee nee ...
Buddhist	*Mbudisti*	m·boo·*dee*·stee
Hindu	*Mhindu*	m·*heen*·doo
Jewish	*Myahudi*	m·ya·*hoo*·dee
Muslim	*Mwislamu*	mwee·*sla*·moo

I'm allergic to ...	*Nina mzio wa ...*	*nee*·na m·*zee*·oh wa ...
dairy produce	*mazao ya maziwa*	ma·*za*·oh ya ma·*zee*·wa
eggs	*mayai*	ma·*ya*·ee
gelatine	*jelatini*	jay·la·*tee*·nee
honey	*asali*	a·*sa*·lee
MSG	*msg*	aym·*ays*·gee
nuts	*kokwa*	*koh*·kwa
peanuts	*karanga*	ka·*ran*·ga
seafood	*vyakula kutoka baharini*	vya·*koo*·la koo·*toh*·ka ba·ha·*ree*·nee
shellfish	*kombe*	*kohm*·bay

culinary reader

somo la vyakula

This miniguide to Swahili cuisine lists dishes and ingredients in Swahili alphabetical order. It's designed to help you get the most out of your gastronomic experience by providing you with food terms that you may see on the menu. For certain dishes we've marked the region or city where they're most popular.

A

achari a·*cha*·ree *pickles • chutney • relish*
aiskrimu a·ee·*skree*·moo *ice cream*
alizeti a·lee·*zay*·tee *sunflower seeds*
asali a·*sa*·lee *honey*

B

balungi ba·*loon*·gee *grapefruit*
bamia ba·*mee*·a *okra*
barafu ba·*ra*·foo *ice*
baridi ba·*ree*·dee *cold* ⓐ
bata *ba*·ta *duck*
— **mdogo** m·*doh*·goh *duckling*
bekoni bay·*koh*·nee *bacon*
bia *bee*·a *beer*
— **baridi** ba·*ree*·dee *cold*
— **ya moto** ya *moh*·toh *warm*
biriani bee·ree·*a*·nee *Indian & Pakistani-inspired dish – a mixture of rice & spices, usually with meat or beans*
biringani bee·reen·*ga*·nee *eggplant • aubergine*
biskuti bees·*koo*·tee *biscuit • cookie*
blue bandi bloo *ban*·dee *margarine*
boha *boh*·ha *sugar cane* **pombe**
bokuboku boh·koo·*boh*·koo *festive dish with a pasty texture made from cooked ground wheat & meat cooked in spices, served over fried onion (Zanzibar)*
brokoli *broh*·koh·lee *broccoli*
buni *boo*·nee *coffee beans*
busi *boo*·see *barley* **pombe**

C

chai *cha*·ee *tea*
— **masala** ma·*sa*·la *spiced sweet tea (often with cardamom)*
— **tangawizi** tan·ga·*wee*·zee *tea flavoured with ginger*
— **ya asubuhi** ya a·soo·*boo*·hee *breakfast*
chakula cha·*koo*·la *food*
— **cha jioni** cha jee·*oh*·nee *dinner*
— **cha kichina** cha kee·*chee*·na *Chinese food*
— **cha kihindi** cha kee·*heen*·dee *Indian food*
— **kikuu** kee·*koo* *main courses*
— **cha mchana** cha m·*cha*·na *lunch*
— **kutoka bahari** koo·*toh*·ka ba·*ha*·ree *seafood*
chang'aa chang·*a* *home-brewed firewater – not recommended for health reasons*
chapati cha·*pa*·tee *round bread cooked like a pancake – you tear off pieces to pick up other food*
chaza *cha*·za *oyster*
chenja *chayn*·ja *drink made by soaking uncooked rice in water with sugar*
chenye viungo *chay*·nyay vee·*oon*·goh *spicy*
chenza *chayn*·za *mandarin*
chewa *chay*·wa *rock cod*
chipsi *chee*·psee *deep-fried potatoes (chips or French fries) – commonly used to bulk up a meal*
— **mayai** ma·*ya*·ee *greasy omelette made with chips – very popular fast food*

chizi *chee*·zee *(cottage) cheese (also known as* **jibini***)*
chumvi *choom*·vee *salt*
chungwa *choon*·gwa *orange*

D

dafu *da*·foo *coconut (green)*
dagaa da·*ga* *freshwater sardines fried & eaten whole*
dalasini da·la·*see*·nee *cinnamon*
dengu *dayn*·goo *lentils*

E

embe *aym*·bay *mango*
— **mafuta** ma·*foo*·ta *avocado*

G

gini *gee*·nee *gin*
giligilani gee·lee·gee·*la*·nee *coriander seeds*
glukos *gloo*·kohs *plain sweet biscuits*
gogwe *gohg*·way *tree tomato*
gongo *gohn*·goh *illegal distilled cashew nut drink*

H

halua hal·*oo*·a *Turkish delight*
heringi hay·*reen*·gee *herring*

I

iliki ee·*lee*·ke *cardamom*
irio ee·*ree*·oh *potato, cabbage & beans mashed together (also known as* **kienyeji***)*

J

jibini jee·*bee*·nee *see* **chizi**
jodari joh·*da*·ree *tuna*
jusi *joo*·see *juice*
— **ya makwaju** ya ma·*kwa*·joo *tamarind juice*
— **ya mananasi** ya ma·na·*na*·see *pineapple juice*
— **ya pasheni** ya pa·*shay*·nee *passion fruit juice*

K

kaa ka *crab*
kababu ka·*ba*·boo *small kebabs – a popular snack food*
kabichi ka·*bee*·chee *cabbage*
kahawa ka·*ha*·wa *coffee*
— **baridi yenye barafu** ba·*ree*·dee *yay*·nyay ba·*ra*·foo *iced coffee*
— **ya maziwa** ya ma·*zee*·wa *white coffee*
— **ya rangi** ya *ran*·gee *black coffee*
kamba *kam*·ba *crayfish*
kambakoche kam·ba·*koh*·chay *rock lobster*
kande *kan*·day *stew made with beans & whole kernels of maize*
kangara kan·*ga*·ra *maize & honey* **pombe**
kapile ka·*pee*·lay *cooked food sold in the market*
karafuu ka·ra·*foo* *clove (the spice)*
karanga ka·*ran*·ga *peanut*
karoti ka·*roh*·tee *carrot*
kasezi bong ka·*say*·zee bong *undistilled Ugandan millet-based alcohol (not recommended for health reasons)*
keki *kay*·kee *cake*
kiamsha hamu kee·*am*·sha *ha*·moo *appetisers*
kiazi (ulaya) kee·*a*·zee (oo·*la*·ya) *(European) potato*
— **kikuu** kee·*koo* *yam potato*
— **kitamu** kee·*ta*·moo *sweet potato*
kienyeji kee·ay·*nyay*·jee *see* **irio**
kima *kee*·ma *mincemeat*
kimbo *keem*·boh *cooking fat (brand name)*
kisibiti kee·see·*bee*·tee *cumin*
kisutuo kee·soo·*too*·oh *food received as a thank you for helping someone*
kitindamlo kee·teen·da·*m*·loh *dessert*
kitumbuo kee·toom·*boo*·oh *deep-fried rice bread*

kitunguu kee·toon·*goo* *onion*
— **saumu** sa·*oo*·moo *garlic*
klub soda kloob *soh*·da *soda water*
koko *koh*·koh *cocoa*
kokteli kohk·*tay*·lee *cocktail*
kokwa *koh*·kwa *nut*
komoni *koh*·moh·nee *local millet beer*
konyagi koh·*nya*·gee *general name for locally produced liquor • local gin-like spirit*
korosho koh·*roh*·shoh *cashew nut – often sold roasted as a street food*
kuku *koo*·koo *chicken*
— **choma** *cho*·ma *roast chicken*
kunde *koon*·day *cowpea (tropical pea)*
kupikwa katika majani koo·*peek*·wa ka·*tee*·ka ma·*ja*·nee *baked in leaves*
kwaju *kwa*·joo *tamarind*

L

lager *la*·gayr *lager beer*
limau lee·*ma*·oo *lemon*
lozi *loh*·zee *almond*

M

maandazi man·*da*·zee *semisweet deep-fried doughnut-like pastry, often containing coconut milk & sometimes spiced – popular snack food*
mabuyu ma·*boo*·yoo *sweet & sour baobab seeds*
madafu ma·*da*·foo *fresh juice of a green coconut*
mafuta ma·*foo*·ta *oil*
maharagwe ma·ha·*rag*·way *red kidney beans (often cooked with coconut)*
mahindi ma·*heen*·dee *corn • maize • roast corn cobs*
maji *ma*·jee *water*
— **ya dafu** ya *da*·foo *coconut milk*
— **ya madini** ya ma·*dee*·nee *mineral water*
— **ya machungwa** ya ma·*choon*·gwa *orange juice*
— **ya ndimu** ya n·*dee*·moo *lime juice*
makaroni ma·ka·*roh*·nee *see* **spageti**

manjano man·*ja*·noh *turmeric*
mastafeli ma·sta·*fay*·lee *soursop*
matapa ma·*ta*·pa *cassava leaves cooked in peanut sauce often served with prawns (Mozambique)*
matoke ma·*toh*·kay *green bananas or plantains boiled, steamed or mashed & eaten as a staple*
mayai ma·*ya*·ee *eggs (also called* **yai***)*
— **yaliyochemshwa** ya·lee·yoh·*chem*·shwa *hard-boiled eggs*
— **yaliyokaangwa** ya·lee·yo·ka·*ang*·wa *fried eggs*
— **yaliyovurugwa** ya·lee·yo·voo·*roog*·wa *scrambled eggs*
maziwa ma·*zee*·wa *milk*
— **ganda** *gan*·da *yoghurt*
— **ya unga** ya *oon*·ga *powdered milk*
maziwalala ma·zee·wa·*la*·la *'sleeping milk' – yoghurt-like fermented milk*
mbege m·*bay*·gay *banana beer*
mbichi m·*bee*·chee *raw*
mbivu m·*bee*·voo *ripe*
mboga m·*boh*·ga *vegetable • vegetables or relish served as a side dish with* **ugali**
mchaichai m·cha·ee·*cha*·ee *lemongrass*
mchele m·*chay*·lay *uncooked white rice*
mchicha m·*chee*·cha *spinach – sometimes cooked with onion & tomato*
mchuzi m·*choo*·zee *sauce (often spicy) eaten with* **ugali***, containing either fish, meat, beans or spinach • any sauce • curry*
— **wa nyama** wa *nya*·ma *beef stew – in Zanzibar, can be a curry with lemon juice & spices including turmeric*
— **wa nyanya** wa *nya*·nya *tomato sauce*
— **wa pilipili hoho** wa pee·lee·*pee*·lee *hoh*·hoh *chilli sauce*
mgiligilani m·gee·lee·gee·*la*·nee *fresh coriander leaves*
miche ya mianzi *mee*·chay ya mee·*an*·zee *bamboo shoots*
mishikaki mee·shee·*ka*·kee *meat on a skewer grilled until crisp – popular roadside snack served with salt & possibly chilli*

mkate m·*ka*·tay *bread*
— **mayai** ma·*ya*·ee *'egg bread' – dough wrapped around minced meat & fried egg*
— **wa mayai** wa ma·*ya*·ee *mixture of eggs, ground meat, onion & spices fried until brown and eaten hot (popular on the East African Coast)*
— **wa ngano asilia** wa n·*ga*·noh a·see·*lee*·a *wholemeal bread*
mkizi m·*kee*·zee *grey mullet*
mlenda m·*layn*·da *green sticky vegetable similar to okra*
mnofu m·*noh*·foo *beefsteak (also known as* **steki***)*
mpishi m·*pee*·shee *flavoured cooking fat (brand name) • cook (chef)*
mtama m·*ta*·ma *sorghum • millet (often cooked into a gruel as a breakfast food)*
mtande m·*tan*·day *food hung to dry*
mtindi m·*teen*·dee *cultured milk product similar to yoghurt • cream (usually skim from boiled milk)*
mtori m·*toh*·ree *banana soup*
muhogo moo·*hoh*·goh *cassava • grilled cassava topped with chilli sauce (a roadside snack)*
muwa *moo*·wa *sugar cane*
mvinyo m·*vee*·nyoh *wine*
— **mwekundu** mway·*koon*·doo *red wine*
— **mwenye povu** *mway*·nyay *poh*·voo *sparkling wine*
— **mweupe** mway·*oo*·pay *white wine*

N

nanasi na·*na*·see *pineapple*
nazi *na*·zee *coconut (ripe)*
ndimu n·*dee*·moo *lime*
ndizi n·*dee*·zee *banana*
— **ko kastad** koh *ka*·stad *custard made from sliced bananas & chopped peanuts, spiced with cloves, cinnamon & nutmeg (Zanzibar)*
— **ya kupika** ya koo·*pee*·ka *plantain*
nduwalo n·doo·*wa*·loh *sailfish*
ngisi n·*gee*·see *squid*
njegere n·jay·*gay*·ray *pigeon pea*
nusu *noo*·soo *half portion*
nyama *nya*·ma *meat*
— **choma** *choh*·ma *grilled meat – often goat meat – cooked over a charcoal pit & sold in bite-sized pieces*
— **mamba** *mam*·ba *crocodile meat*
— **mbuni** m·*boo*·nee *ostrich meat*
— **mbuzi** m·*boo*·zee *goat meat • mutton*
— **ng'ombe** ng·*ohm*·bay *beef*
— **nguruwe** n·goo·*roo*·way *pork – not widely available as many of the Swahili-speaking areas are Muslim*
— **punda milia** *poon*·da mee·*lee*·a *zebra meat*
— **swala** *swa*·la *impala meat*
— **twiga** *twee*·ga *giraffe meat*
— **ya mkebe** ya m·*kay*·bay *tinned meat*
— **ya kopo** ya *koh*·poh *tinned meat*
— **ya wanyama pori** ya wa·*nya*·ma *poh*·ree *game meat – may be legally farmed or illegally poached*
nyanya *nya*·nya *tomato*
— **ya mkebe** ya m·*kay*·bay *tomato paste*

O

oluwombo o·loo·*wohm*·boh *dish made from meat or even peanuts mixed with mushrooms (Uganda)*
omlet ohm·*layt* *omelette*

P

papa *pa*·pa *shark*
papai pa·*pa*·ee *papaya • pawpaw*
parachichi pa·ra·*chee*·chee *avocado*
pasheni pa·*shay*·nee *passion fruit*
pera *pay*·ra *guava*
peremende pay·ray·*mayn*·day *sweet* ⓝ
pilau pee·*la*·oo *rice, vegetables & meat cooked in a seasoned broth*
pilipili pee·lee·*pee*·lee *pepper*
— **hoho** *hoh*·hoh *hot pepper • chilli • chilli sauce*
— **manga** *man*·ga *black pepper • black peppercorn*
— **mbichi** m·*bee*·chee *green pepper*

pipi *pee*·pee *candy*
piripiri pee·ree·*pee*·ree *very hot sauce made from chilli pepper & lemon juice, eaten with meat, fish & shellfish*
pojo *poh*·joh *mung beans*
pombe *pohm*·bay *popular home-made beer-like brew made from maize, millet, banana, or other local produce*
— **kali** *ka*·lee *spirits*
popkon *pohp*·kohn *popcorn*
posho *poh*·shoh *see* **ugali**
pweza *pway*·za *octopus*

R

rasiberi ra·see·*bay*·ree *raspberry*
rojorojo roh·joh·*roh*·joh *viscous food (especially sauce)*
rubisi roo·*bee*·see *banana wine*
rumi *roo*·mee *rum*

S

saladi sa·*la*·dee *lettuce • salad*
samaki sa·*ma*·kee *fish*
— **ya kupaka** ya koo·*pa*·ka *fish cooked in a spicy coconut sauce*
— **ya kuwonga** ya koo·*wohn*·ga *fish croquettes (Zanzibar)*
— **ya mkebe/kopo** ya m·*kay*·bay/*koh*·poh *tinned sardines*
sambusa sam·*boo*·sa *mixture of meat, onion, vegetables & spices fried in a triangular-shaped pastry & eaten as a snack (also known as* **samosa***)*
samosa sa·*moh*·sa *see* **sambusa**
sandwichi sand·*wee*·chee *sandwich*
shampeni sham·*pay*·nee *champagne*
shayiri sha·*yee*·ree *barley • oats*
siagi see·*a*·gee *butter*
siki *see*·kee *vinegar*
simsim *seem*·seem *sesame seeds • sesame candy (Zanzibar)*
slaisi sla·*ee*·see *slice (see also* **tosti***)*
soda *soh*·da *soft drink*
sorpotel sohr·poh·*tayl* *stew of beef & pork flavoured with a rich spice mix (Zanzibar)*
soseji ya nyama nguruwe soh·*say*·jee ya *nya*·ma n·goo·*roo*·way *pork sausage*

spageti spa·*gay*·tee *spaghetti (see also* **makaroni***)*
stauti sta·*oo*·tee *stout beer*
steki *stay*·kee *see* **mnofu**
stroberi *stroh*·bay·ree *strawberry*
sukari soo·*ka*·ree *sugar*
sukuma wiki soo·*koo*·ma *wee*·kee *mixture of basic greens (eg spinach) often served with meat dishes*
supu *soo*·poo *soup • broth (sometimes spicy) made from pieces of chicken, meat or fish*
— **ya kuku** ya *koo*·koo *chicken soup with onion, cabbage, tomato & celery*

T

tangawizi tan·ga·*wee*·zee *ginger*
tembo *taym*·boh *palm wine*
tende *tayn*·day *date*
tikiti (maji) tee·*kee*·tee (*ma*·jee) *melon • watermelon*
tilapia tee·la·*pee*·a *tilapia (Nile perch)*
tofaa toh·*fa* *apple*
topetope toh·pay·*toh*·pay *cherimoya • custard apple*
tosti *toh*·stee *slice of bread (often toasted), also known as* **slaisi**
tunda *toon*·da *fruit*

U

ubwabwa oo·*bwa*·bwa *rice cooked with coconut*
ugali oo·*ga*·lee *traditional dish made by mixing maize and/or cassava flour in hot water until it becomes like a stiff porridge & eaten by rolling it in the hand to form a small ball which is then dipped in sauce before eating (also known as* **posho** *in Uganda)*
uji *oo*·jee *thin sweet porridge*
ulanzi oo·*lan*·zee *bamboo juice* **pombe**
umanga oo·*man*·ga *plain food (without relish)*
unga wa kahawa wa moja kwa moja *oon*·ga wa ka·*ha*·wa wa *moh*·ja kwa *moh*·ja *instant coffee*

unga wa mahindi *oon*·ga wa ma·*heen*·dee *maize/corn meal*
unga wa pilipili hoho *oon*·ga wa pee·lee·*pee*·lee *hoh*·hoh *chilli powder*
unga wa viazi vikuu *oon*·ga wa vee·*a*·zee vee·*ku*·*u* *yam flour*
uraka oo·*ra*·ka *brewed cashew nut drink*
utumbo wa nyama oo·*toom*·boh wa *nya*·ma *offal • intestines*

V

vinginevyo veen·gee·*nay*·vyo *side dishes*
vinywaji veeny·*wa*·jee *drinks*
vitambua vee·tam·*boo*·a *small cakes made with rice flour*

W

wanzuki wan·*zoo*·kee *honey beer*
wali *wa*·lee *cooked rice (available with a variety of meats or sauces)*
— **maharagwe** ma·ha·*ra*·gway *cooked rice and beans*
waragi wa·*ra*·gee *millet-based alcohol (Uganda)*

Y

yai *see* **mayai**
ya kuchemshwa ya koo·*chaym*·shwa *boiled*
ya kuchomwa ya koo·*choh*·mwa *broiled • grilled*
ya kuiva kidogo ya koo·ee·va kee·*doh*·goh *rare (meat)*
ya kuiva kubisa/sana ya koo·*ee*·va koo·*bee*·sa/*sa*·na *well-done*
ya kuiva wastani ya koo·*ee*·va wa·*sta*·nee *medium (meat)*
ya kukaanga ya koo·ka·*a*·nga *fried*
ya kuoka ya koo·*oh*·ka *roasted*
ya kuokwa ya koo·*ok*·wa *baked*
ya kupikwa ya koo·*peek*·wa *cooked • heated*

Z

zabibu za·*bee*·boo *grapes*
— **nyeupe zilizokaushwa** nyay·*oo*·pay zee·lee·zoh·ka·*oo*·shwa *sultanas*
zabibubata za·bee·boo·*ba*·ta *cape gooseberries (Kenya)*

emergencies

dharura

Careful!	*Angalia!*	an·ga·*lee*·a
Help!	*Saidia!*	sa·ee·*dee*·a
Stop!	*Simama!*	see·*ma*·ma
Go away!	*Toka!*	*toh*·ka
Thief!	*Mwizi!*	*mwee*·zee
Fire!	*Moto!*	*moh*·toh
Watch out!	*Angalia!*	an·ga·*lee*·a

Leave me alone!
Niache! nee·*a*·chay

I won't give you any money!
Sitakupa hela! see·ta·*koo*·pa *hay*·la

It's an emergency.
Ni dharura. nee dha·*roo*·a

There's been an accident.
Ajali imetokea. a·*ja*·lee ee·may·toh·*kay*·a

Call the police.
Waite polisi. wa·*ee*·tay poh·*lee*·see

Call a doctor.
Mwite daktari. m·*wee*·tay dak·*ta*·ree

Call an ambulance.
Ita gari la hospitali. *ee*·ta *ga*·ree la ho·spee·*ta*·lee

signs

Dharura	dha·*roo*·ra	**Emergency Department**
Hospitali	hoh·spee·*ta*·lee	**Hospital**
Polisi	poh·*lee*·see	**Police**

Could you please help?
Saidia, tafadhali. sa·ee·*dee*·a ta·fa·*dha*·lee

Can I use your phone?
Naomba kutumia simu yako. na·*ohm*·ba koo·too·*mee*·a *see*·moo *ya*·koh

I'm lost.
Nimejipotea. nee·may·jee·poh·*tay*·a

Where are the toilets?
Vyoo viko wapi? vyoh *vee*·ko *wa*·pee

Is it safe ...?	*Ni salama ...?*	nee sa·*la*·ma ...
at night	*usikuni*	oo·see·*koo*·nee
for gay people	*kwa wasenge*	kwa wa·*sayn*·gay
for travellers	*kwa watalii*	kwa wa·ta·*lee*
for women	*kwa wanawake*	kwa wa·na·*wa*·kay
on your own	*kuwa pekee*	*koo*·wa pay·*kay*

police

polisi

Where's the police station?
Kituo cha polisi kiko wapi? kee·*too*·oh cha poh·*lee*·see *kee*·koh *wa*·pee

I want to report an offence.
Nataka kutoa taarifa ya jinai. na·*ta*·ka koo·*toh*·a ta·*ree*·fa ya jee·*na*·ee

Can I see your police identification card?
Nionyeshe kadi ya kitambulisho ya polisi. nee·oh·*nyay*·shay *ka*·dee ya kee·tam·boo·*lee*·shoh ya poh·*lee*·see

It was him/her.
Alikuwa yeye. a·lee·*koo*·wa *yay*·yay

I have insurance.
Nina bima. *nee*·na *bee*·ma

My (backpack) was stolen.
(Shanta) iliibwa. (*shan*·ta) ee·lee·*ee*·bwa

I've been …

assaulted	*Nilishambuliwa.*	nee·lee·sham·boo·*lee*·wa
mugged	*Nilivamiwa.*	nee·lee·va·*mee*·wa
raped	*Nilibakwa.*	nee·lee·*ba*·kwa
robbed	*Niliibiwa.*	nee·lee·ee·*bee*·wa

He/She tried to … me.	*Alijaribu …*	a·lee·ja·*ree*·boo …
assault	*kunishambulia*	koo·nee·sham·boo·*lee*·a
rape	*kunibaka*	koo·nee·*ba*·ka
rob	*kuniibia*	koo·nee·ee·*bee*·a
trick	*kunidanganya*	koo·nee·dan·*ga*·nya

I've lost my …	*Nilipoteza …*	nee·lee·poh·*tay*·za …
bags	*mizigo yangu*	mee·*zee*·goh *yan*·goo
car	*gari langu*	*ga*·ree *lan*·goo
credit card	*kadi ya benki*	*ka*·dee ya *bayn*·kee
money	*pesa yangu*	*pay*·sa *yan*·goo
passport	*pasipoti yangu*	pa·see·*poh*·tee *yan*·goo

What am I accused of?
Nashtakiwa na nini? — na·shta·*kee*·wa na *nee*·nee

I'm sorry.
Nasikia majuto. — na·see·*kee*·a ma·*joo*·toh

I didn't realise I was doing anything wrong.
Nilikuwa sielewi kwamba nilifanya kosa lolote. — nee·lee·*koo*·wa see·ay·*lay*·wee *kwam*·ba nee·lee·*fa*·nya *koh*·sa loh·*loh*·tay

I didn't do it.
Sikuifanya. — see·koo·ee·*fa*·nya

Can I pay an on-the-spot fine?
Naweza kulipa faini hapa hapa? — na·*way*·za koo·*lee*·pa fa·*ee*·nee *ha*·pa *ha*·pa

Can I make a phone call?
Naweza kutumia simu? — na·*way*·za koo·too·*mee*·a *see*·moo

I want to contact my embassy/consulate.
Nataka kuwasiliana na ubalozi wangu. — na·*ta*·ka koo·wa·see·lee·*a*·na na oo·ba·*loh*·zee *wan*·goo

Can I have a lawyer (who speaks English)?

Naomba mwanasheria (anayesema Kiingereza).	na·*ohm*·ba mwa·na·shay·*ree*·a (a·na·yay·*say*·ma kee·een·gay·*ray*·za)

This drug is for personal use.

Dawa hili ni kwa matumizi yangu mwenyewe.	*da*·wa *hee*·lee nee kwa ma·too·*mee*·zee *yan*·goo mway·*nyay*·way

I have a prescription for this drug.

Nina agizo la daktari kwa dawa hili.	*nee*·na a·*gee*·zoh la dak·*ta*·ree kwa *da*·wa *hee*·lee

the police may say ...

Unashitakiwa na ...	oo·na·shee·ta·*kee*·wa na ...	**You're charged with ...**
Anashitakiwa na ...	a·na·shee·ta·*kee*·wa na ...	**He/She is charged with ...**
kubaki baada ya visa kuisha	koo·*ba*·kee ba·*a*·da ya *vee*·sa koo·*ee*·sha	**overstaying your visa**
kuiba dukani	koo·*ee*·ba doo·*ka*·nee	**shoplifting**
kutokuwa na visa	koo·toh·*koo*·wa na *vee*·sa	**not having a visa**
kuvuruka amani	koo·voo·*roo*·ka a·*ma*·nee	**disturbing the peace**
kuwa na (kitu kinyume cha sheria)	*koo*·wa na (*kee*·too kee·*nyoo*·may cha shay·*ree*·ya)	**possession (of illegal substances)**
shambulio	sham·boo·*lee*·oh	**assault**

Ni faini ya kuegesha gari.
nee fa·*ee*·nee ya koo·ay·*gay*·sha *ga*·ree — **It's a parking fine.**

Ni faini ya kwenda mwendo kubwa mno.
nee fa·*ee*·nee ya *kwayn*·da *mwayn*·do *koob*·wa *m*·noh — **It's a speeding fine.**

doctor

daktari

Where's the nearest ...?	*... hapo karibuni iko wapi?*	... *ha*·poh ka·ree·*boo*·nee *ee*·koh *wa*·pee
dentist	*Daktari wa meno*	dak·*ta*·ree wa *may*·noh
doctor	*Daktari*	dak·*ta*·ree
emergency department	*Wadi ya dharura*	*wa*·dee ya dha·*roo*·ra
hospital	*Hospitali*	hoh·spee·*ta*·lee
medical centre	*Kituo cha afya*	kee·*too*·oh cha *af*·ya
(night) pharmacist	*Duka la madawa (la saa za manane)*	*doo*·ka la ma·*da*·wa (la sa za ma·*na*·nay)
optometrist	*Daktari wa macho*	dak·*ta*·ree wa *ma*·choh
rural clinic	*Kliniki*	klee·*nee*·kee

I need a doctor (who speaks English).
Nahitaji daktari (anayesema Kiingereza). — na·hee·*ta*·jee dak·*ta*·ree (a·na·yay·*say*·ma kee·een·gay·*ray*·za)

Could I see a female doctor?
Inawezekana nione daktari mwanamke? — ee·na·way·zay·*ka*·na nee·*oh*·nay dak·*ta*·ree mwa·*nam*·kay

Could the doctor come here?
Daktari anaweza kuja hapa? — dak·*ta*·ree a·na·*way*·za *koo*·ja *ha*·pa

Is there an after-hours emergency number?
Kuna simu ya dharura kupiga baada ya saa za kazi? — *koo*·na *see*·moo ya dha·*roo*·ra koo·*pee*·ga ba·*a*·da ya sa za *ka*·zee

I've run out of my medication.
Dawa langu limekwisha. — *da*·wa *lan*·goo lee·may·*kwee*·sha

This is my usual medicine.

Hili ni dawa langu la kawaida.	*hee*·lee nee *da*·wa *lan*·goo la ka·wa·*ee*·da

My child weighs (20 kilos).

Mtoto wangu ana uzito wa (kilo ishirini).	m·*toh*·toh *wan*·goo *a*·na oo·*zee*·toh wa (*kee*·loh ee·shee·*ree*·nee)

What's the correct dosage?

Niambie kipimo halisi?	nee·am·*bee*·ay kee·*pee*·moh ha·*lee*·see

I don't want a blood transfusion.

Sitaki damu kutoka mtu mwengine.	see·*ta*·kee *da*·moo koo·*toh*·ka *m*·too mwayn·*gee*·nay

Please use a new syringe.

Tumia sindano mpya.	too·*mee*·a seen·*da*·noh *m*·pya

I have my own syringe.

Nina sindano yangu.	*nee*·na seen·*da*·noh *yan*·goo

the doctor may say ...

Kuna shida gani? koo·na *shee*·da *ga*·nee	**What's the problem?**
Una maumivu wapi? oo·na ma·oo·*mee*·voo *wa*·pee	**Where does it hurt?**
Una homa? oo·na *hoh*·ma	**Do you have a temperature?**
Umekuwa hivyo kwa muda gani? oo·may·*koo*·wa *heev*·yoh kwa *moo*·da *ga*·nee	**How long have you been like this?**
Imetokea kabla? ee·may·toh·*kay*·a *ka*·bla	**Have you had this before?**
Umekunywa maji yasiyo salama? oo·may·*koony*·wa *ma*·jee ya·*see*·yoh sa·*la*·ma	**Have you drunk any unsafe water?**
Umekula chakula kisicho salama? oo·may·*koo*·la cha·*koo*·la kee·*see*·choh sa·*la*·ma	**Have you eaten any unsafe food?**

the doctor may say ...

Wewe hufanya mapenzi? *way*·way hoo·*fa*·nya ma·*payn*·zee	**Are you sexually active?**
Umewahi kufanya mapenzi bila kinga? oo·may·*wa*·hee koo·*fa*·nya ma·*payn*·zee *bee*·la *keen*·ga	**Have you had unprotected sex?**
Unakunywa? oo·na·*koony*·wa	**Do you drink?**
Unavuta sigara? oo·na·*voo*·ta see·*ga*·ra	**Do you smoke?**
Unatumia madawa ya kulevya? oo·na·too·*mee*·a ma·*da*·wa ya koo·*lay*·vya	**Do you take drugs?**
Una mzio wa kitu chochote? *oo*·na m·*zee*·oh wa *kee*·too choh·*choh*·tay	**Are you allergic to anything?**
Unatumia dawa lolote? oo·na·too·*mee*·a *da*·wa loh·*loh*·tay	**Are you on medication?**
Unasafiri kwa muda gani? oo·na·sa·*fee*·ree kwa *moo*·da *ga*·nee	**How long are you travelling for?**
Inabidi ulazwe hospitalini. ee·na·*bee*·dee oo·*laz*·way hoh·spee·ta·*lee*·nee	**You need to be admitted to hospital.**
Inatakiwa daktari akuangalie ukifika nyumbani. ee·na·ta·*kee*·wa dak·*ta*·ree a·koo·an·ga·*lee*·ay oo·kee·*fee*·ka nyoom·*ba*·nee	**You should have it checked when you go home.**
Afadhali urudi kwenu kwa matibabu. a·fa·*dha*·lee oo·*roo*·dee *kway*·noo kwa ma·tee·*ba*·boo	**You should return home for treatment.**
Wewe huwaza magonjwa yasiyoonekana. *way*·way hoo·*wa*·za ma·*gohn*·jwa ya·see·yoh·oh·nay·*ka*·na	**You're a hypochondriac.**

I'm vaccinated against …	*Nimechanjwa kwa …*	nee·may·*chan*·jwa kwa …
hepatitis A/B/C	*uvimbe wa ini A/B/C*	oo·*veem*·bay wa *ee*·nee a/bay/say
meningitis	*homa ya uti wa mgongo*	*hoh*·ma ya *oo*·tee wa m·*gohn*·goh
rabies	*kichaa cha mbwa*	kee·*cha* cha *m*·bwa
tetanus	*pepopunda*	pay·poh·*poon*·da
typhoid	*homa ya matumbo*	*hoh*·ma ya ma·*toom*·boh
yellow fever	*homa ya manjano*	*hoh*·ma ya man·*ja*·noh

I need new …	*Nahitaji … mpya.*	na·hee·*ta*·jee … *m*·pya
contact lenses	*lenzi mboni*	*layn*·zee m·*boh*·nee
glasses	*miwani*	mee·*wa*·nee

My prescription is …
Agizo la daktari ni … a·*gee*·zoh la dak·*ta*·ree nee …

Can I have a receipt for my insurance?
Niandikie risiti kwa kampuni yangu ya bima. nee·an·dee·*kee*·ay ree·*see*·tee kwa kam·*poo*·nee *yan*·goo ya *bee*·ma

symptoms & conditions

dalili na uhali

I'm sick.
Mimi ni mgonjwa. *mee*·mee nee m·*gohn*·jwa

My friend is (very) sick.
Rafiki yangu ni mgonjwa (sana). ra·*fee*·kee *yan*·goo nee m·*gohn*·jwa (*sa*·na)

My child is (very) sick.
Mwanangu ni mgonjwa (sana). mwa·*nan*·goo nee m·*gohn*·jwa (*sa*·na)

He/She is having a/an …

allergic reaction	*Ana matatizo ya mzio.*	*a*·na ma·ta·*tee*·zoh ya m·*zee*·oh
asthma attack	*Anashambuliwa na pumu.*	a·na·sham·boo·*lee*·wa na *poo*·moo
baby	*Anajifungua.*	a·na·jee·foon·*goo*·a
epileptic fit	*Anashambuliwa na kifafa.*	a·na·sham·boo·*lee*·wa na kee·*fa*·fa
heart attack	*Ameshambuliwa na maradhi ya moyo.*	a·may·sham·boo·*lee*·wa na ma·*ra*·dhee ya *moh*·yoh

I've been …

injured	*Nimejeruhiwa.*	nee·may·jay·roo·*hee*·wa
vomiting	*Nimekuwa natapika.*	nee·may·*koo*·wa na·ta·*pee*·ka

I feel …	*Nasikia …*	na·see·*kee*·a …
anxious	*wasiwasi*	wa·see·*wa*·see
better	*afadhali*	a·fa·*dha*·lee
depressed	*huzuni*	hoo·*zoo*·nee
dizzy	*kizunguzungu*	kee·zoon·goo·*zoon*·goo
hot and cold	*joto na baridi*	*joh*·toh na ba·*ree*·dee
nauseous	*kichefuchefu*	kee·chay·foo·*chay*·foo
shivery	*mitetemeko*	mee·tay·tay·*may*·koh
strange	*siyo kawaida*	*see*·yoh ka·wa·*ee*·da
weak	*hafifu*	ha·*fee*·foo
worse	*mbaya zaidi*	m·*ba*·ya za·*ee*·dee

It hurts here.
Inauma hapa. ee·na·*oo*·ma *ha*·pa

I'm dehydrated.
Nimekausha maji. nee·may·ka·*oo*·sha *ma*·jee

I can't sleep.
Siwezi kulala. see·*way*·zee koo·*la*·la

I think it's the medication I'm on.
Nadhani ni dawa ninalomeza. na·*dha*·nee nee *da*·wa nee·na·loh·*may*·za

I'm on medication for …
Ninameza dawa kwa … nee·na·*may*·za *da*·wa kwa …

He/She is on medication for …
Anameza dawa kwa … a·na·*may*·za *da*·wa kwa …

I have (a/an) …
Nina … *nee*·na …

He/She has (a/an) …
Ana … *a*·na …

AIDS	*ukimwi*	oo·*keem*·wee
amoebic dysentery	*ugonjwa wa amoeba*	oo·*gohn*·jwa wa a·moh·*ay*·ba
asthma	*pumu*	*poo*·moo
bedbugs	*kunguni*	koon·*goo*·nee
bilharzia	*kichocho*	kee·*choh*·choh
cholera	*kipindupindu*	kee·peen·doo·*peen*·doo
cold n	*mafua*	ma·*foo*·a
constipation	*hali ya kufunga choo*	*ha*·lee ya koo·*foon*·ga cho
cough	*kikohozi*	kee·koh·*hoh*·zee
diabetes	*kisukari*	kee·soo·*ka*·ree
diarrhoea	*kuhara*	koo·*ha*·ra
fever	*homa*	*hoh*·ma
headache	*maumivu ya kichwa*	ma·oo·*mee*·voo ya *kee*·chwa
HIV	*VVU*	vee·vee·*yoo*
malaria	*malaria*	ma·*la*·ree·a
meningitis	*homa ya uti wa mgongo*	*hoh*·ma ya *oo*·tee wa m·*gohn*·goh
nausea	*kichefuchefu*	kee·chay·foo·*chay*·foo
pain	*maumivu*	ma·oo·*mee*·voo
runny nose	*pua yenye makamasi*	*poo*·a *yay*·nyay ma·ka·*ma*·see
sore throat	*koo lenye maumivu*	koh *lay*·nyay ma·oo·*mee*·voo
intestinal worms	*minyoo*	mee·*nyoh*
typhoid	*homa ya matumbo*	*hoh*·ma ya ma·*toom*·boh

women's health

afya ya wanawake

(I think) I'm pregnant.
(Nafikiri) mimi ni mja mzito. — (na·fee·*kee*·ree) *mee*·mee nee *m*·ja m·*zee*·toh

I'm on the pill.
Natumia vidonge vya uzazi wa mpango. — na·too·*mee*·a vee·*dohn*·gay vya oo·*za*·zee wa m·*pan*·goh

I haven't had my period for (six) weeks.
Sijaingia mwezini kwa wiki (sita). — see·ja·een·*gee*·a mway·*zee*·nee kwa *wee*·kee (*see*·ta)

I've noticed a lump here.
Nimegundua uvimbe hapa. — nee·may·goon·*doo*·a oo·*veem*·bee *ha*·pa

Do you have something for (period pain)?
Una dawa kwa (maumivu ya mwezini)? — *oo*·na *da*·wa kwa (ma·oo·*mee*·voo ya mway·*zee*·nee)

the doctor may say ...

Ulipopata hedhi ilikuwa lini?
oo·lee·poh·*pa*·ta *hay*·dhee ee·lee·*koo*·wa *lee*·nee — **When did you last have your period?**

Umepata hedhi?
oo·may·*pa*·ta *hay*·dhee — **Are you menstruating?**

Unatumia uzazi wa mpango?
oo·na·too·*mee*·a oo·*za*·zee wa m·*pan*·goh — **Are you using contraception?**

Wewe ni mja mzito?
way·way nee *m*·ja m·*zee*·toh — **Are you pregnant?**

Wewe ni mja mzito.
way·way nee *m*·ja m·*zee*·toh — **You're pregnant.**

I have a …	*Nina …*	*nee*·na …
urinary tract infection	*ambukizo la mfumo wa mkojo*	am·boo·*kee*·zoh la m·*foo*·moh wa m·*koh*·joh
yeast infection	*ambukizo la hamira*	am·boo·*kee*·zoh la ha·*mee*·ra

I need …	*Nahitaji …*	na·hee·*ta*·jee …
a pregnancy test	*kupima kama mimi ni mja mzito*	koo·*pee*·ma *ka*·ma *mee*·mee nee *m*·ja m·*zee*·toh
contraception	*uzuiaji mimba*	oo·zoo·ee·*a*·jee *meem*·ba
the morning-after pill	*kidonge cha kuzuia mimba kumeza baada ya mahusiano*	kee·*dohn*·gay cha koo·zoo·*ee*·a *meem*·ba koo·*may*·za ba·*a*·da ya ma·hoo·see·*a*·noh

allergies

mzio

I'm allergic to …	*Nina mzio wa …*	*nee*·na m·*zee*·oh wa …
He/She is allergic to …	*Ana mzio wa …*	*a*·na m·*zee*·oh wa …
antibiotics	*viuavija-sumu*	vee·oo·a·vee·ja·*soo*·moo
anti-inflammatories	*madawa ya kupunguza uvimbe*	ma·*da*·wa ya koo·poon·*goo*·za oo·*veem*·bee
aspirin	*aspirini*	as·pee·*ree*·nee
bees	*nyuki*	*nyoo*·kee
penicillin	*penisilini*	pay·nee·see·*lee*·nee
pollen	*chavua*	cha·*voo*·a
sulphur-based drugs	*madawa yenye sulfa ndani*	ma·*da*·wa *yay*·nyay *sool*·fa n·*da*·nee

I have a skin allergy.
Nina mzio wa ngozi. *nee*·na m·*zee*·oh wa n·*goh*·zee

inhaler	*kivutia pumzi*	kee·voo·*tee*·a *poom*·zee
injection	*sindano*	seen·*da*·noh
antimalarials	*madawa kuzuia malaria*	ma·*da*·wa koo·zoo·*ee*·a ma·*la*·ree·a

For food-related allergies, see **vegetarian & special meals**, page 172.

alternative treatments

matibabu mengine

I don't use (Western medicine).
Situmii (uganga wa Ulaya). — see·too·*mee* (oo·*gan*·ga wa oo·*la*·ya)

Can I see someone who practices acupuncture?
Naomba kuona mtaalamu wa tiba ya kuchoma sindano. — na·*ohm*·ba koo·*oh*·na m·ta·*la*·moo wa *tee*·ba ya koo·*choh*·ma seen·*da*·noh

Can I see someone who practices naturopathy?
Naomba kuona mtaalamu wa matibabu asilia. — na·*ohm*·ba koo·*oh*·na m·ta·*la*·moo wa ma·tee·*ba*·boo a·see·*lee*·a

better safe than sorry

Here are a few terms you might need to know while you're in East Africa, just to be on the safe side:

(DEET) insect repellent
dawa la kufukuza wadudu (aina ya dit) — *da*·wa la koo·foo·*koo*·za wa·*doo*·doo (a·*ee*·na ya deet)

(permethrin) insect repellent
dawa la kufukuza wadudu (aina ya permethrin) — *da*·wa la koo·foo·*koo*·za wa·*doo*·doo (a·*ee*·na ya payr·*may*·threen)

water purification tablets
vidonge vya kusafisha maji — vee·*dohn*·gay vya koo·sa·*fee*·sha *ma*·jee

parts of the body

sehemu za mwili

My … hurts.
… yangu inauma. … *yan*·goo ee·na·*oo*·ma

I can't move my …
Siwezi kuhamisha … yangu. see·*way*·zee koo·ha·*mee*·sha … *yan*·goo

I have a cramp in my …
Nina mkakamao kwenye … yangu. *nee*·na m·ka·ka·*ma*·oh *kway*·nyay … *yan*·goo

My … is swollen.
… yangu imevimba. … *yan*·goo ee·may·*veem*·ba

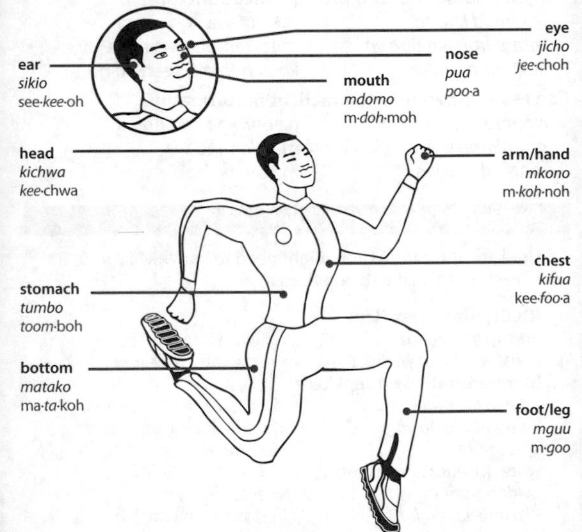

pharmacist

duka la madawa

I need something for (a headache).
Nahitaji dawa kwa (maumivu ya kichwa). — na·hee·*ta*·jee *da*·wa kwa (ma·oo·*mee*·voo ya *kee*·chwa)

Do I need a prescription for ...?
Inabidi niwe na agizo la daktari kwa ...? — ee·na·*bee*·dee *nee*·way na a·*gee*·zoh la dak·*ta*·ree kwa ...

I have a prescription.
Nina agizo la daktari. — *nee*·na a·*gee*·zoh la dak·*ta*·ree

How many times a day?
Mara ngapi kwa siku? — *ma*·ra n·*ga*·pee kwa *see*·koo

Will it make me drowsy?
Itanisinzisha? — ee·ta·nee·seen·*zee*·sha

antiseptic n	*dawa ya kusafisha jeraha*	*da*·wa ya koo·sa·*fee*·sha jay·*ra*·ha
condoms	*kondom*	*kohn*·dohm
contraceptives	*kingamimba*	keen·ga·*meem*·ba
iodine	*iodini*	ee·oh·*dee*·nee
painkillers	*viondoa maumivu*	vee·ohn·*doh*·a ma·oo·*mee*·voo
rehydration salts	*dawa ya kuongeza maji mwilini*	*da*·wa ya koo·ohn·*gay*·za *ma*·jee mwee·*lee*·nee

the pharmacist may say ...

Mara mbili kwa siku (pamoja na chakula).
ma·ra m·*bee*·lee kwa *see*·koo (pa·*moh*·ja na cha·*koo*·la) — **Twice a day (with food).**

Umewahi kumeza hili?
oo·may·*wa*·hee koo·*may*·za *hee*·lee — **Have you taken this before?**

Ni lazima umalize kosi.
nee *la*·zee·ma oo·ma·*lee*·zay *koh*·see — **You must complete the course.**

dentist

daktari wa meno

I have a …	*Nina …*	*nee*·na …
broken tooth	*jino lililovunjika*	*jee*·noh lee·lee·loh·voon·*jee*·ka
cavity	*kutokoka kwa jino*	koo·toh·*koh*·ka kwa *jee*·noh
toothache	*maumivu ya jino*	ma·oo·*mee*·voo ya *jee*·noh

I need (a/an) …	*Nahitaji …*	na·hee·*ta*·jee …
anaesthetic	*ganzi*	*gan*·zee
filling	*kijazio*	kee·ja·*zee*·oh

I've lost a filling.
Nimepoteza kijazio. nee·may·poh·*tay*·za kee·ja·*zee*·oh

My gums hurt.
Ufizi unaniumiza. oo·*fee*·zee oo·na·nee·oo·*mee*·za

I don't want it extracted.
Sitaki ung'oaji. see·*ta*·kee oong·oh·*a*·jee

the dentist may say …

Fumbua sana. foom·*boo*·a *sa*·na	**Open wide.**
Haitauma hata kidogo. ha·ee·ta·*oo*·ma *ha*·ta kee·*doh*·goh	**This won't hurt a bit.**
Tafuna na kamata. ta·*foo*·na na ka·*ma*·ta	**Bite down on this.**
Usihame. oo·see·*ha*·may	**Don't move.**
Sukutua! soo·koo·*too*·a	**Rinse!**
Rejea, sijamaliza. ray·*jay*·a see·ja·ma·*lee*·za	**Come back, I haven't finished.**

What is sustainable travel and responsible tourism?

Being a responsible tourist in East Africa means acknowledging that travel inevitably impacts on the host communities and environment you visit. When you travel, you're not only embracing the diversity of this big, wide, wonderful world – you're adding your footprints to those left by some of the 700-million-plus people who travel internationally each year. This runaway juggernaut affects wilderness, native species and traditional cultures. The goal is to make the impact as positive as possible by giving back to local communities and acting to minimise negative outcomes. In doing so, you're helping to make your steps lighter, greener and friendlier.

How can travel to East Africa have a positive effect on local industries and wildlife?

A region of stunning geography, all-night partying and wondrous architecture, East Africa is also the ultimate destination to observe the 'Big Five' (elephant, rhinoceros, leopard, lion and Cape buffalo) in their natural habitat. However, with the global inequities of wealth distribution so pronounced in East Africa, it's particularly important to ensure that your travel enjoyment is not at the expense of locals and their environment.

At one level, the impact of tourism can be positive – it can provide an incentive for locals to preserve environments and wildlife by generating employment, while enabling them to maintain their traditional lifestyles. However, the negative impacts of tourism can be substantial and contribute to the gradual erosion of traditional life. You can try to keep your impact as low as possible by following these tips:

- Support local enterprise. Use locally owned hotels and restaurants and buy souvenirs directly from the tradespeople and craftspeople who make them.
- Don't buy items made from natural materials such as ivory, skins and shells.
- Choose safari and trekking operators that treat local communities as equal partners, and that are committed to protecting local ecosystems.
- Question any so-called ecotourism operators about what they're really doing to protect the environment and the people who live there.
- Instead of giving cash, food or medicines to locals, make a donation to a recognised project such as a health centre or school.
- Try to get a balanced view of life in developing countries, and focus on the strong points of local culture.
- Resist the local tendency to be indifferent to littering. On treks, in parks or when camping, carry out your litter and leave areas cleaner than you found them.
- In order to help minimise land degradation, keep to the tracks when walking or when on safari, or encourage your driver to do so.

What are the main safari regions in East Africa?

East Africa has a clutch of popular parks showcasing some of the greatest wildlife spectacles on earth. Highlights are the magnificent Serengeti–Masai Mara ecosystem; the wildlife-packed Ngorongoro Crater and Tarangire National Park in Tanzania; Parc National de Volcans, Rwanda's original Gorillas in the Mist backdrop; and the hippo-, crocodile- and elephant-filled Murchison Falls and Budongo Central Forest Reserve with its chimpanzees and dense forest, in Uganda.

the big five

buffalo	*mbogo*	m·*boh*·goh
elephant	*ndovu/tembo*	n·*doh*·voo/*teym*·boh
leopard	*chui*	*choo*·ee
lion	*simba*	*seem*·baa
rhinoceros	*kifaru*	kee·*faa*·roo

For more on East African wildlife, see the box **local plants & animals** on page 152.

I'd like to visit a native-style tourist station.
Ningependa kufikia kwenye kituo cha kitalii cha kienyeji. — neen·gey·*peyn*·daa koo·*fee*·kaa *kweyn*·yey kee·*too*·oh chaa kee·taa·*lee* chaa kee·eyn·*yey*·jee

Are there any local-style guesthouses in the park?
Kuna nyumba za wageni za kienyeji ndani ya hifadhi? — *koo*·naa *nyoom*·baa zaa waa·*gey*·nee zaa kee·eyn·*yey*·jee n·*daa*·nee yaa hee·*faa*·dhee

Are there fair working standards at this park?
Kuna viwango vya kazi za kistaarabu ndani ya hifadhi? — *koo*·naa vee·*waan*·goh vyaa *kaa*·zee zaa kee·staa·*raa*·boo n·*daa*·nee yaa hee·*faa*·dhee

Is your business involved in tourism activities that protect the environment?
Biashara yako inajihusisha na shughuli za kitalii kuhifadhi mazingira? — bee·aa·*shaa*·raa *yaa*·koh ee·naa·jee·hoo·*see*·shaa naa shoo·*goo*·lee zaa kee·taa·*lee* koo·hee·*faa*·dhee maa·zeen·*gee*·raa

I'd like to hire a local guide.
Nataka kuajiri kiongozi kutoka hapo jirani. — naa·*taa*·kaa koo·aa·*jee*·ree kee·ohn·*goh*·zee koo·*toh*·kaa *haa*·poh jee·*raa*·nee

I'd like to go somewhere off the beaten track.

Nataka kuenda	naa·*taa*·kaa koo·*eyn*·daa
mahali ambapo	maa·*haa*·lee aam·*baa*·poh
siyo kawaida	*see*·yoh kaa·waa·*ee*·daa
kwa watalii.	kwaa waa·taa·*lee*

Is it safe to walk around this section of the park?

Ni salama	nee saa·*laa*·maa
nikitembea kwa	nee·kee·teym·*bey*·aa kwaa
miguu katika	mee·*goo* kaa·*tee*·kaa
sehemu hii ya	sey·*hey*·moo hee yaa
hifadhi?	hee·*faa*·dhee

Do you have information about the preservation of wildlife at this park?

Je, unazo taarifa	jey oo·*naa*·zoh taa·*ree*·faa
zinazohusiana	zee·naa·zoh·hoo·see·*aa*·naa
na utunzaji wa	naa oo·toon·*zaa*·jee waa
wanyama pori	waan·*yaa*·maa *poh*·ree
ndani ya hifadhi hii?	n·*daa*·nee yaa hee·*faa*·dhee hee

Do you have any endangered species at this park?

Je, unao viumbe	jey oo·*naa*·oh vee·*oom*·bey
walioko hatarini	waa·lee·*oh*·koh haa·taa·*ree*·nee
katika hifadhi hii?	kaa·*tee*·kaa hee·*faa*·dhee hee

Do you have the Big Five animals at this park?

Je, unao wanyama	jey oo·*naa*·oh waan·*yaa*·maa
wakuu watano katika	waa·*koo* waa·*taa*·noh kaa·*tee*·kaa
hifadhi hii?	hee·*faa*·dhee hii

Can you recommend a company that organises safaris?

Unaweza	oo·naa·*wey*·zaa
kupendekeza	koo·peyn·dey·*key*·zaa
kampuni ya safari	kaam·*poo*·nee yaa saa·*faa*·ree
kwa miguu?	kwaa mee·*goo*

For more practical phrases, see also **tours/safaris**, page 97, and **outdoors**, page 147.

Verbs are shown in the dictionary in their root forms, with a hyphen in front. To express a series of functions in a sentence, the verb can have several prefixes, infixes and suffixes. Some adjectives will also have a hyphen in front as they take different prefixes depending on certain characteristics of the thing being described. For more details on verbs and adjectives, see the **phrasebuilder**. You'll also find words marked as adjective ⓐ, noun ⓝ, verb ⓥ, singular sg or plural pl where necessary. A Swahili dictionary is also available online at www.kamusiproject.org.

A

aboard *chomboni* chohm·*boh*·nee
abortion *kutoa mimba* koo·*toh*·a *meem*·ba
about *kuhusu* koo·*hoo*·soo
above *juu ya* joo ya
abroad *nchi za nje* n·chee za *n*·jay
accident *ajali* a·*ja*·lee
accommodation *malazi* ma·*la*·zee
account (bank) *akaunti* a·ka·*oon*·tee
across *ng'ambo* ng·*am*·boh
activist *mhamisishaji* m·ha·mee·see·*sha*·jee
actor *mwigizaji* mwee·gee·*za*·jee
acupuncture *tiba ya kuchoma na sindano* *tee*·ba ya koo·*choh*·ma na seen·*da*·noh
adaptor *adapta* a·*dap*·ta
address *anwani* an·*wa*·nee
administration *usimamizi* oo·see·ma·*mee*·zee
admission (price) *bei ya kuingia* bay ya koo·een·*gee*·a
admit *·laza* ·*la*·za
adult ⓝ *mtu mzima* *m*·too m·*zee*·ma
advertisement *tangazo* tan·*ga*·zoh
advice *ushauri* oo·sha·*oo*·ree
aeroplane *ndege* n·*day*·gay
Africa *Afrika* a·*free*·ka
after *baada ya* ba·*a*·da ya
afternoon *mchana* m·*cha*·na
aftershave *losheni baada ya kunyoa ndevu* loh·*shay*·nee ba·*a*·da ya koo·*nyoh*·a n·*day*·voo
again *tena* *tay*·na
age *umri* *oom*·ree
agree *-kubali* ·koo·*ba*·lee
agriculture *kilimo* kee·*lee*·moh
ahead *mbele* m·*bay*·lay
AIDS *ukimwi* oo·*keem*·wee
air (outside) *hewa* *hay*·wa
air (in a tyre) *upepo* oo·*pay*·poh
air-conditioned *kwenye a/c* *kway*·nyay ay·*see*
air conditioning *a/c* ay·*see*
airline *kampuni ya ndege* kam·*poo*·nee ya n·*day*·gay
airmail *barua kwa ndege* ba·*roo*·a kwa n·*day*·gay
airplane *ndege* n·*day*·gay
airport *uwanja wa ndege* oo·*wan*·ja wa n·*day*·gay
airport tax *kodi ya uwanja wa ndege* *koh*·dee ya oo·*wan*·ja wa n·*day*·gay
aisle (on plane) *njia* n·*jee*·a
alarm clock *saa yenye kengele* sa *yay*·nyay kayn·*gay*·lay
alcohol *kilevi* kee·*lay*·vee
alcoholic drink *pombe* *pohm*·bay
all *zote* *zoh*·tay
allergy *mzio* m·*zee*·oh
almond *lozi* *loh*·zee
almost *karibu na* ka·*ree*·boo na
alone *pekee* pay·*kay*
already *tayari* ta·*ya*·ree
also *pia* *pee*·a
altar *madhahabu* ma·dha·*ha*·boo
altitude *kimo* *kee*·moh
always *daima* da·*ee*·ma
ambassador *balozi* ba·*loh*·zee
ambulance *gari la hospitali* *ga*·ree la hoh·spee·*ta*·lee
America *Marekani* ma·ray·*ka*·nee

American football *futbol ya kimarekani* *foot*·bohl ya kee·ma·ray·*ka*·nee
anaemia *upungufu wa damu* oo·poon·*goo*·foo wa *da*·moo
anarchist *mshabiki wa utawala huria* m·sha·*bee*·kee wa oo·ta·*wa*·la hoo·*ree*·a
ancient *ya kale* ya *ka*·lay
and *na* na
angry *mwenye hasira* *mway*·nyay ha·*see*·ra
animal *mnyama* m·*nya*·ma
ankle *kiwiko cha mguu* kee·*wee*·koh cha m·*goo*
another *nyingine* nyeen·*gee*·nay
answer *jibu* *jee*·boo
ant *sungusungu* soon·goo·*soon*·goo
antelope *palahala* pa·la·*ha*·la
antibiotic *kiuavijasumu* kee·oo·a·vee·ja·*soo*·moo
antinuclear *dhidi ya nyuklia* *dhee*·dee ya *nyoo*·klee·a
antique ⓝ *ya zamani* ya za·*ma*·nee
antiseptic ⓝ *dawa ya kusafisha jeraha* *da*·wa ya koo·sa·*fee*·sha jay·*ra*·ha
any *yoyote* yoh·*yoh*·tay
apartment *fleti* *flay*·tee
appendix (body) *kibole* kee·*boh*·lay
apple *tofaa* to·*fa*
appointment *miadi* mee·*a*·dee
April *mwezi wa nne* *mway*·zee wa *n*·nay
archaeological *ya elimu kale* ya ay·*lee*·moo *ka*·lay
architect *msanifu wa majengo* m·sa·*nee*·foo wa ma·*jayn*·goh
architecture *ujenzi* oo·*jayn*·zee
argue *-bisha* ·*bee*·sha
arm *mkono* m·*koh*·noh
aromatherapy *tiba ya harufu* *tee*·ba ya ha·*roo*·foo
arrest *-kamata* ·ka·*ma*·ta
arrivals *wanaofika* wa·na·oh·*fee*·ka
arrive *-fika* ·*fee*·ka
art *sanaa* sa·*na*
art gallery *nyumba ya sanaa* *nyoom*·ba ya sa·*na*
artist *msanii* m·sa·*nee*
ashtray *chombo cha majivu* *chohm*·boh cha ma·*jee*·voo
Asia *Asia* a·*see*·a
ask (a question) *-uliza* ·oo·*lee*·za
ask (for something) *-omba* ·*ohm*·ba
aspirin *aspirini* a·spee·*ree*·nee
asthma *pumu* *poo*·moo
at *kwenye* *kway*·nyay
athletics *michezo ya riadha* mee·*chay*·zoh ya ree·*a*·dha
atmosphere *hewa* *hay*·wa
aubergine *biringani* bee·reen·*ga*·nee
August *mwezi wa nane* *mway*·zee wa *na*·nay
aunt *shangazi* shan·*ga*·zee
Australia *Australia* a·oo·*stra*·lee·a
automated teller machine (ATM) *mashine ya kutolea pesa* ma·*shee*·nay ya koo·toh·*lay*·a *pay*·sa
autumn *kipindi cha baridi kidogo* kee·*peen*·dee cha ba·*ree*·dee kee·*doh*·goh
avenue *barabara* ba·ra·*ba*·ra
avocado *embe mafuta* *aym*·bay ma·*foo*·ta
awful *mbaya sana* m·*ba*·ya *sa*·na

B

B&W (film) *nyeusi na nyeupe* nyay·*oo*·see na nyay·*oo*·pay
baboon *nyani* *nya*·nee
baby *mtoto mchanga* m·*toh*·toh m·*chan*·ga
baby food *chakula cha mtoto mchanga* cha·*koo*·la cha m·*toh*·toh m·*chan*·ga
baby powder *pauda kwa mtoto* pa·*oo*·da kwa m·*toh*·toh
babysitter *yaya* *ya*·ya
back (body) *mgongo* m·*gohn*·goh
back (position) *nyuma* *nyoo*·ma
backpack *shanta* *shan*·ta
bacon *bekoni* bay·*koh*·nee
bad *mbaya* m·*ba*·ya
bag *mfuko* m·*foo*·koh
baggage *mizigo* mee·*zee*·goh
baggage allowance *uzito usiolipiwa* oo·*zee*·toh oo·see·oh·lee·*pee*·wa
baggage claim *sehemu ya kuchukulia mizigo* say·*hay*·moo ya koo·choo·koo·*lee*·a mee·*zee*·goh
bakery *duka la mkate* *doo*·ka la m·*ka*·tay
balance (account) *urari* oo·*ra*·ree
balcony *ubaraza* oo·ba·*ra*·za
ball *mpira* m·*pee*·ra
ballet *ngoma ya kuigiza hadithi* n·*goh*·ma ya koo·ee·*gee*·za ha·*dee*·thee
banana *ndizi* n·*dee*·zee
band (music) *kikundi* kee·*koon*·dee
bandage *plasta* *pla*·sta

Band-Aid *elasto* ay·*la*·stoh
bank *benki* *bayn*·kee
bank account *akaunti ya benki* a·ka·*oon*·tee ya *bayn*·kee
banknote *noti* *noh*·tee
baptism *ubatizo* oo·ba·*tee*·zoh
bar *baa* ba
bar work *kazi kwenye baa* *ka*·zee *kway*·nyay ba
barber *kinyozi* kee·*nyoh*·zee
basket *kikapu* kee·*ka*·poo
basketball *mpira wa kikapu* m·*pee*·ra wa kee·*ka*·poo
bath *bafu* *ba*·foo
bathing suit *nguo za kuogelea* n·*goo*·oh za koo·oh·gay·*lay*·a
bathroom (for bathing) *bafuni* ba·*foo*·nee
bathroom (toilet) *choo* chooh
battery *betri* *bay*·tree
be *-wa* ·wa
beach *ufukwe* oo·*fook*·way
beach volleyball *mpira wa wavu ufukoni* m·*pee*·ra wa *wa*·voo oo·foo·*koh*·nee
beans *maharagwe* ma·ha·*rag*·way
beansprouts *miche ya maharagwe* *mee*·chay ya ma·ha·*rag*·way
beautiful *ya kupendeza* ya koo·payn·*day*·za
beauty salon *saloni* sa·*loh*·nee
because *kwa sababu* kwa sa·*ba*·boo
bed *kitanda* kee·*tan*·da
bed linen *shuka* *shoo*·ka
bedding *shuka na tandiko* *shoo*·ka na tan·*dee*·koh
bedroom *chumba cha kulala* *choom*·ba cha koo·*la*·la
bee *nyuki* *nyoo*·kee
beef *nyama ng'ombe* *nya*·ma ng·*ohm*·bay
beer *bia* *bee*·a
beetroot *kiazisukari* kee·a·zee·soo·*ka*·ree
before *kabla* *ka*·bla
beggar *mwombaji* mwohm·*ba*·jee
behind *nyuma* *nyoo*·ma
Belgium *Ubelgiji* oo·bayl·*gee*·jee
below *chini* *chee*·nee
beside *jirani* jee·*ra*·nee
best *nzuri kabisa* n·*zoo*·ree ka·*bee*·sa
bet *dau* *da*·oo
better *afadhali* a·fa·*dha*·lee
between *katikati* ka·tee·*ka*·tee
Bible *Biblia* beeb·*lee*·a
bicycle *baisikeli* ba·ee·see·*kay*·lee

big *kubwa* *koob*·wa
bigger *kubwa zaidi* *koob*·wa za·*ee*·dee
biggest *kubwa kabisa* *koob*·wa ka·*bee*·sa
bike *baisikeli* ba·ee·see·*kay*·lee
bike chain *mnyororo wa baisikeli* m·nyoh·*roh*·roh wa ba·ee·see·*kay*·lee
bike lock *kufuli ya baisikeli* koo·*foo*·lee ya ba·ee·see·*kay*·lee
bike path *njia ya baisikeli* n·*jee*·a ya ba·ee·see·*kay*·lee
bike shop *duka la baisikeli* *doo*·ka la ba·ee·see·*kay*·lee
bill (restaurant etc) *bili* *bee*·lee
binoculars *darubini* da·roo·*bee*·nee
bird *ndege* n·*day*·gay
birth certificate *cheti cha kuzaliwa* *chay*·tee cha koo·za·*lee*·wa
birthday *sikukuu ya kuzaliwa* see·koo·*koo* ya koo·za·*lee*·wa
biscuit *biskuti* bee·*skoo*·tee
bite (dog, insect etc) ⓝ *uma* *oo*·ma
bitter *chungu* *choon*·goo
black *nyeusi* nyay·*oo*·see
bladder *kibofu* kee·*boh*·foo
blanket *blanketi* blan·*kay*·tee
blind *kipofu* kee·*poh*·foo
blister *lengelenge* layn·gay·*layn*·gay
blockage *kizuizi* kee·zoo·*ee*·zee
blood *damu* *da*·moo
blood group *aina ya damu* a·*ee*·na ya *da*·moo
blood pressure *shinikizo la damu* shee·nee·*kee*·zoh la *da*·moo
blood test *kipimo cha damu* kee·*pee*·moh cha *da*·moo
blue *buluu* boo·*loo*
board (a plane, ship etc) *-panda* ·*pan*·da
boarding house *nyumba ya wageni* *nyoom*·ba ya wa·*gay*·nee
boarding pass *pasi ya kupanda ndege* *pa*·see ya koo·*pan*·da n·*day*·gay
boat *boti* *boh*·tee
body *mwili* *mwee*·lee
boiled *ya kuchemshwa* ya koo·*chaym*·shwa
bone *mfupa* m·*foo*·pa
book ⓝ *kitabu* kee·*ta*·boo
book ⓥ *-fanya buking* ·*fa*·nya *boo*·keeng
booked out *hakuna nafasi* ha·*koo*·na na·*fa*·see
bookshop *duka la vitabu* *doo*·ka la vee·*ta*·boo
boots (footwear) *mabuti* ma·*boo*·tee

border *mpaka* m·*pa*·ka
bored *-choshwa* ·*choh*·shwa
boring *ya kuchosha* ya koo·*choh*·sha
borrow *-kopa* ·*koh*·pa
botanic garden *bustani ya kibotania* boo·*sta*·nee ya kee·boh·ta·*nee*·a
both *mbili* m·*bee*·lee
bottle *chupa* *choo*·pa
bottle opener *kifungua chupa* kee·foon·*goo*·a *choo*·pa
bottle shop *duka la pombe kali* *doo*·ka la *pohm*·bay *ka*·lee
bottom (body) *matako* ma·*ta*·koh
bottom (position) *chini* *chee*·nee
bowl *bakuli* ba·*koo*·lee
box *sanduku* san·*doo*·koo
boxer shorts *chupi* *choo*·pee
boxing *ndondi* n·*dohn*·dee
boy *mvulana* m·voo·*la*·na
boyfriend *mpenzi* m·*payn*·zee
bra *sidiria* see·dee·*ree*·a
brakes *breki* *bray*·kee
brandy *brandi* *bran*·dee
brave *shupavu* shoo·*pa*·voo
bread *mkate* m·*ka*·tay
bread rolls *skonzi* *skohn*·zee
break *-vunja* ·*voon*·ja
break down *-vunjika* ·voon·*jee*·ka
breakfast *chai ya asubuhi* *cha*·ee ya a·soo·*boo*·hee
breast (body) *titi* *tee*·tee
breast-feed *-nyonyesha* ·nyoh·*nyay*·sha
breathe *-pumua* ·poo·*moo*·a
bribe *-toa rushwa* ·*toh*·a *roosh*·wa
bridge *daraja* da·*ra*·ja
briefcase *mkoba* m·*koh*·ba
bring *-leta* ·*lay*·ta
brochure *kijitabu* kee·jee·*ta*·boo
broken *ya kuvunjika* ya koo·voon·*jee*·ka
broken down *ya kuharibika* ya koo·ha·ree·*bee*·ka
bronchitis *mkamba* m·*kam*·ba
brother *kaka* *ka*·ka
brown *kahawia* ka·ha·*wee*·a
bruise *jeraha* jay·*ra*·ha
brush *burashi* boo·*ra*·shee
bucket *ndoo* n·*doh*
Buddhist *Mbudisti* m·boo·*dee*·stee
budget *bajeti* *ba*·jay·tee
buffalo *nyati* *nya*·tee
buffet *meza kujihudumia* *may*·za koo·jee·hoo·doo·*mee*·a
bug *mdudu* m·*doo*·doo
build *-jenga* ·*jayn*·ga
builder *mjenzi* m·*jayn*·zee
building *jengo* *jayn*·goh
burn ⓝ *jeraha la moto* jay·*ra*·ha la *moh*·toh
burnt *ya kuchomwa* ya koo·*chohm*·wa
Burundi *Burundi* boo·*roon*·dee
bus (city) *daladala/matatu* Tan/Ken da·la·*da*·la/ma·*ta*·too
bus (intercity) *basi* *ba*·see
bus station *stendi ya basi* *stayn*·dee ya *ba*·see
bus stop *kituo cha basi* kee·*too*·oh cha *ba*·see
business *biashara* bee·a·*sha*·ra
business class *daraja la wafanyabiashara* da·*ra*·ja la wa·fa·nya·bee·a·*sha*·ra
business person *mfanyabiashara* m·fa·nya·bee·a·*sha*·ra
business trip *safari kwa biashara* sa·*fa*·ree kwa bee·a·*sha*·ra
busker *mwimbaji barabarani* mweem·*ba*·jee ba·ra·ba·*ra*·nee
busy (person) *mwenye shughuli nyingi* *mway*·nyay shoo·*goo*·lee *nyeen*·gee
but *lakini* la·*kee*·nee
butcher *bucha* *boo*·cha
butcher's shop *bucha* *boo*·cha
butter *siagi* see·*a*·gee
butterfly *kipepeo* kee·pay·*pay*·oh
button *kifungo* kee·*foon*·goh
buy *-nunua* ·noo·*noo*·a

C

cabbage *kabichi* ka·*bee*·chee
café *mgahawa* m·ga·*ha*·wa
cake *keki* *kay*·kee
cake shop *duka la keki* *doo*·ka la *kay*·kee
calculator *kikokotoo* kee·koh·koh·*toh*·oh
calendar *kalenda* ka·*layn*·da
call *-ita* ·*ee*·ta
camel *ngamia* n·ga·*mee*·a
camera *kemra* *kaym*·ra
camera shop *duka la kemra* *doo*·ka la *kaym*·ra
camp *-piga kambi* ·*pee*·ga *kam*·bee
camp site *kiwanja cha kupigia kambi* kee·*wan*·ja cha kuu·pee·*gee*·a *kam*·bee
camping ground *uwanja wa kupigia kambi* oo·*wan*·ja cha kuu·pee·*gee*·a *kam*·bee

camping store *duka la vifaa vya kambi* *doo*·ka la vee·*fa* vya *kam*·bee
can (be able) *-weza* ·*way*·za
can (have permission) *-ruhusiwa* ·roo·hoo·*see*·wa
can (tin) *mkebe/kopo* m·*kay*·bay/*koh*·poh
can opener *opena ya kopo* *oh*·pay·na ya *koh*·poh
Canada *Kanada* *ka*·na·da
cancel *-futa* ·*foo*·ta
cancer *kansa* *kan*·sa
candle *mshumaa* m·shoo·*ma*
candy *pipi* *pee*·pee
cantaloupe *tikiti maji ndogo la rangi ya machungwa* tee·*kee*·tee *ma*·jee n·*doh*·goh *la ran*·gee ya ma·*choon*·gwa
capsicum *pilipili hoho* *pee*·lee·*pee*·lee *hoh*·hoh
car *gari* *ga*·ree
car hire *kukodi gari* koo·*koh*·dee *ga*·ree
car owner's title *haki ya kisheria ya mmiliki wa gari* *ha*·kee ya kee·shay·*ree*·a ya m·mee·*lee*·kee wa *ga*·ree
car park *sehemu ya kuegeshea magari* say·*hay*·moo ya koo·ay·gay·*shay*·a ma·*ga*·ree
car registration *usajili wa gari* oo·*sa*·jee·lee wa *ga*·ree
caravan *lori la wasafiri* *loh*·ree la wa·sa·*fee*·ree
cardiac arrest *kusimama kwa mapigo ya moyo* koo·see·*ma*·ma kwa ma·*pee*·goh ya *moh*·yoh
cards (playing) *karata* ka·*ra*·ta
care (for someone) *-tunza* ·*toon*·za
carpenter *seremala* say·ray·*ma*·la
carrot *karoti* ka·*roh*·tee
carry *-beba* ·*bay*·ba
carton *katoni* ka·*toh*·nee
cash ⓝ *fedha* *fay*·dha
cash register *rejista* ray·*gee*·sta
cash (a cheque) *-lipwa fedha kwa kutoa hundi* ·*leep*·wa *fay*·dha kwa koo·*toh*·a *hoon*·dee
cashew *korosho* koh·*roh*·shoh
cashier *keshia* kay·*shee*·a
casino *kasino* ka·*see*·noh
cassette *kanda* *kan*·da
castle *husuni* hoo·*soo*·nee
casual work *kibarua* kee·ba·*roo*·a
cat *paka* *pa*·ka
cathedral *kanisa kuu* ka·*nee*·sa koo
Catholic (denomination) *Romani* roh·*ma*·nee
Catholic (person) *Mkatoliki* m·ka·toh·*lee*·kee
cauliflower *koliflawa* koh·lee·*fla*·wa
cave *pango* *pan*·goh
CD *CD* see·*dee*
CD-ROM *cd-rom* see·dee·*rohm*
celebration *sherehe* shay·*ray*·hay
cell phone *simu ya mkononi* *see*·moo ya m·koh·*noh*·nee
cemetery *makaburini* ma·ka·boo·*ree*·nee
cent *senti* *sayn*·tee
centimetre *sentimita* sayn·tee·*mee*·ta
Central Africa *Afrika ya Kati* a·*free*·ka ya *ka*·tee
centre *katikati* ka·tee·*ka*·tee
ceramics *ufinyanzi* oo·fee·*nyan*·zee
cereal *nafaka* na·*fa*·ka
certificate *cheti* *chay*·tee
chain *mnyororo* m·nyoh·*roh*·roh
chair *kiti* *kee*·tee
championships *mashindano ya ubingwa* ma·sheen·*da*·noh ya oo·*been*·gwa
chance *nafasi* na·*fa*·see
change (coins) *sarafu* sa·*ra*·foo
change (money) *-badilisha hela* ·ba·dee·*lee*·sha *hay*·la
changing room (in shop) *chumba cha kubadilisha nguo* *choom*·ba cha koo·ba·dee·*lee*·sha n·*goo*·oh
charming *mwenye haiba* *mway*·nyay ha·*ee*·ba
cheap *rahisi* ra·*hee*·see
cheat ⓝ *mdanganyi* m·dan·*ga*·nyee
check (banking) *hundi* *hoon*·dee
check (bill) *bili* *bee*·lee
check *-kagua* ·ka·*goo*·a
check-in (desk) *mapokezi* ma·poh·*kay*·zee
checkpoint *kituo cha ukaguzi* kee·*too*·oh cha oo·ka·*goo*·zee
cheese *jibini* jee·*bee*·nee
cheetah *duma* *doo*·ma
chef *mpishi* m·*pee*·shee
chemist (pharmacy) *duka la dawa* *doo*·ka la *da*·wa
chemist (person) *mfamasia* m·fa·ma·*see*·a
cheque (banking) *hundi* *hoon*·dee
cheque (bill) *bili* *bee*·lee
cherry *cheri* *chay*·ree
chess *sataranji* sa·ta·*ran*·jee
chessboard *ubao wa sataranji* oo·*ba*·oh wa sa·ta·*ran*·jee
chest (body) *kufua* koo·*foo*·a

chewing gum *mpira* m·*pee*·ra
chicken *kuku* *koo*·koo
chicken pox *tetekuwanga* tay·tay·koo·*wan*·ga
child *mtoto* m·*toh*·toh
child seat *kiti cha mtoto* *kee*·tee cha m·*toh*·toh
childminding *ulezi wa mtoto* oo·*lay*·zee wa m·*toh*·toh
children *watoto* wa·*toh*·toh
chilli *pilipili hoho* pee·lee·*pee*·lee *hoh*·hoh
chilli sauce *mchuzi wa pilipili hoho* m·*choo*·zee wa pee·lee·*pee*·lee *hoh*·hoh
China *China* *chee*·na
chiropractor *tabibu wa maungo* ta·*bee*·boo wa ma·*oon*·goh
choose *-chagua* ·cha·*goo*·a
chopping board *bao la kukatia* *ba*·oh la koo·ka·*tee*·a
Christian *Mkristo* m·*kree*·stoh
Christian name *jina la kwanza* *jee*·na la *kwan*·za
Christmas *Krismasi* krees·*ma*·see
church *kanisa* ka·*nee*·sa
cigar *biri* *bee*·ree
cigarette *sigara* see·*ga*·ra
cigarette lighter *kiwashio* kee·wa·*shee*·oh
cinema *sinema* see·*nay*·ma
circus *sarakasi* sa·ra·*ka*·see
citizenship *uraia* oo·ra·*ee*·a
city *mji* *m*·jee
city centre *katikati ya mji* ka·tee·*ka*·tee ya *m*·jee
civil rights *haki za binadamu* *ha*·kee za been·a·*da*·moo
class (category) *tabaka* ta·*ba*·ka
class system *mfumo wa matabaka* m·*foo*·moh wa ma·ta·*ba*·ka
classical *ya jadi* ya *ja*·dee
clay *udongo* oo·*dohn*·goh
clean ⓐ *safi* *sa*·fee
clean *-safisha* ·sa·*fee*·sha
cleaning *usafi* oo·*sa*·fee
client *mteja* m·*tay*·ja
cliff *mwamba* *mwam*·ba
climb *-panda* ·*pan*·da
cloakroom *chumba cha makoti* *choom*·ba cha ma·*koh*·tee
clock *saa* sa
close *-funga* ·*foon*·ga
closed *ya kufungwa* ya koo·*foon*·gwa
clothesline *kamba ya kukausha nguo* *kam*·ba ya koo·ka·*oo*·sha n·*goo*·oh
clothing *nguo* n·*goo*·oh
clothing store *duka la nguo* *doo*·ka la n·*goo*·oh
cloud *wingu* *ween*·goo
cloudy *kuna mawingu* *koo*·na ma·*ween*·goo
clutch (car) *klachi* *kla*·chee
coach (bus) *basi* *ba*·see
coast *pwani* *pwa*·nee
coat *koti* *koh*·tee
cobra *koboko* koh·*boh*·koh
cocaine *kokeini* koh·kay·*ee*·nee
cockroach *mende* *mayn*·day
cocoa *kakao* ka·*ka*·oh
coconut *nazi* *na*·zee
coffee *kahawa* ka·*ha*·wa
coins *sarafu* sa·*ra*·foo
cold ⓐ *baridi* ba·*ree*·dee
cold (illness) *ugonjwa* oo·*gon*·jwa
colleague *mwenzi wangu* *mwayn*·zee *wan*·goo
collect call *gharama kwa mpigiwa simu* gha·*ra*·ma kwa m·pee·*gee*·wa *see*·moo
college *chuo* *choo*·oh
colour *rangi* *ran*·gee
comb *chanuo* cha·*noo*·oh
come *-ja* ·ja
comedy *ya kuchekesha* ya koo·chay·*kay*·sha
comfortable *ya starehe* ya sta·*ray*·hay
commission *kamisheni* ka·mee·*shay*·nee
communications (profession) *mawasiliano* ma·wa·see·lee·*a*·noh
communion *komunyo* koh·*moo*·nyoh
(The) Comoros Islands *Visiwa vya Komoros* vee·*see*·wa vya koh·*moh*·rohs
companion *mwenzi* *mwayn*·zee
company *kampuni* kam·*poo*·nee
compass *dira* *dee*·ra
complaint *lalamiko* la·la·*mee*·koh
complimentary (free) *bure* *boo*·ray
computer *kompyuta* kohm·*pyoo*·ta
computer game *mchezo kwenye kompyuta* m·*chay*·zoh *kway*·nyay kom·*pyoo*·ta
concert *onyesho la muziki* oh·*nyay*·shoh la moo·*zee*·kee
concussion *mshtuko wa ubongo* m·*shtoo*·koh wa oo·*bohn*·goh
conditioner (hair) *dawa la kuboresha nywele* *da*·wa la koo·boh·*ray*·sha *nyway*·lay
condom *kondom* *kohn*·dohm
conference (big) *mikutano* mee·koo·*ta*·noh

conference (small) *mkutano* m·koo·*ta*·noh
confession *ungamo* oon·*ga*·moh
confirm (a booking) *-hakikisha* ·ha·kee·*kee*·sha
congratulations *hongera* hohn·*gay*·ra
conjunctivitis *uvimbe wa mboni* oo·*veem*·bay wa m·*boh*·nee
connection *kiungo* kee·*oon*·goh
conservative *muhafidhina* moo·ha·fee·*dhee*·na
constipation *uyabisi wa tumbo* oo·ya·*bee*·see wa *toom*·boh
consulate *ubalozi mdogo* oo·ba·*loh*·zee m·*doh*·goh
contact lenses *lenzi mboni* *layn*·zee m·*boh*·nee
contact lenses solution *myeyuko wa lenzi mboni* m·yay·*yoo*·koh wa *layn*·zee m·*boh*·nee
contraceptives *kingamimba* keen·ga·*meem*·ba
contract *mkataba* m·ka·*ta*·ba
convenience store *duka la bidhaa mbalimbali* *doo*·ka la bee·*dha* m·ba·lee·m·*ba*·lee
convent *jumuiya ya masista* joo·moo·*ee*·ya ya ma·*see*·sta
cook ⓝ *mpishi* m·*pee*·shee
cook ⓥ *-pika* ·*pee*·ka
cookie *biskuti* bee·*skoo*·tee
cooking *kupika* koo·*pee*·ka
cool (temperature) *ya baridi* ya ba·*ree*·dee
copper *shaba* *sha*·ba
corkscrew *kizibuo* kee·zee·*boo*·oh
corn *mahindi* ma·*heen*·dee
corner *kona* *koh*·na
corrupt *ya kula rushwa* ya *koo*·la *roosh*·wa
cost *gharama* ga·*ra*·ma
cotton *pamba* *pam*·ba
cotton balls *mafusha ya pamba* pl ma·*foo*·sha ya *pam*·ba
cotton buds *vijiti vya pamba safi* pl vee·*jee*·tee vya *pam*·ba *sa*·fee
cough *kikohozi* kee·koh·*hoh*·zee
cough medicine *dawa la kukohoa* *da*·wa la koo·koh·*hoh*·a
count *-hesabu* ·hay·*sa*·boo
counter (at bar) *kaunta* ka·*oon*·ta
country *nchi* *n*·chee
countryside *nyika* *nyee*·ka
coupon *kuponi* koo·*pohn*·ee
courgette *mumunye ya kula* moo·*moo*·nyay ya *koo*·la
court (legal) *mahakama* ma·*ha*·ka·ma
court (tennis) *kiwanja* kee·*wan*·ja
cover charge *bei ya kuingia* bay ya koo·een·*gee*·a
cow *ng'ombe* ng·*ohm*·bay
cracker (biscuit) *mkate mkavu* m·*ka*·tay m·*ka*·voo
crafts *vitu vya sanaa* *vee*·too vya sa·*na*
crash *mgongano* m·gohn·*ga*·noh
crazy *mwenye kichaa* *mway*·nyay kee·*cha*
cream *mtindi* m·*teen*·dee
credit *mkopo* m·*koh*·poh
credit card *kadi ya benki* *ka*·dee ya *bayn*·kee
crocodile *mamba* *mam*·ba
crop *zao* *za*·oh
cross (religious) *msalaba* m·sa·*la*·ba
crowded *ya kujazana* ya koo·ja·*za*·na
cucumber *tango* *tan*·goh
cup *kikombe* kee·*kohm*·bay
cupboard *kabati* ka·*ba*·tee
currency exchange *kubadilisha hela* koo·ba·dee·*lee*·sha *hay*·la
current (electricity) *mkondo* m·*kohn*·doh
curry *bizari* bee·*za*·ree
custom (tradition) *mila* *mee*·la
customs *forodha* foh·*roh*·dha
cut *-kata* ·*ka*·ta
cutlery *visu* *vee*·soo
CV *maelezo binafsi ya ujuzi* ma·ay·*lay*·zoh bee·*naf*·see ya oo·*joo*·zee
cycle *-panda baisikeli* ·*pan*·da ba·ee·see·*kay*·lee
cycling *kupanda baisikeli* koo·*pan*·da ba·ee·see·*kay*·lee
cyclist *mpanda baisikeli* m·*pan*·da ba·ee·see·*kay*·lee
cystitis *kuvimba kibofu* koo·*veem*·ba kee·*boh*·foo

D

dad *baba* *ba*·ba
daily *kila siku* *kee*·la *see*·koo
dance *-cheza densi* ·*chay*·za *dayn*·see
dancing *densi* *dayn*·see
dangerous *hatari* ha·*ta*·ree
dark (at night) *giza* *gee*·za
dark (of colour) *nyeusi* nyay·*oo*·see
date (appointment) *miadi* mee·*a*·dee

date (fruit) *tende* tayn·day
date (day) *tarehe* ta·*ray*·hay
date (a person) *-wa marafiki* ·wa ma·ra·*fee*·kee
date of birth *tarehe ya kuzaliwa* ta·*ray*·hay ya koo·za·*lee*·wa
daughter *binti* *been*·tee
dawn *kucha* *koo*·cha
day *siku* *see*·koo
(the) day after tomorrow *kesho kutwa* *kay*·shoh *koot*·wa
(the) day before yesterday *juzi* *joo*·zee
dead *amekufa* a·may·*koo*·fa
deaf *ziwi* *zee*·wee
December *mwezi wa kumi na mbili* *mway*·zee wa *koo*·mee na m·*bee*·lee
decide *-amua* ·a·*moo*·a
deep *-refu* ·*ray*·foo
deforestation *kuharibu misitu* koo·ha·*ree*·boo mee·*see*·too
degrees (temperature) *nyuzi* *nyoo*·zee
delay *ucheleweshaji* oo·chay·lay·way·*sha*·jee
deliver *-fikisha* ·fee·*kee*·sha
democracy *demokrasia* day·moh·*kra*·see·a
demonstration (protest) *maandamano* ma·an·da·*ma*·noh
Denmark *Denmarki* dayn·*mar*·kee
dental floss *uzi wa meno* *oo*·zee wa *may*·noh
dentist *daktari wa meno* dak·*ta*·ree wa *may*·noh
deodorant *diodorani* dee·oh·doh·*ra*·nee
depart *-ondoka* ·ohn·*doh*·ka
department store *duka lenye vitu vingi* *doo*·ka *lay*·nyay *vee*·too *veen*·gee
departure *kuondoka* koo·ohn·*doh*·ka
departure gate *mlango wa kuondoka* m·*lan*·goh wa koo·ohn·*doh*·ka
deposit (bank) *amana* a·*ma*·na
desert *jangwa* *jan*·gwa
design *rasimu* ra·*see*·moo
dessert *kitindamlo* kee·teen·da·*m*·loh
destination *kifiko* kee·*fee*·koh
details *vipengele* vee·payn·*gay*·lay
diabetes *kisukari* kee·soo·*ka*·ree
dial tone *mlio wa simu* m·*lee*·oh wa *see*·moo
diaper *nepi* *nay*·pee
diaphragm (contraceptive) *kiwambo cha kizuia mimba* kee·*wam*·boh cha kee·zoo·*ee*·a *meem*·ba
diarrhoea *kuhara* koo·*ha*·ra
diary *kitabu cha kumbukumbu* kee·*ta*·boo cha koom·boo·*koom*·boo
dice *dadu* *da*·doo
dictionary *kamusi* ka·*moo*·see
die *-fa* ·fa
diet ⓝ *mlo* *m*·loh
different *tofauti* to·fa·*oo*·tee
difficult *vigumu* vee·*goo*·moo
digital *dijiti* dee·*jee*·tee
dining car *bogi la kulia chakula* *boh*·gee la koo·*lee*·a cha·*koo*·la
dinner *chakula cha jioni* cha·*koo*·la cha jee·*oh*·nee
direct *moja kwa moja* *moh*·ja kwa *moh*·ja
direct dial *kupiga simu moja kwa moja* koo·*pee*·ga *see*·moo *moh*·ja kwa *moh*·ja
direction *uelekeo* oo·ay·lay·*kay*·oh
director *mkurugenzi* m·koo·roo·*gayn*·zee
dirty *chafu* *cha*·foo
disabled *wasiojiweza* wa·see·oh·jee·*way*·za
disco *disko* *dees*·koh
discount *punguzo* poon·*goo*·zoh
discrimination *ubaguzi* oo·ba·*goo*·zee
disease *maradhi* ma·*ra*·dhee
dish *chakula* cha·*koo*·la
disk *diski* *dee*·skee
disk (floppy) *disketi* dees·*kay*·tee
diving *kuzamia* koo·za·*mee*·a
diving equipment *vifaa vya kuzamia* vee·*fa* vya koo·za·*mee*·a
divorced *kutalikiwa* koo·ta·lee·*kee*·wa
dizzyness *kizunguzungu* kee·zoon·goo·*zoon*·goo
do *-fanya* ·*fa*·nya
doctor *daktari* dak·*ta*·ree
documentary (film) *filamu ya hali halisi* fee·*la*·moo ya *ha*·lee ha·*lee*·see
dog *mbwa* *m*·bwa
dole *posho* *poh*·shoh
doll *mwanasesere* mwa·na·say·*say*·ray
dollar *dola* *doh*·la
door *mlango* m·*lan*·goh
dope (drugs) *madawa ya kulevya* ma·*da*·wa ya koo·*lay*·vya
double *mbilimbili* m·bee·lee·m·*bee*·lee
double bed *kitanda cha watu wawili* kee·*tan*·da cha *wa*·too wa·*wee*·lee
double room *chumba cha watu wawili* *choom*·ba cha *wa*·too wa·*wee*·lee
down *chini* *chee*·nee
downhill *kwa kuteremka* kwa koo·tay·*raym*·ka

dozen *kumi na mbili* *koo*·mee na m·*bee*·lee
drama *hadithi kama riwaya* ha·*dee*·thee *ka*·ma ree·*wa*·ya
dream *ndoto* n·*doh*·toh
dress *vazi* *va*·zee
dried *ya kukaushwa* ya koo·ka·*oosh*·wa
dried fruit *matunda yaliyokaushwa* ma·*toon*·da ya·lee·yoh·ka·*oosh*·wa
drink ⓝ *kinywaji* kee·*nywa*·jee
drink *-nywa* ·nywa
drink (alcoholic) ⓝ *pombe* *pohm*·bay
drive *-endesha* ·ayn·*day*·sha
drivers license *leseni ya kuendesha gari* lay·*say*·nee ya koo·ayn·*day*·sha *ga*·ree
drug *dawa* *da*·wa
drug addiction *utegemezi wa madawa ya kulevya* oo·tay·gay·*may*·zee wa ma·*da*·wa ya koo·*lay*·vya
drug dealer *mwuzaji wa madawa ya kulevya* mwoo·*za*·jee wa ma·*da*·wa ya koo·*lay*·vya
drug trafficking *kuuza madawa ya kulevya* koo·*oo*·za ma·*da*·wa ya koo·*lay*·vya
drug user *mtumiaji wa madawa ya kulevya* m·too·mee·*a*·jee wa ma·*da*·wa ya koo·*lay*·vya
(illegal) drugs *madawa (ya kulevya)* ma·*da*·wa (ya koo·*lay*·vya)
drum *ngoma* n·*goh*·ma
(be) drunk *-lewa* ·*lay*·wa
dry *-kausha* ·ka·*oo*·sha
dry ⓐ *kavu* *ka*·voo
duck *bata* *ba*·ta
dummy (pacifier) *nyonyo bandia* *nyoh*·nyoh ban·*dee*·a
DVD *dvd* dee·vee·*dee*

E

each *kila* *kee*·la
ear *sikio* see·*kee*·oh
early *mapema* ma·*pay*·ma
earn *-pata* ·*pa*·ta
earplugs *vizibo vya masikio* vee·*zee*·boh vya ma·see·*kee*·oh
earrings *herini* hay·*ree*·nee
Earth *Dunia* doo·*nee*·a
earthquake *tetemeko la ardhi* tay·tay·*may*·koh la *ar*·dhee
east *mashariki* ma·sha·*ree*·kee
East Africa *Afrika ya Mashariki* a·*free*·ka ya ma·sha·*ree*·kee
Easter *Pasaka* pa·*sa*·ka
easy *rahisi* ra·*hee*·see
eat *-la* ·la
economy class *daraja la tatu* da·*ra*·ja la *ta*·too
ecstacy (drug) *ekstasi* *ayk*·sta·see
eczema *ukurutu* oo·koo·*roo*·too
education *elimu* ay·*lee*·moo
egg *yai* *ya*·ee
eggplant *biringani* bee·reen·*ga*·nee
election *uchaguzi* oo·cha·*goo*·zee
electrical store *duka la bidhaa za umeme* *doo*·ka la bee·*dha* za oo·*may*·may
electricity *umeme* oo·*may*·may
elephant *ndovu/tembo* n·*doh*·voo/*taym*·boh
elevator *lifti* *leef*·tee
email *barua pepe* ba·*roo*·a *pay*·pay
embarrassment *aibu* a·*ee*·boo
embassy *ubalozi* oo·ba·*loh*·zee
emergency *dharura* dha·*roo*·ra
emotional *mwenye hisia* *mway*·nyay hee·*see*·a
employee *mfanyakazi* m·fa·nya·*ka*·zee
employer *mwajiri* mwa·*jee*·ree
empty *tupu* *too*·poo
end *mwisho* *mwee*·shoh
endangered species *spishi zilizo hatarini* *spee*·shee zee·*lee*·zoh ha·ta·*ree*·nee
(I'm) engaged *nimechumbiwa* nee·may·choom·*bee*·wa
engagement (to be married) *uchumba* oo·*choom*·ba
engine *injini* een·*jee*·nee
engineer *mhandisi* m·han·*dee*·see
engineering *uhandisi* oo·han·*dee*·see
England *Uingereza* oo·een·gay·*ray*·za
English (language) *Kiingereza* kee·een·gay·*ray*·za
enjoy oneself *-furahia* ·foo·ra·*hee*·a
enough *ya kutosha* ya koo·*toh*·sha
enter *-ingia* ·een·*gee*·a
entertainment guide *mwongozo wa burudani* mwohn·*goh*·zoh wa boo·roo·*da*·nee
entry (access) *mwingilio* mween·gee·*lee*·oh
envelope *bahasha* ba·*ha*·sha
environment *mazingira* ma·zeen·*gee*·ra
epilepsy *kifafa* kee·*fa*·fa
equal opportunity *fursa sawa* *foor*·sa *sa*·wa
equality *usawa* oo·*sa*·wa

equipment *vifaa* vee·*fa*
escalator *eskaleta* ays·ka·*lay*·ta
estate agency *wakala wa shamba* wa·*ka*·la wa *sham*·ba
Ethiopia *Uhabeshi* oo·ha·*bay*·shee
euro *euro* ay·*oo*·roh
Europe *Ulaya* oo·*la*·ya
euthanasia *eutanasia* ay·oo·ta·*na*·see·a
evening *jioni* jee·*oh*·nee
every *kila* *kee*·la
everyone *wote* *woh*·tay
everything *kila kitu* *kee*·la *kee*·too
exactly *kamili* ka·*mee*·lee
example *mfano* m·*fa*·noh
excellent *barabara* ba·*ra*·ba·ra
excess baggage *mizigo ziada* mee·*zee*·goh zee·*a*·da
exchange *-badilisha* ·ba·dee·*lee*·sha
exchange rate *kiwango cha kubadiishia fedha* kee·*wan*·goh cha koo·ba·dee·*lee*·shee·a *fay*·dha
excluded *ya kuachwa* ya koo·*ach*·wa
exhaust (car) *mchemuo* m·chay·*moo*·oh
exhibition *maonyesho* ma·oh·*nyay*·shoh
exit *kutoka* koo·*toh*·ka
expensive *ghali* *ga*·lee
experience *uzoefu* oo·zoh·*ay*·foo
exploitation *utumiaji* oo·too·mee·*a*·jee
express ⓐ *ekspres* *ayk*·sprays
express mail *barua ya haraka* ba·*roo*·a ya ha·*ra*·ka
extension (visa) *uongezaji wa visa* oo·ohn·gay·*za*·jee wa *vee*·sa
eye *jicho* *jee*·choh
eye drops *matone ya macho* ma·*toh*·nay ya *ma*·choh
eyes *macho* *ma*·choh

F

fabric *kitambaa* kee·tam·*ba*
face (body) *uso* *oo*·soh
face cloth *kitambaa cha mkono* kee·tam·*ba* cha m·*koh*·noh
factory *kiwanda* kee·*wan*·da
factory worker *mfanyakazi wa kiwandani* m·fa·nya·*ka*·zee wa kee·wan·*da*·nee
fall (autumn) *kipindi cha baridi kidogo* kee·*peen*·dee cha ba·*ree*·dee kee·*doh*·goh
fall (down) *-anguka* ·an·*goo*·ka
family *familia* fa·mee·*lee*·a
family name *jina la familia* *jee*·na la fa·mee·*lee*·a
famous *maarufu* ma·a·*roo*·foo
fan (machine) *feni* *fay*·nee
fan (sport, etc) *mshabiki* m·sha·*bee*·kee
fanbelt *mkanda wa feni* m·*kan*·da wa *fay*·nee
far *mbali* m·*ba*·lee
fare *nauli* na·*oo*·lee
farm *shamba* *sham*·ba
farmer *mkulima* m·koo·*lee*·ma
fashion *mtindo* m·*teen*·doh
fast *ya kasi* ya *ka*·see
fat ⓐ *nene* *nay*·nay
father *baba* *ba*·ba
father-in-law *babamkwe* ba·ba·*m*·kway
faucet *bomba* *bohm*·ba
(someone's) fault *kosa* *koh*·sa
faulty *yenye kosa* *yay*·nyay *koh*·sa
fax machine *faksi* *fak*·see
February *mwezi wa pili* *mway*·zee wa *pee*·lee
feed *-lisha* ·*lee*·sha
feel (touch) *-hisi* ·*hee*·see
feeling (physical) *hisia* hee·*see*·a
feelings *hisia* hee·*see*·a
female *ya kike* ya *kee*·kay
fence *wigo* *wee*·goh
ferry *kivuko* kee·*voo*·koh
festival *tamasha* ta·*ma*·sha
fever *homa* *hoh*·ma
few *chache* *cha*·chay
fiancé *mchumba* m·*choom*·ba
fiancée *mchumba* m·*choom*·ba
fiction *uzushi* oo·*zoo*·shee
fig *tini* *tee*·nee
fight *pigano* pee·*ga*·noh
fill *-jaza* ·*ja*·za
fillet *sarara* sa·*ra*·ra
film (cinema) *filamu* fee·*la*·moo
film (for camera) *mkanda wa picha* m·*kan*·da wa *pee*·cha
film speed *mwendo wa mkanda* *mwayn*·doh wa m·*kan*·da
filtered *ya chujwa* ya *chooj*·wa
find *-gundua* ·goon·*doo*·a
fine ⓝ *faini* fa·*ee*·nee
fine ⓐ *nzuri* n·*zoo*·ree
finger *kidole* kee·*doh*·lay
finish ⓝ *mwisho* *mwee*·shoh
finish *-maliza* ·ma·*lee*·za
Finland *Ufini* oo·*fee*·nee
fire *moto* *moh*·toh

firewood *kuni* koo·nee
first *ya kwanza* ya *kwan*·za
first class *daraja la kwanza* da·*ra*·ja la *kwan*·za
first-aid kit *kisanduku cha huduma ya kwanza* kee·san·*doo*·koo cha hoo·*doo*·ma ya *kwan*·za
first name *jina la kwanza* *jee*·na la *kwan*·za
fish *samaki* sa·*ma*·kee
fishing *uvuvi* oo·*voo*·vee
fish shop *duka la samaki* *doo*·ka la sa·*ma*·kee
flag *bendera* bayn·*day*·ra
flamingo *heroe* hay·*roh*·ay
flashlight (torch) *tochi* *toh*·chee
flat ⓝ *fleti* *flay*·tee
flat ⓐ *tambalale* tam·ba·*la*·lay
flea *kiroboto* kee·roh·*boh*·toh
fleamarket *mnada* m·*na*·da
flight (of a bird) *mruko* m·*roo*·koh
flight (plane) *ndege* n·*day*·gay
flood *mafuriko* ma·foo·*ree*·koh
floor *sakafu* sa·*ka*·foo
floor (storey) *ghorofa* go·*ro*·fa
florist *duka la maua* *doo*·ka la ma·*oo*·a
flour *unga* *oon*·ga
flower *ua* *oo*·a
flu *fluu* floo
fly *-ruka* ·*roo*·ka
fog *ukungu* oo·*koon*·goo
follow *-fuata* ·foo·*a*·ta
food *chakula* cha·*koo*·la
food supplies *akiba za chakula* a·*kee*·ba ya za·*koo*·la
food vendor *mwuzaji wa chakula* mwoo·*za*·jee wa cha·*koo*·la
foot *mguu* m·*goo*
football (soccer) *soka* *soh*·ka
footpath *njia ya miguu* n·*jee*·a ya mee·*goo*
foreign *ya kigeni* ya kee·*gay*·nee
forest *msitu* m·*see*·too
forever *milele* mee·*lay*·lay
forget *-sahau* ·sa·*ha*·oo
forgive *-samehe* ·sa·*may*·hay
fork *uma* *oo*·ma
fortnight *wiki mbili* *wee*·kee m·*bee*·lee
fortune teller *mtabiri* m·ta·*bee*·ree
foul (sport) *faulo* fa·*oo*·loh
foyer *sebule* say·*boo*·lay
fragile *ya kuvunjika kirahisi* ya koo·voon·*jee*·ka kee·ra·*hee*·see
France *Ufaransa* oo·fa·*ran*·sa
free (available) *kupatikana* koo·pa·tee·*ka*·na
free (gratis) *bure* *boo*·ray
free (not bound) *huru* *hoo*·roo
freeze *-ganda* ·*gan*·da
fresh *bichi* *bee*·chee
Friday *Ijumaa* ee·joo·*ma*
fridge *friji* *free*·jee
fried *ya kukaangwa* ya koo·ka·*an*·gwa
friend *rafiki* ra·*fee*·kee
from *kutoka* koo·*toh*·ka
frost *sakitu* sa·*kee*·too
frozen *ya kugandwa* ya koo·*gan*·dwa
fruit *tunda* *toon*·da
fry *-kaanga* ·ka·*an*·ga
frying pan *kikaango* kee·ka·*an*·goh
full *ya kujaa* ya koo·*ja*
full-time *ya muda kamili* ya *moo*·da ka·*mee*·lee
fun *burudani* boo·roo·*da*·nee
funeral *kilio* kee·*lee*·oh
funny *ya kuchekesha* ya koo·chay·*kay*·sha
furniture *fenicha* fay·*nee*·cha
future ⓝ *mbeleni* m·bay·*lay*·nee

G

game (sport) *mchezo* m·*chay*·zoh
game park *hifadhi ya wanyama* hee·*fa*·dhee ya wa·*nya*·ma
garage *gereji* gay·*ray*·jee
garbage *takataka* ta·ka·*ta*·ka
garbage can *pipa la taka* *pee*·pee la *ta*·ka
garden *bustani* boo·*sta*·nee
gardener *mtunza bustani* m·*toon*·za boo·*sta*·nee
gardening *kilimo cha bustani* kee·*lee*·moh cha boo·*sta*·nee
garlic *kitunguu saumu* kee·toon·*goo* sa·*oo*·moo
gas (for cooking) *mafuta ya taa* ma·*foo*·ta ya ta
gas (petrol) *mafuta* ma·*foo*·ta
gas cartridge *mtungi wa gesi* m·*toon*·gee wa *gay*·see
gate (airport, etc) *mlango* m·*lan*·goh
gauze *shashi* *sha*·shee
gay *msenge* m·*sayn*·gay
gazelle *swala* *swa*·la
Germany *Ujerumani* oo·jay·roo·*ma*·nee
get *-pata* ·*pa*·ta

get off (a train, etc) *-shuka ·shoo*·ka
gift *zawadi* za·*wa*·dee
gig (musical) *onyesho* oh·*nyay*·shoh
giraffe *twiga* *twee*·ga
girl *msichana* m·see·*cha*·na
girlfriend *mpenzi* m·*payn*·zee
give *-pa* ·pa
given name *jina la kwanza* *jee*·na la *kwan*·za
glandular fever *homa ya matezi* *hoh*·ma ya ma·*tay*·zee
glass (drinking) *glesi* *glay*·see
glasses (spectacles) *miwani* mee·*wa*·nee
gloves *maglavu* ma·*gla*·voo
glue *gundi* *goon*·dee
go *-enda* ·*ayn*·da
go out *-enda nje* ·*ayn*·da *n*·jay
go out with *-rafikiana* ·ra·fee·kee·*a*·na
go shopping *-enda dukani* ·*ayn*·da doo·*ka*·nee
goal *goli* *goh*·lee
goalkeeper *kipa* *kee*·pa
goat *mbuzi* m·*boo*·zee
God *Mungu* *moon*·goo
goggles (swimming) *miwani ya kuogelea* mee·*wa*·nee ya koo·oh·gay·*lay*·a
gold *dhahabu* dha·*ha*·boo
golf ball *mpira wa gofu* m·*pee*·ra wa *goh*·foo
golf course *uwanja wa gofu* oo·*wan*·ja wa *goh*·foo
good *nzuri* n·*zoo*·ree
government *serikali* say·ree·*ka*·lee
gram *gramu* *gra*·moo
grandchild *mjukuu* m·joo·*koo*
grandfather *babu* *ba*·boo
grandmother *bibi* *bee*·bee
grapefruit *balungi* ba·*loon*·gee
grapes *zabibu* za·*bee*·boo
grass *nyasi* *nya*·see
grateful *mwenye shukrani* *mway*·nyay shook·*ra*·nee
grave *kaburi* ka·*boo*·ree
gray *kijivu* kee·*jee*·voo
great (fantastic) *nzuri sana* n·*zoo*·ree *sa*·na
green *kijani* kee·*ja*·nee
greengrocer *duka la mboga* *doo*·ka la m·*boh*·ga
grey *kijivu* kee·*jee*·voo
groceries *vyakula* vya·*koo*·la
groundnut *karanga* ka·*ran*·ga
grow *-mea* ·*may*·a

guarantee *dhamana* dha·*ma*·na
guess *-buni* ·*boo*·nee
guesthouse *gesti* *gay*·stee
guide (audio) *mwongozo wa sauti* mwohn·*goh*·zoh (wa sa·*oo*·tee)
guide (person) *kiongozi* kee·ohn·*goh*·zee
guide dog *mbwa wa kuongoza* *m*·bwa wa koo·ohn·*goh*·za
guidebook *kitabu cha mwongozo* kee·*ta*·boo cha mwohn·*goh*·zoh
guided tour *safari yenye kiongozi* sa·*fa*·ree *yay*·nyay kee·ohn·*goh*·zee
guilty *mwenye hatia* *mway*·nyay ha·*tee*·a
guitar *zeze* *zay*·zay
gum *mpira* m·*pee*·ra
gun *bunduki* boon·*doo*·kee
gym (fitness room) *ukumbi* oo·*koom*·bee
gymnastics *sarakasi* sa·ra·*ka*·see
gynaecologist *daktari wa akina mama* dak·*ta*·ree wa a·*kee*·na *ma*·ma

H

hair *nywele* *nyway*·lay
hairbrush *burashi ya nywele* boo·*ra*·shee ya *nyway*·lay
haircut *kukata nywele* koo·*ka*·ta *nyway*·lay
hairdresser *msusi* m·*soo*·see
halal *halali* ha·*la*·lee
half *nusu* *noo*·soo
hallucination *wazimu* wa·*zee*·moo
ham *nyama nguruwe* *nya*·ma n·goo·*roo*·way
hammer *nyundo* *nyoon*·doh
hammock *machela* ma·*chay*·la
hand *mkono* m·*koh*·noh
handbag *mkoba* m·*koh*·ba
handball *mpira wa mikono* m·*pee*·ra wa mee·*koh*·noh
handicrafts *kazi ya mikono* *ka*·zee ya mee·*koh*·noh
handkerchief *kitambaa cha mkono* kee·tam·*ba* cha m·*koh*·noh
handlebars *usukani* pl oo·soo·*ka*·nee
handmade *kutengenezwa kwa mkono* koo·tayn·gay·*nayz*·wa kwa m·*koh*·noh
handsome *mrembo* m·*raym*·boh
happy *mwenye furaha* *mway*·nyay foo·*ra*·ha
harassment *usumbufu* oo·soom·*boo*·foo
harbour *bandari* ban·*da*·ree

hard (not soft) *ngumu* n·*goo*·moo
hard-boiled egg *yai lililochemshwa* *ya*·ee lee·lee·loh·*chaym*·shwa
hardware store *duka la vifaa vya ujenzi* *doo*·ka la vee·*fa* vya oo·*jayn*·zee
hash *bangi* *ban*·gee
hat *kofia* koh·*fee*·a
have *-wa na* ·wa na
have a cold *-wa mgonjwa* ·wa m·*gohn*·jwa
have fun *-furahia* ·foo·ra·*hee*·a
hawker *mchuuzi* m·choo·*oo*·zee
hay fever *homa ya mzio* *hoh*·ma ya m·*zee*·oh
he *yeye* *yay*·yay
head *kichwa* *keech*·wa
headache *maumivu ya kichwa* ma·oo·*mee*·voo ya *keech*·wa
headlights *taa za mbele* ta za m·*bay*·lay
health *afya* *af*·ya
hear *-sikia* ·see·*kee*·a
hearing aid *chombo cha kusaidia kusikia* *chohm*·boh cha koo·sa·ee·*dee*·a koo·see·*kee*·a
heart *moyo* *moh*·yoh
heart attack *kushambuliwa na maradhi ya moyo* koo·sham·boo·*lee*·wa na ma·*ra*·dhee ya *moh*·yoh
heart condition *ugonjwa wa moyo* oo·*gohn*·jwa wa *moh*·yoh
heat *joto* *joh*·toh
heated *ya moto* ya *moh*·toh
heater *kipasha moto* kee·*pa*·sha *moh*·toh
heating *joto* *joh*·toh
heavy *nzito* n·*zee*·toh
helmet *helmeti* hayl·*may*·tee
help ⓝ *msaada* m·sa·*a*·da
help *-saidia* ·sa·ee·*dee*·a
hepatitis *uvimbi wa ini* oo·*veem*·bee wa *ee*·nee
her (ownership) *yake* *ya*·kay
herbs *mboga za majani* m·*boh*·ga za ma·*ja*·nee
herbalist *mganga wa madawa ya kienyeji* m·*gan*·ga wa ma·*da*·wa ya kee·ay·*nyay*·jee
here *hapa* *ha*·pa
heroin *heroini* hay·roh·*ee*·nee
high *juu* joo
high school *shule ya msingi* *shoo*·lay ya m·*seen*·gee
highchair *kiti juu cha mtoto* *kee*·tee joo cha m·*toh*·toh
highway *barabara* ba·ra·*ba*·ra
hike *-tembea porini* ·taym·*bay*·a poh·*ree*·nee
hiking *kutembea porini* koo·taym·*bay*·a poh·*ree*·nee
hiking boots *mabuti ya kutembea porini* ma·*boo*·tee ya koo·taym·*bay*·a poh·*ree*·nee
hiking route *njia ya kutembea porini* n·*jee*·a ya koo·taym·*bay*·a poh·*ree*·nee
hill *mlima* m·*lee*·ma
Hindu *Mhindu* m·*heen*·doo
hippopotamus *kiboko* kee·*boh*·koh
hire *-kodi* ·*koh*·dee
his *yake* *ya*·kay
historical *ya kihistoria* ya kee·hee·stoh·*ree*·a
history *historia* hee·stoh·*ree*·a
hitchhike *-omba lifti* ·*ohm*·ba *leef*·tee
HIV *VVU* vee·vee·*yoo*
holiday *sikukuu* see·koo·*koo*
holidays *likizo* lee·*kee*·zoh
home *nyumbani* nyoom·*ba*·nee
home brew *pombe ya kienyeji* *pohm*·bay ya kee·ay·*nyay*·jee
homeless *bila nyumba* *bee*·la *nyoom*·ba
homemaker *mke anayekaa nyumbani* *m*·kay a·na·yay·*ka* nyoom·*ba*·nee
homosexual *msenge* m·*sayn*·gay
honey *asali* a·*sa*·lee
honeymoon *fungate* foon·*ga*·tay
hoodlum *mhuni* m·*hoo*·nee
horn *honi* *hoh*·nee
horoscope *falaki* fa·*la*·kee
horse *farasi* fa·*ra*·see
horse riding *kupanda farasi* koo·*pan*·da fa·*ra*·see
hospital *hospitali* hoh·spee·*ta*·lee
hospitality *ukarimu* oo·ka·*ree*·moo
hot *joto* *joh*·toh
hot water *maji ya moto* *ma*·jee ya *moh*·toh
hotel *gesti* *gay*·stee
hour *saa* sa
house *nyumba* *nyoom*·ba
housework *kazi ya nyumbani* *ka*·zee ya nyum·*ba*·nee
how *namna* *nam*·na
how much *kiasi gani* kee·*a*·see *ga*·nee
hug *-kumbatia* ·koom·ba·*tee*·a
huge *kubwa sana* *koob*·wa *sa*·na
human resources *uwezo wa watu* oo·*way*·zoh wa *wa*·too

human rights *haki za binadamu* *ha*·kee za bee·na·*da*·moo
humanities *sayansi za jamii* sa·*yan*·see za ja·*mee*
hundred *mia mee*·a
hunger *njaa* n·*ja*
hunting *uwindaji* oo·ween·*da*·jee
hurt *-uma* ·*oo*·ma
husband *mume moo*·may
hyena *fisi fee*·see

I

I *mimi mee*·mee
ice *barafu* ba·*ra*·foo
ice axe *kishota cha kukatia barafu* kee·*shoh*·ta cha koo·ka·*tee*·a ba·*ra*·foo
ice cream *aiskrimu* a·ee·*skree*·moo
ice hockey *hoki ya barafuni* *hoh*·kee ya ba·ra·*foo*·nee
identification card (ID) *kitambulisho* kee·tam·boo·*lee*·shoh
idiot *mjinga* m·*jeen*·ga
if *kama ka*·ma
ill *mgonjwa* m·*gohn*·jwa
immigration *uhamiaji* oo·ha·mee·*a*·jee
impala *swalapala* swa·la·*pa*·la
important *muhimu* moo·*hee*·moo
impossible *haiwezekani* ha·ee·way·zay·*ka*·nee
in *katika* ka·*tee*·ka
in a hurry *kwa haraka* kwa ha·*ra*·ka
in front of *mbele ya* m·*bay*·lay ya
included *ndani yake* n·*da*·nee *ya*·kay
income tax *kodi ya mapato* *koh*·dee ya ma·*pa*·toh
India *Uhindi* oo·*heen*·dee
Indian Ocean *Bahari Hindi* ba·*ha*·ree *heen*·dee
indicator *kionyeshi* kee·oh·*nyay*·shee
indigestion *kuvimbiwa* koo·veem·*bee*·wa
indoor *ndani* n·*da*·nee
industry *kiwanda* kee·*wan*·da
infection *ambukizo* am·boo·*kee*·zoh
inflammation *uvimbe* oo·*veem*·bay
influenza *fluu* floo
information *taarifa* ta·a·*ree*·fa
ingredient *kiambato* kee·am·*ba*·toh
inject *-choma sindano* ·*choh*·ma seen·*da*·noh
injection *dawa la sindano* *da*·wa la seen·*da*·noh
injury *jeraha* jay·*ra*·ha
inner tube *tyubu tyoo*·boo
innocent *asiye na hatia* a·*see*·yay na ha·*tee*·a
inside *ndani* n·*da*·nee
instructor *mwalimu* mwa·*lee*·moo
insurance *bima bee*·ma
interesting *ya kuvutia* ya koo·voo·*tee*·a
intermission *mapumziko* ma·poom·*zee*·koh
international *ya kimataifa* ya kee·ma·ta·*ee*·fa
Internet *mtandao wa kompyuta* m·tan·*da*·oh wa kohm·*pyoo*·ta
Internet café *intanet kafe* een·ta·*nayt* ka·*fay*
interpreter *mkalimani* m·ka·lee·*ma*·nee
interview *mahojiano* ma·hoh·jee·*a*·noh
invite *-karibisha* ·ka·ree·*bee*·sha
Ireland *Irelandi* ee·ray·*layn*·dee
iron (for clothes) *pasi pa*·see
island *kisiwa* kee·*see*·wa
Israel *Israeli* ees·ra·*ay*·lee
it *hii* hee
IT *teknolojia ya maarifa* tayk·noh·loh·*jee*·a ya ma·a·*ree*·fa
Italy *Italia* ee·*ta*·lee·a
itch *mwasho mwa*·shoh
itemised *kuandikwa kitu kimoja kimoja* koo·an·*deek*·wa *kee*·too kee·*moh*·ja kee·*moh*·jah
itinerary *ratiba ya safari* ra·*tee*·ba ya sa·*fa*·ree
IUD *kitanzi cha kuzuia kuzaa* kee·*tan*·zee cha koo·zoo·*ee*·a koo·*za*

J

jacket *jaketi* ja·*kay*·tee
jail *gereza* gay·*ray*·za
jam *jamu ja*·moo
January *mwezi wa kwanza* *mway*·zee wa *kwan*·za
Japan *Japani* ja·*pa*·nee
jar *chupa choo*·pa
jaw *taya ta*·ya
jealous *mwenye wivu* *mway*·nyay *wee*·voo
jeans *jinzi jeen*·zee
jeep *jipi jee*·pee
jet lag *kizunguzungu cha saa kutokana na kusafiri kwa ndege* kee·zoon·goo·*zoon*·goo cha sa koo·toh·*ka*·na na koo·sa·*fee*·ree kwa n·*day*·gay

jewellery *vipuli* vee·*poo*·lee
jewellery store *duka la vipuli* *doo*·ka la vee·*poo*·lee
Jewish *Myahudi* m·ya·*hoo*·dee
job *kazi* *ka*·zee
jogging *kukimbia taratibu* koo·keem·*bee*·a ta·ra·*tee*·boo
joke *soga* *soh*·ga
journalist *mwandishi wa habari* mwan·*dee*·shee wa ha·*ba*·ree
journey *safari* sa·*fa*·ree
judge *hakimu* ha·*kee*·moo
juice *jusi* *joo*·see
July *mwezi wa saba* *mway*·zee wa *sa*·ba
jump *-ruka* ·*roo*·ka
jumper (sweater) *sweta* *sway*·ta
jumper leads *kebo za kuwashia* *kay*·boh za koo·wa·*shee*·a
June *mwezi wa sita* *mway*·zee wa *see*·ta

K

Kenya *Kenya* *kayn*·ya
ketchup *mchuzi wa nyanya* m·*choo*·zee wa *nya*·nya
key *ufunguo* oo·foon·*goo*·oh
keyboard *kichapishi* kee·cha·*pee*·shee
kick *-piga teke* ·*pee*·ga *tay*·kay
kidney *figo* *fee*·goh
kilogram *kilo* *kee*·loh
kilometre *kilomita* kee·loh·*mee*·ta
kind (nice) *mkarimu* m·ka·*ree*·moo
kindergarten *chekechea* chay·kay·*chay*·a
king *mfalme* m·*fal*·may
kiosk *kioski* kee·*oh*·skee
kiss ⓝ *busu* *boo*·soo
kiss *-busu* ·*boo*·soo
kitchen *jiko* *jee*·koh
knee *goti* *goh*·tee
knife *kisu* *kee*·soo
know *-jua* ·*joo*·a
kosher *halali* ha·*la*·lee

L

labourer *mfanyakazi* m·fa·nya·*ka*·zee
laces *kamba za viatu* *kam*·ba za vee·*a*·too
lake *ziwa* *zee*·wa
lamb *mwanakondoo* mwa·na·kohn·*doh*
land *ardhi* *ar*·dhee
landlady/landlord *mwenye nyumba* *mway*·nyay *nyoom*·ba
language *lugha* *loo*·gha
laptop *kompyuta ya kubeba* kohm·*pyoo*·ta ya koo·*bay*·ba
large *kubwa* *koob*·wa
last (previous) *ya kabla* ya *kab*·la
last (final) *ya mwisho* ya *mwee*·shoh
last week *wiki iliyopita* *wee*·kee ee·lee·yoh·*pee*·ta
late *ya kuchelewa* ya koo·chay·*lay*·wa
later *baadaye* ba·a·*da*·yay
laugh *-cheka* ·*chay*·ka
launderette *dobi* *doh*·bee
laundry (clothes) *nguo kufua* n·*goo*·oh koo·*foo*·a
laundry (place) *udobi* oo·*doh*·bee
laundry (room) *chumba cha dobi* *choom*·ba cha *doh*·bee
law *sheria* shay·*ree*·a
lawyer *mwanasheria* mwa·na·shay·*ree*·a
laxative *dawa la kuendesha* *da*·wa la koo·ayn·*day*·sha
lazy *mvivu* m·*vee*·voo
leader *kiongozi* kee·ohn·*goh*·zee
leaf *jani* *ja*·nee
learn *-jifunza* ·jee·*foon*·za
leather *ngozi* n·*goh*·zee
lecturer *mhadhiri* m·ha·*dhee*·ree
ledge *mwamba* *mwam*·ba
left (direction) *kushoto* koo·*shoh*·toh
left luggage *mizigo iliyowekwa* mee·*zee*·goh ee·lee·yoh·*wayk*·wa
left-luggage office *chumba cha kuwekea mizigo* *choom*·ba cha koo·way·*kay*·a mee·*zee*·goh
left-wing *mrengo wa kushoto* m·*rayn*·goh wa koo·*shoh*·toh
leg *mguu* m·*goo*
legal *halali* ha·*la*·lee
legislation *sheria* shay·*ree*·a
legume *kundekunde* koon·day·*koon*·day
lemon *limau* lee·*ma*·oo
lemonade *maji ya limau* *ma*·jee ya lee·*ma*·oo
leopard *chui* *choo*·ee
lens (eye) *mboni* m·*boh*·nee
lentil *dengu* *dayn*·goo
lesbian *msagaji* m·sa·*ga*·jee
less *chache* *cha*·chay
letter (mail) *barua* ba·*roo*·a
lettuce *saladi* sa·*la*·dee
liar *mwongo* *mwohn*·goh
library *maktaba* mak·*ta*·ba
lice *chawa* *cha*·wa

license *laiseni* la·ee·*say*·nee
licence plate number *namba ya gari* *nam*·ba ya *ga*·ree
lie (not stand) *-lala* ·*la*·la
life *maisha* ma·*ee*·sha
life jacket *jaketi la kuokolea* ja·*kay*·tee la koo·oh·koh·*lay*·a
lift (elevator) *lifti* *leef*·tee
light (brightness) *mwanga* *mwan*·ga
light (lamp) *taa* ta
light (colour) *nyeupe* nyay·*oo*·pay
light (not heavy) *nyepesi* nyay·*pay*·see
light bulb *balbu ya taa* *bal*·boo ya *ta*
light meter *kipima mwanga* kee·*pee*·ma *mwan*·ga
lighter (match) *kibiriti* kee·bee·*ree*·tee
lighter (cigarette) *kiwashio* kee·wa·*shee*·oh
like *-penda* ·*payn*·da
lime (fruit) *ndimu* n·*dee*·moo
linen (material) *kitani* kee·*ta*·nee
linen (sheets etc) *mashuka* ma·*shoo*·ka
lion *simba* *seem*·ba
lip balm *dawa la midomo* *da*·wa la mee·*doh*·moh
lips *midomo* mee·*doh*·moh
lipstick *rangi ya mdomo* *ran*·gee ya m·*doh*·moh
liquor store *duka la pombe* *doo*·ka la *pohm*·bay
listen *-sikiliza* ·see·kee·*lee*·za
little (not much) *chache* *cha*·chay
little (small) *-dogo* ·*doh*·goh
live (somewhere) *-ishi* ·*ee*·shee
liver *ini* *ee*·nee
lizard *mjusi* m·*joo*·see
local ⓐ *ya kienyeji* ya kee·ayn·*nyay*·jee
lock ⓝ *kufuli* koo·*foo*·lee
lock *-funga kwa ufunguo* ·*foon*·ga kwa oo·foon·*goo*·oh
locked *ya kufungwa* ya koo·*foon*·gwa
lollies *pipi* *pee*·pee
long *ndefu* n·*day*·foo
look *-angalia* ·an·ga·*lee*·a
look after *-tunza* ·*toon*·za
look for *-tafuta* ·ta·*foo*·ta
lookout *lindo* *leen*·doh
loose *kejekeje* kay·jay·*kay*·jay
loose change *pesa kichele* *pay*·sa kee·*chay*·lay
lose *-potea* ·poh·*tay*·a
lost *ya kupotezwa* ya koo·poh·tayz·wa
lost property office *chumba cha mali ya kuokota* choom·ba cha ma·lee ya koo·oh·koh·ta
(a) lot *nyingi* nyeen·gee
loud *kwa sauti* kwa sa·oo·tee
love ⓝ *upendo* oo·payn·doh
love ⓥ *-penda* ·payn·da
lover *mpenzi* m·*payn*·zee
low *chini* *chee*·nee
lubricant *kilainishio* kee·la·ee·nee·shee·oh
luck *bahati* ba·*ha*·tee
lucky *mwenye bahati* *mway*·nyay ba·*ha*·tee
luggage *mizigo* mee·zee·goh
luggage locker *sanduku la kuhifadhia mizigo* san·doo·koo la koo·hee·fa·dhee·a mee·zee·goh
luggage tag *tiketi ya mzigo* tee·*kay*·tee ya m·*zee*·goh
lump *uvimbe* oo·*veem*·bay
lunch *chakula cha mchana* cha·koo·la cha m·cha·na
lung *pafu* *pa*·foo
luxury *anasa* a·na·sa

M

machine *mashine* ma·*shee*·nay
Madagascar *Madagascar* ma·da·*ga*·skar
magazine *gazeti* ga·*zay*·tee
mail (letters) *barua* ba·*roo*·a
mail (postal system) *posta* *poh*·sta
mailbox *sanduku la posta* san·*doo*·koo la *poh*·sta
main *-kuu* ·koo
main road *barabara kuu* ba·ra·*ba*·ra *koo*
make *-tengeneza* ·tayn·gay·*nay*·za
make-up *kipodozi* kee·poh·*doh*·zee
malaria *malaria* ma·*la*·ree·a
Malawi *Malawi* ma·*la*·wee
man *mwanamume* mwa·na·*moo*·may
manager (restaurant, hotel) *meneja* may·*nay*·ja
manager (sales, sports) *mkurugenzi* m·koo·roo·*gayn*·zee
mandarin *chenza* *chayn*·za
mango *embe* *aym*·bay
manual worker *mfanyakazi wa kutumia mikono* m·fa·nya·*ka*·zee wa koo·too·*mee*·a mee·*koh*·noh
many *nyingi* *nyeen*·gee

map *ramani* ra·*ma*·nee
March *mwezi wa tatu*
mway·zee wa *ta*·too
margarine *blue bandi* bloo·*ban*·dee
marijuana *bangi ban*·gee
marital status *hadhi ya kindoa*
ha·dhee ya kee·n·*doh*·a
market *soko soh*·koh
marmalade *jamu ya machungwa*
ja·moo ya ma·*choon*·gwa
marriage *ndoa* n·*doh*·a
(I'm) married (man) *nimeoa*
nee·may·*oh*·a
(I'm) married (woman) *nimeolewa*
nee·may·oh·*lay*·wa
marry (man) *-oa* ·*oh*·a
marry (woman) *-olewa* ·oh·*lay*·wa
martial arts *mieleka* mee·ay·*lay*·ka
mass (Catholic) *misa mee*·sa
massage *kuchuliwa* koo·choo·*lee*·wa
masseur/masseuse *mchuaji* m·choo·*a*·jee
mat *mkeka* m·*kay*·ka
match (sports) *mechi may*·chee
matches (for lighting) *vibiriti*
vee·bee·*ree*·tee
mattress *godolo* goh·*doh*·loh
May *mwezi wa tano mway*·zee wa *ta*·noh
maybe *labda lab*·da
mayonnaise *mayonezi* ma·yoh·*nay*·zee
mayor *mwenyekiti* mway·nyay·*kee*·tee
me *mimi mee*·mee
meal *mlo m*·loh
measles *surua* soo·*roo*·a
meat *nyama nya*·ma
mechanic *fundi foon*·dee
media *vyombo vya habari*
vyohm·boh vya ha·*ba*·ree
medicine (study, profession) *udaktari*
oo·dak·*ta*·ree
medicine (medication) *dawa da*·wa
meditation *kutaamali* koo·ta·a·*ma*·lee
meet *-kuta* ·*koo*·ta
melon *tikiti maji* tee·*kee*·tee *ma*·jee
member *mwanachama* mwa·na·*cha*·ma
menstruation *hedhi hay*·dhee
menu *menyu may*·nyoo
message *ujumbe* oo·*joom*·bay
metal ⓝ *metali* may·*ta*·lee
metre *mita mee*·ta
microwave (oven) *joko la mikrowevu*
joh·koh la mee·kroh·*way*·voo
midday (noon) *saa sita mchana*
sa *see*·ta m·*cha*·na
midnight *saa sita usiku*
sa *see*·ta oo·*see*·koo
migraine *kipandauso* kee·pan·da·*oo*·soh
military ⓝ *jeshi jay*·shee
military service *kutumikia jeshi*
koo·too·mee·*kee*·a *jay*·shee
milk *maziwa* ma·*zee*·wa
millimetre *milimita* mee·lee·*mee*·ta
million *milioni* mee·lee·*oh*·nee
mince *nyama ya kusaga*
nya·ma ya koo·*sa*·ga
mineral water *maji ya madini*
ma·jee ya ma·*dee*·nee
minute *dakika* da·*kee*·ka
mirror *kioo* kee·*oh*
miscarriage *kuharibu mimba*
koo·ha·*ree*·boo *meem*·ba
Miss *Bibi bee*·bee
miss (feel absence of) *-kosa* ·*koh*·sa
mistake *kosa koh*·sa
mix *-changanyika* ·chan·ga·*nyee*·ka
mobile phone *simu ya mkononi*
see·moo ya m·koh·*noh*·nee
modem *modemu* moh·*day*·moo
modern *ya kisasa* ya kee·*sa*·sa
moisturiser *krimu ya kulainisha ngozi*
kree·moo ya koo·la·ee·*nee*·sha n·*goh*·zee
monastery *nyumba ya utawa wa*
wanaume nyoom·ba ya oo·*ta*·wa wa
wa·na·*oo*·may
Monday *Jumatatu* joo·ma·*ta*·too
money *pesa pay*·sa
monk *mtawa* m·*ta*·wa
monkey *tumbili* toom·*bee*·lee
month *mwezi mway*·zee
monument *mnara* m·*na*·ra
moon *mwezi mway*·zee
more *zaidi* za·*ee*·dee
morning *asubuhi* a·soo·*boo*·hee
morning sickness *kichefuchefu cha*
asubuhi kee·chay·foo·*chay*·foo cha
a·soo·*boo*·hee
mosque *msikiti* m·see·*kee*·tee
mosquito *mbu* m·boo
mosquito net *chandarua* chan·da·*roo*·a
motel *gesti gay*·stee
mother *mama ma*·ma
mother-in-law *mamamkwe*
ma·ma·*m*·kway
motorbike *pikipiki* pee·kee·*pee*·kee
motorboat *motaboti* moh·ta·*boh*·tee
motorcycle *pikipiki* pee·kee·*pee*·kee
motorway *barabara* ba·ra·*ba*·ra

mountain *mlima* m·*lee*·ma
mountain bike *baisikeli kwenye gia*
ba·ee·see·*kay*·lee *kway*·nyay *gee*·a
mountain path *njia ya kupanda mlimani*
n·*jee*·a ya koo·*pan*·da m·lee·*ma*·nee
mountain range *safu ya milima*
sa·foo ya mee·*lee*·ma
mountaineering *kupanda milima*
koo·*pan*·da mee·*lee*·ma
mouse *panya pa*·nya
mouth *mdomo* m·*doh*·moh
movie *filamu* fee·*la*·moo
Mozambique *Msumbiji* m·soom·*bee*·jee
Mr *Bwana bwa*·na
Mrs *Bi* bee
Ms (Miss) *Bibi bee*·bee
mud *matope* ma·*toh*·pay
mum *mama ma*·ma
mumps *machumbwichumbwi*
ma·choom·bwee·*choom*·bwee
murder ⓝ *mauaji* ma·oo·*a*·jee
murder ⓥ *-ua ·oo*·a
muscle *musuli* moo·*soo*·lee
museum *makumbusho*
ma·koom·*boo*·shoh
mushroom *uyoga* oo·*yoh*·ga
music *muziki* moo·*zee*·kee
music shop *duka la muziki*
doo·ka la moo·*zee*·kee
musician *mwanamuziki*
mwa·na·moo·*zee*·kee
Muslim *Mwislamu* mwee·*sla*·moo
mussel *kome koh*·may
mustard *mastadi* ma·*sta*·dee
mute *bubu boo*·boo
my *yangu yan*·goo

N

nail clippers *mkasi wa kucha*
m·*ka*·see wa *koo*·cha
name *jina jee*·na
napkin *kitambaa cha mkono*
kee·tam·*ba* cha m·*koh*·noh
nappy *nepi nay*·pee
nappy rash *upele wa nepi*
oo·*pay*·lay wa *nay*·pee
national park *hifadhi ya wanyama*
hee·*fa*·dhee ya wa·*nya*·ma
nationality *raia* ra·ee·a
nature *hali asili ha*·le a·*see*·lee
naturopathy *matibabu asilia*
ma·tee·*ba*·boo a·see·*lee*·a

nausea *kichefuchefu*
kee·chay·foo·*chay*·foo
near *karibu* ka·*ree*·boo
nearby *hapo karibuni ha*·poh ka·ree·*boo*·nee
nearest *karibu zaidi* ka·*ree*·boo za·*ee*·dee
necessary *lazima* la·*zee*·ma
necklace *mkufu* m·*koo*·foo
need *-hitaji* ·hee·*ta*·jee
needle (sewing) *sindano (ya kushonea)*
seen·*da*·noh (ya koo·shoh·*nay*·a)
needle (syringe) *sindano (ya dawa)*
seen·*da*·noh (ya *da*·wa)
negative ⓐ *ya kukana* ya koo·*ka*·na
neither *wala wa*·la
net *neti nay*·tee
Netherlands *Uholanzi* oo·hoh·*lan*·zee
never *kamwe kam*·way
new *mpya m*·pya
New Year's Day *Siku ya Mwaka Mpya*
see·koo ya *mwa*·ka *m*·pya
New Year's Eve *Mkesha wa Mwaka Mpya*
m·*kay*·sha wa *mwa*·ka *m*·pya
New Zealand *New Zealandi*
noo zee·*lan*·dee
news *habari* ha·*ba*·ree
newsstand *duka la magazeti*
doo·ka la ma·ga·*zay*·tee
newsagency *shirika la habari*
shee·*ree*·ka la ha·*ba*·ree
newspaper *gazeti* ga·*zay*·tee
newspaper vendor *mwuzaji wa magazeti*
mwoo·*za*·jee wa ma·ga·*zay*·tee
next *ijayo* ee·*ja*·yoh
next (month) *(mwezi) ujao*
(*mway*·zee) oo·*ja*·oh
next to *kando ya kan*·doh ya
nice *mwema mway*·ma
nickname *jina la utani jee*·na la oo·*ta*·nee
night *usiku* oo·*see*·koo
night out *usiku nje* oo·*see*·koo *n*·jay
nightclub *klabu ya usiku*
kla·boo ya oo·*see*·koo
no *hapana* ha·*pa*·na
no vacancy *hakuna nafasi*
ha·*koo*·na na·*fa*·see
noisy *yenye kelele yay*·nyay kay·*lay*·lay
none *hakuna* ha·*koo*·na
nonsmoking *hakuna sigara*
ha·*koo*·na see·*ga*·ra
noodles *tambi tam*·bee
noon *saa sita mchana* sa *see*·ta m·*cha*·na
north *kaskazini* kas·ka·*zee*·nee
North Africa *Afrika ya Kaskazini*
a·*free*·ka ya ka·ska·*zee*·nee

Norway *Norwei* nohr·*way*·ee
nose *pua* *poo*·a
not *hapana* ha·*pa*·na
not yet *bado* *ba*·doh
notebook *daftari* daf·*ta*·ree
nothing *hakuna kitu* ha·*koo*·na *kee*·too
November *mwezi wa kumi na moja* *mway*·zee wa *koo*·mee na *moh*·ja
now *sasa* *sa*·sa
nuclear energy *nishati ya nyuklia* *nee*·sha·tee ya *nyook*·lee·a
nuclear testing *majaribio ya nyuklia* ma·ja·ree·*bee*·oh ya *nyook*·lee·a
nuclear waste *takataka za nyuklia* ta·ka·*ta*·ka za *nyook*·lee·a
number *namba* *nam*·ba
numberplate *kipande cha namba ya gari* kee·*pan*·day cha *nam*·ba ya *ga*·ree
nun *sista* *see*·sta
nurse *mwuguzi* mwoo·*goo*·zee
nut *kokwa* *kohk*·wa

O

ocean *bahari* ba·*ha*·ree
October *mwezi wa kumi* *mway*·zee wa *koo*·mee
off (spoiled) *mbaya* m·*ba*·ya
office *ofisi* oh·*fee*·see
office worker *mfanyakazi ofisini* m·fa·nya·*ka*·zee o·fee·*see*·nee
often *mara nyingi* *ma*·ra *nyeen*·gee
oil *mafuta* ma·*foo*·ta
old ⓐ *ya zamani* ya za·*ma*·nee
old person ⓝ *mzee* m·*zay*
olive *zaituni* za·ee·*too*·nee
olive oil *mafuta ya zaituni* ma·*foo*·ta ya za·ee·*too*·nee
Olympic Games *Michezo ya Olimpiki* mee·*chay*·zoh ya oh·leem·*pee*·kee
omelette *omlet* *ohm*·layt
on *juu ya* joo ya
on time *kuwahi* koo·*wa*·hee
once *mara moja* *ma*·ra *moh*·ja
one *moja* *moh*·ja
one-way ticket *tiketi ya kwenda tu* tee·*kay*·tee ya *kwayn*·da too
onion *kitunguu* kee·toon·*goo*
only *tu* too
open ⓥ *-fungua* ·foon·*goo*·a
open ⓐ *wazi* *wa*·zee
opening hours *masaa ya kufunguliwa* ma·*sa* ya koo·foon·goo·*lee*·wa
opera *opera* *oh*·pay·ra
opera house *jumba la opera* *joom*·ba la *oh*·pay·ra
operation (medical) *operesheni* oh·pay·ray·*shay*·nee
operator *opareta* oh·pa·*ray*·ta
opinion *maoni* ma·*oh*·nee
opposite *kinyume* kee·*nyoo*·may
optometrist *daktari wa macho* dak·*ta*·ree wa *ma*·choh
or *au* *a*·oo
orange (fruit) *chungwa* *choon*·gwa
orange (colour) *rangi ya machungwa* *ran*·gee ya ma·*choon*·gwa
orange juice *maji ya machungwa* *ma*·jee ya ma·*choon*·gwa
orchestra *okestra* oh·*kay*·stra
order ⓝ *agizo* a·*gee*·zoh
order ⓥ *-agiza* ·a·*gee*·za
ordinary *kawaida* ka·wa·*ee*·da
orgasm *mshushio* m·shoo·*shee*·oh
original *ya awali* ya *a*·wa·lee
oryx *choroa* choh·*roh*·a
ostrich *mbuni* m·*boo*·nee
other *nyingine* nyeen·*gee*·nay
our *yetu* *yay*·too
out of order *imevunjika* ee·may·voon·*jee*·ka
outside *nje* *n*·jay
ovarian cyst *uvimbe wa ovari* oo·*veem*·bay wa oh·*va*·ree
ovary *ovari* oh·*va*·ree
oven *joko* *joh*·koh
overcoat *kabuti* ka·*boo*·tee
overdose *dozi kubwa mno ya dawa* *doh*·zee *koob*·wa *m*·noh ya *da*·wa
overnight *kwa usiku mmoja* kwa oo·*see*·koo m·*moh*·ja
overseas *nchi za nje* *n*·chee za *n*·jay
owe *-wa na deni* ·wa na *day*·nee
owner *mwenye* *mway*·nyay
oxygen *oksijeni* ohk·see·*jay*·nee
oyster *chaza* *cha*·za
ozone layer *tabaka la hewa ya ozoni* ta·*ba*·ka la *hay*·wa ya oh·*zoh*·nee

P

pacemaker *kirekebisho moyo* kee·ray·kay·*bee*·shoh *moh*·yoh
pacifier (dummy) *nyonyo bandia* *nyoh*·nyoh ban·*dee*·a
package *furushi* foo·*roo*·shee

packet (general) *pakiti* pa·*kee*·tee
padlock *kufuli* koo·*foo*·lee
page *ukurasa* oo·koo·*ra*·sa
pain *maumivu* ma·oo·*mee*·voo
painful *ya kuumiza* ya koo·oo·*mee*·za
painkiller *kiondoa maumivu* kee·ohn·*doh*·a ma·oo·*mee*·voo
painter *msanii wa rangi* m·sa·*nee* wa *ran*·gee
painting (a work) *picha* *pee*·cha
painting (the art) *sanaa ya uchoraji wa rangi* sa·*na* ya oo·choh·*ra*·jee wa *ran*·gee
pair (couple) *wawili wawili* wa·*wee*·lee wa·*wee*·lee
palace *jumba* *joom*·ba
pan *kikaango* kee·ka·*an*·goh
pants (trousers) *suruali* soo·roo·*a*·lee
panty liners *kibandiko cha chupi* pl kee·ban·*dee*·koh cha *choo*·pee
paper *karatasi* ka·ra·*ta*·see
paperwork *kazi ya ukarani* *ka*·zee ya oo·ka·*ra*·nee
paraplegic *kilema* kee·*lay*·ma
parcel *kifurushi* kee·foo·*roo*·shee
parents *wazazi* wa·*za*·zee
park ⓝ *hifadhi* hee·*fa*·dhee
park (a car) *-egesha* ·ay·*gay*·sha
parliament *bunge* *boon*·gay
part (component) *sehemu* say·*hay*·moo
part-time *kibarua* kee·ba·*roo*·a
party (night out) *sherehe* shay·*ray*·hay
party (politics) *chama* *cha*·ma
pass *-pita* ·*pee*·ta
passenger *abiria* a·bee·*ree*·a
passionfruit *pasheni* pa·*shay*·nee
passport *pasipoti* pa·see·*poh*·tee
passport number *namba ya pasipoti* *nam*·ba ya pa·see·*poh*·tee
past ⓝ *zamani* za·*ma*·nee
pasta *tambi* *tam*·bee
pastry *kitobosha* kee·toh·*boh*·sha
path *njia* n·*jee*·a
pay *-lipa* ·*lee*·pa
payment *malipo* ma·*lee*·poh
pea *njegere* n·jay·*gay*·ray
peace *amani* a·*ma*·nee
peach *pichi* *pee*·chee
peak (mountain) *kilele* kee·*lay*·lay
peanut *karanga* ka·*ran*·ga
pear *pea* *pay*·a
pedal *pedeli* pay·*day*·lee
pedestrian *mtembezi* m·taym·*bay*·zee
pen (ballpoint) *kalamu* ka·*la*·moo
pencil *pensili* payn·*see*·lee
penis *mboo* m·*boh*
penknife *kisu cha mfukoni* *kee*·soo cha m·foo·*koh*·nee
pensioner *mzee* m·*zay*
people *watu* *wa*·too
pepper *pilipili* pee·lee·*pee*·lee
pepper (bell) *pilipili mbichi* pee·lee·*pee*·lee m·*bee*·chee
per (day) *kwa* kwa
per cent *asilimia* a·see·lee·*mee*·a
perfect *kamili* ka·*mee*·lee
performance *onyesho* oh·*nyay*·shoh
perfume *marashi* ma·*ra*·shee
period pain *maumivu ya mwezini* ma·oo·*mee*·voo ya mway·*zee*·nee
permission *ruhusa* roo·*hoo*·sa
permit *kibali* kee·*ba*·lee
person *mtu* *m*·too
petition *ombi* *ohm*·bee
petrol *mafuta* ma·*foo*·ta
petrol station *kituo cha mafuta* kee·*too*·oh cha ma·*foo*·ta
pharmacist *mfamasia* m·fa·ma·*see*·a
pharmacy *duka la dawa* *doo*·ka la *da*·wa
phone book *kitabu cha namba za simu* kee·*ta*·boo cha *nam*·ba za *see*·moo
phone box *kibanda cha simu* kee·*ban*·da cha *see*·moo
phonecard *kadi ya simu za vibandani* *ka*·dee ya *see*·moo za vee·ban·*da*·nee
photo *picha* *pee*·cha
photographer *mpigapicha* m·pee·ga·*pee*·cha
photography *upigaji picha* oo·pee·*ga*·jee *pee*·cha
phrasebook *kitabu cha misemo* kee·*ta*·boo cha mee·*say*·moh
pickaxe *sururu* soo·*roo*·roo
pickles *achari* a·*cha*·ree
picnic *mandari* man·*da*·ree
pie *pai* *pa*·ee
piece *kipande* kee·*pan*·day
pig *nguruwe* n·goo·*roo*·way
pill *kidonge* kee·*dohn*·gay
(the) pill *kidonge cha kuzuia mimba* kee·*dohn*·gay cha koo·zoo·*ee*·a *meem*·ba
pillow *mto* *m*·toh
pillowcase *foronya* foh·*roh*·nya
pineapple *nanasi* na·*na*·see
pink *pinki* *peen*·kee

place *mahali* ma·*ha*·lee
place of birth *mahali pa kuzaliwa* ma·*ha*·lee pa koo·za·*lee*·wa
plane *ndege* n·*day*·gay
planet *sayari* sa·*ya*·ree
plant *mmea* m·*may*·a
plastic *plastiki* pla·*stee*·kee
plate *sahani* sa·*ha*·nee
plateau *uwanda wa juu* oo·*wan*·da wa *joo*
platform *jukwaa* joo·kwa
play (in theatre) *mchezo wa kuigiza* m·*chay*·zoh wa koo·ee·*gee*·za
play cards *-cheza karata* ·*chay*·za ka·*ra*·ta
play guitar *-cheza gitaa* ·*chay*·za gee·*taa*
plug (bath) *kizibo* kee·*zee*·boh
plug (electricity) *plagi* *pla*·gee
plum *plamu* *pla*·moo
poached (game) *ujangili* oo·jan·*gee*·lee
pocket *mfuko* m·*foo*·koh
pocket knife *kisu cha mfukoni* *kee*·soo cha m·foo·*koh*·nee
poetry *shairi* pl sha·*ee*·ree
point ⓝ *nukta* *nook*·ta
point ⓥ *-elekeza* ·ay·lay·*kay*·za
poisonous *yenye sumu* *yay*·nyay *soo*·moo
police *polisi* poh·*lee*·see
police officer *polisi* poh·*lee*·see
police station *kituo cha polisi* kee·*too*·oh cha poh·*lee*·see
policy *sera* *say*·ra
politician *mwanasiasa* mwa·na·see·*a*·sa
politics *siasa* see·*a*·sa
pollen *chavua* cha·*voo*·a
pollution *uchafuzi* oo·cha·*foo*·zee
pool (game) *biliadi* bee·lee·*a*·dee
pool (swimming) *bwawa* *bwa*·wa
poor *maskini* mas·*kee*·nee
popular *ya kupendwa* ya koo·*payn*·dwa
pork *nyama nguruwe* *nya*·ma n·goo·*roo*·way
port (sea) *bandari* ban·*da*·ree
positive *ya hakika* ya ha·*kee*·ka
possible *ya kuwezekana* ya koo·way·zay·*ka*·na
postage *stempu* *staym*·poo
postcard *postikadi* poh·stee·*ka*·dee
post code *simbo ya posta* *seem*·boh ya *poh*·sta
poster *bango* *ban*·goh
post office *posta* *poh*·sta
pot (ceramics) *chungu* *choon*·goo
pot (dope) *bangi* *ban*·gee
potato *kiazi* kee·*a*·zee
pottery *vyombo vya udongo* *vyohm*·boh vya oo·*dohn*·goh
pound (money, weight) *paundi* pa·*oon*·dee
poverty *umaskini* oo·ma·*skee*·nee
powder *poda* *poh*·da
power *nguvu* n·*goo*·voo
prawn *kamba* *kam*·ba
pray *-sali* ·*sa*·lee
prayer *sala* *sa*·la
prefer *-pendelea* ·payn·day·*lay*·a
pregnancy test kit *upimaji mimba* oo·pee·*ma*·jee *meem*·ba
pregnant *mjamzito* m·ja·m·*zee*·toh
premenstrual tension *zingizi* zeen·*gee*·zee
prepare *-andaa* ·an·*da*
prescription *agizo la daktari* a·*gee*·zoh la dak·*ta*·ree
present (gift) *zawadi* za·*wa*·dee
present (time) *sasa* *sa*·sa
president *rais* ra·*ees*
pressure *shinikizo* shee·nee·*kee*·zoh
pretty *ya kupendeza* ya koo·payn·*day*·za
price *bei* bay
priest *padri* *pa*·dree
prime minister *waziri mkuu* wa·*zee*·ree m·*koo*
printer (computer) *printa* *preen*·ta
prison *gereza* gay·*ray*·za
prisoner *mfungwa* m·*foon*·gwa
private *binafsi* bee·*naf*·see
profit *faida* fa·*ee*·da
program *mradi* m·*ra*·dee
projector *projekta* proh·*jayk*·ta
promise *-ahidi* ·a·*hee*·dee
prostitute *malaya* ma·*la*·ya
protect *-kinga* ·*keen*·ga
protected species *spishi zilizo hifadhiwa* *spee*·shee zee·lee·zoh hee·fa·*dhee*·wa
protest ⓝ *maandamano* ma·an·da·*ma*·noh
protest ⓥ *-pinga* ·*peen*·ga
provisions *maakuli* ma·a·*koo*·lee
prune *plamu kavu* *pla*·moo *ka*·voo
pub (bar) *baa* ba
public relations *uhusiano wa jamii* oo·hoo·see·*a*·noh wa ja·*mee*
public telephone *simu ya mtaani* *see*·moo ya m·*ta*·nee
public toilet *choo cha hadhara* choh cha *ha*·dha·ra
pull *-vuta* ·*voo*·ta

pump ⓝ *pampu pam*·poo
pumpkin *boga boh*·ga
puncture *pancha pan*·cha
pure *halisi* ha·*lee*·see
purple *zambarau* zam·ba·*ra*·oo
purse *mkoba* m·*koh*·ba
push *-sukuma* ·soo·*koo*·ma
put *-weka* ·*way*·ka

Q

qualifications *sifa za kielimu see*·fa za kee·ay·*lee*·moo
quality *sifa see*·fa
quarantine *karantini* ka·ran·*tee*·nee
quarter *robo roh*·boh
queen *malkia* mal·*kee*·a
question *swali swa*·lee
queue *mstari* m·*sta*·ree
quick *nyepesi* nyay·*pay*·see
quiet *-tulivu* ·too·*lee*·voo
quit *-acha* ·*a*·cha

R

rabbit *sungura* soon·*goo*·ra
race (sport) *shindano* sheen·*da*·noh
racetrack *uwanja wa mbio* oo·*wan*·ja wa m·*bee*·oh
racing bike *baisikeli ya mashindano* ba·ee·see·*kay*·lee ya ma·sheen·*da*·noh
racism *ubaguzi wa rangi* oo·ba·*goo*·zee wa *ran*·gee
racquet *raketi* ra·*kay*·tee
radiator *kinururishi* kee·noo·roo·*ree*·shee
radio *redio* ray·*dee*·oh
radish *figili* fee·*gee*·lee
railway station *stesheni ya treni* stay·*shay*·nee ya *tray*·nee
rain *mvua* m·*voo*·a
raincoat *koti la mvua koh*·tee la m·*voo*·a
raisin *zabibu kavu* za·*bee*·boo *ka*·voo
rally (public meeting) *mkutano wa hadhara* m·koo·*ta*·noh wa *ha*·dha·ra
rape ⓝ *ubakaji* oo·ba·*ka*·jee
rape ⓥ *-baka* ·*ba*·ka
rare (food) *ya kuiva kidogo* ya koo·*ee*·va kee·*doh*·goh
rare (uncommon) *nadra na*·dra
rash *upele* oo·*pay*·lay
rat *panya pa*·nya
raw *-bichi* ·*bee*·chee
razor *wembe waym*·bay
razor blade *wembe waym*·bay
read *-soma* ·*soh*·ma
reading *somo soh*·moh
ready *tayari* ta·*ya*·ree
real estate agent *wakala wa maeneo* wa·*ka*·la wa ma·ay·*nay*·oh
rear (location) *nyuma nyoo*·ma
reason (explanation) *sababu* sa·*ba*·boo
receipt *risiti* ree·*see*·tee
recently *hivi karibuni hee*·vee ka·ree·*boo*·nee
recommend *-pendekeza* ·payn·day·*kay*·za
record (music) *-rekodi (muziki)* ·ray·*koh*·dee (moo·*zee*·kee)
recording (musical) *kanda kan*·da
recyclable *ya kurejeleza* ya koo·ray·jay·*lay*·za
red *nyekundu* nyay·*koon*·doo
referee *mwamuzi* mwa·*moo*·zee
reference *marejeo* ma·ray·*jay*·oh
refrigerator *friji free*·jee
refugee *mkimbizi* m·keem·*bee*·zee
refund *kurudisha pesa* koo·roo·*dee*·sha *pay*·sa
refuse *-kataa* ·ka·*ta*
regional *ya mkoa* ya m·*koh*·a
registered mail/post *barua ya rejista* ba·*roo*·a ya *ray*·jee·sta
rehydration salts *dawa ya kuongeza maji mwilini da*·wa ya koo·ohn·*gay*·za *ma*·jee mwee·*lee*·nee
relationship *uhusiano* oo·hoo·see·*a*·noh
relax *-jiburudisha* ·jee·boo·roo·*dee*·sha
relic *mabaki* ma·*ba*·kee
religion *dini dee*·nee
religious *ya kidini* ya kee·*dee*·nee
remote *mbali* m·*ba*·lee
remote control *rimoti* ree·*moh*·tee
rent *-kodi* ·*koh*·dee
repair *-tengeneza* ·tayn·gay·*nay*·za
republic *jamhuri* jam·*hoo*·ree
reservation (booking) *buking boo*·keeng
rest *-pumzika* ·poom·*zee*·ka
restaurant *mgahawa* m·ga·*ha*·wa
résumé (CV) *muhtasari* mooh·*ta*·sa·ree
retired *aliyestaafu* a·lee·yay·sta·*a*·foo
return (come back) *-rudi* ·*roo*·dee
return ticket *tiketi ya kwenda na kurudi* tee·*kay*·tee ya *kwayn*·da na koo·*roo*·dee
review *mapitio* ma·pee·*tee*·oh
rhinoceros *kifaru* kee·*fa*·roo
rhythm *mahadhi* ma·*ha*·dhee

rib *ubavu* oo·*ba*·voo
rice (cooked) *wali* *wa*·lee
rice (uncooked) *mchele* m·*chay*·lay
rich (wealthy) *tajiri* ta·*jee*·ree
ride ⓝ *lifti* *leef*·tee
ride (horse) ⓥ *-panda (farasi)* ·*pan*·da (fa·*ra*·see)
right (correct) *sawa* *sa*·wa
right (direction) *kulia* koo·*lee*·a
right-wing *mrengo wa kulia* m·*rayn*·goh wa koo·*lee*·a
ring (on finger) *pete* *pay*·tay
ring (phone) *-piga simu* ·*pee*·ga *see*·moo
rip-off *wizi* *wee*·zee
risk *hatari* ha·*ta*·ree
river *mto* *m*·toh
road *barabara* ba·ra·*ba*·ra
road map *ramani* ra·*ma*·nee
rob *-iba* ·*ee*·ba
rock *jiwe* *jee*·way
rock climbing *upandaji miamba* oo·pan·*da*·jee mee·*am*·ba
rock group *kundi ya roki* *koon*·dee ya *roh*·kee
rock music *roki* *roh*·kee
roll (bread) *skonzi* *skohn*·zee
romantic *kwa wapenzi* kwa wa·*payn*·zee
room *chumba* *choom*·ba
room number *namba ya chumba* *nam*·ba ya *choom*·ba
rope *kamba* *kam*·ba
round *duara* doo·*a*·ra
roundabout *kiplefti* keep·*layf*·tee
route *njia* n·*jee*·a
rowing *kuvuta makasia* koo·*voo*·ta ma·ka·*see*·a
rubbish *takataka* ta·ka·*ta*·ka
rug *zulia* zoo·*lee*·a
rugby *ragbi* *rag*·bee
ruins *magofu* ma·*goh*·foo
rule *utawala* oo·ta·*wa*·la
run *-kimbia* ·keem·*bee*·a
running *kukimbia* koo·keem·*bee*·a
Rwanda *Rwanda* r·*wan*·da

S

sad *masikitiko* ma·see·kee·*tee*·koh
saddle *tandiko* tan·*dee*·koh
safe (for money) ⓝ *kasha la fedha* *ka*·sha la *fay*·dha
safe ⓐ *salama* sa·*la*·ma
safe sex *mapenzi salama* ma·*payn*·zee sa·*la*·ma
saint *mtakatifu* m·ta·ka·*tee*·foo
salad *saladi* sa·*la*·dee
salary *mshahara* m·sha·*ha*·ra
sale *seli* *say*·lee
sales tax *kodi ya mauzo* *koh*·dee ya ma·*oo*·zoh
salmon *samoni* sa·*moh*·nee
salt *chumvi* *choom*·vee
same *sawasawa* sa·wa·*sa*·wa
sand *mchanga* m·*chan*·ga
sandal *ndala* n·*da*·la
sanitary napkin *sodo* *soh*·doh
sardine *dagaa* da·*ga*
Saturday *Jumamosi* joo·ma·*moh*·see
sauce *mchuzi* m·*choo*·zee
saucepan *sufuria* soo·foo·*ree*·a
sauna *sauna* sa·*oo*·na
sausage *soseji* soh·*say*·jee
say *-sema* ·*say*·ma
scalp *ngozi ya kichwa* n·*goh*·zee ya *keech*·wa
scarf *skafu* *ska*·foo
school *shule* *shoo*·lay
science *sayansi* sa·*yan*·see
scientist *mwanasayansi* mwa·na·sa·*yan*·see
scissors *mkasi* m·*ka*·see
score *alama* a·*la*·ma
scoreboard *ubao wa matokeo* oo·*ba*·oh wa ma·toh·*kay*·oh
Scotland *Skotlandi* skoht·*lan*·dee
scrambled eggs *mayai yaliyovurugwa* ma·*ya*·ee ya·lee·yoh·voo·*roog*·wa
sculpture *uchongaji* oo·chohn·*ga*·jee
sea *bahari* ba·*ha*·ree
seasickness *kichefuchefu cha bahrini* kee·chay·foo·*chay*·foo cha ba·ha·*ree*·nee
seaside *ufukwe* oo·*fook*·way
season *majira* ma·*jee*·ra
seat (place) *kiti* *kee*·tee
seatbelt *mkanda wa kiti* m·*kan*·da wa *kee*·tee
second (time unit) *sekundi* say·*koon*·dee
second ⓐ *ya pili* ya *pee*·lee
second class *daraja la pili* da·*ra*·ja la *pee*·lee
second-hand *mitumba* mee·*toom*·ba
second-hand shop *duka la mitumba* *doo*·ka la mee·*toom*·ba
secretary *karani* ka·*ra*·nee

see *-ona* ·*oh*·na
self-employed *ya kujiajiri* ya koo·jee·a·*jee*·ree
selfish *mwenye choyo* *mway*·nyay *choh*·yoh
self service *ya kujihuduma* ya koo·jee·hoo·*doo*·ma
sell *-uza* ·*oo*·za
send *-peleka* ·pay·*lay*·ka
sensible *yenye busara* *yay*·nyay boo·*sa*·ra
sensual *ya kutamanisha* ya koo·ta·ma·*nee*·sha
separate *mbalimbali* m·ba·lee·m·*ba*·lee
September *mwezi wa tisa* *mway*·zee wa *tee*·sa
serious *makini* ma·*kee*·nee
service *huduma* hoo·*doo*·ma
service charge *malipo ya huduma* ma·*lee*·poh ya hoo·*doo*·ma
service station *kituo cha petroli* kee·*too*·oh cha pay·*troh*·lee
serviette *kitambaa cha mkono* kee·tam·*ba* cha m·*koh*·noh
several *kadhaa* ka·*dha*
sew *-shona* ·*shoh*·na
sex (gender) *jinsia* jeen·*see*·a
sex (intercourse) *mapenzi* ma·*payn*·zee
sexism *ubaguzi wa kijinsia* oo·ba·*goo*·zee wa kee·jeen·*see*·a
sexy *ya kuchochea ashiki* ya koo·choh·*chay*·a a·*shee*·kee
shade *kivuli* kee·*voo*·lee
shadow *kivuli* kee·*voo*·lee
shampoo *shampuu* sham·*poo*
shape *umbo* *oom*·boh
share (a dorm etc) *-gawana* ·ga·*wa*·na
share (with) *-shirikiana* ·shee·ree·kee·*a*·na
shave *-nyoa* ·*nyoh*·a
shaving cream *sabuni ya kunyolea* sa·*boo*·nee ya koo·nyoh·*lay*·a
she *yeye* *yay*·yay
sheep *kondoo* kohn·*doh*
sheet (bed) *shuka* *shoo*·ka
shelf *rafu* *ra*·foo
shingles (illness) *moto ya mungu* *moh*·toh ya *moon*·goo
shiny *almasi* al·*ma*·see
ship *meli* *may*·lee
shirt *shati* *sha*·tee
shoe *kiatu* kee·*a*·too
shoe shop *duka la viatu* *doo*·ka la vee·*a*·too
shoes *viatu* vee·*a*·too
shoot *-piga risasi* ·*pee*·ga ree·*sa*·see
shop ⓝ *duka* *doo*·ka
shop ⓥ *-nunua* ·noo·*noo*·a
shopping *ununuzi* oo·noo·*noo*·zee
shopping centre *madukani* ma·doo·*ka*·nee
short (height) *fupi* *foo*·pee
shortage *upungufu* oo·poon·*goo*·foo
shorts *kaptura* kap·*too*·ra
shoulder *bega* *bay*·ga
shout *-piga kelele* ·*pee*·ga kay·*lay*·lay
show ⓝ *onyesho* oh·*nyay*·shoh
show ⓥ *-onyesha* ·oh·*nyay*·sha
shower *bafuni* ba·*foo*·nee
shrine *ziara* zee·*a*·ra
shut ⓐ *kufungwa* koo·*foon*·gwa
shy *ya aibu* ya a·*ee*·boo
sick *mgonjwa* m·*gohn*·jwa
side *upande* oo·*pan*·day
sign *alama* a·*la*·ma
signature *sahihi* sa·*hee*·hee
silk ⓝ *hariri* ha·*ree*·ree
silver *fedha* *fay*·dha
silver shop *duka la fedha* *doo*·ka la *fay*·dha
SIM card *kadi ya simu (ya mikononi)* *ka*·dee ya *see*·moo (ya mee·koh·*noh*·nee)
similar *yenye kufanana* *yay*·nyay koo·fa·*na*·na
simple *rahisi* ra·*hee*·see
since (May) *tangu (Mei)* *tan*·goo (*may*·ee)
sing *-imba* ·*eem*·ba
Singapore *Singapore* seen·ga·*poh*·ray
singer *mwimbaji* mweem·*ba*·jee
single (person) *kapera* ka·*pay*·ra
single room *chumba kwa mtu mmoja* *choom*·ba kwa *m*·too m·*moh*·ja
singlet *fulana ya ndani* foo·*la*·na ya n·*da*·nee
sister *dada* *da*·da
sit *-kaa* ·ka
size (general) *saizi* sa·*ee*·zee
skate *-teleza* ·tay·*lay*·za
skateboarding *ubao wa kuteleza* oo·*ba*·oh wa koo·tay·*lay*·za
ski *-skii* ·skee
skiing *kuskii* koo·*skee*
skim milk *machunda* ma·*choon*·da
skin *ngozi* n·*goh*·zee
skirt *skati* *ska*·tee
skull *fuvu* *foo*·voo
sky *mbingu* m·*been*·goo
sleep *-sinzia* ·seen·*zee*·a
sleeping bag *mfuko wa kulalia* m·*foo*·koh wa koo·la·*lee*·a

sleeping berth *kitanda katika behewa* kee·*tan*·da ka·*tee*·ka bay·*hay*·wa
sleeping car *gari la vitanda* *ga*·ree la vee·*tan*·da
sleeping pills *vidonge vya usingizi* vee·*dohn*·gay vya oo·seen·*gee*·zee
sleepy *mwenye usingizi* *mway*·nyay oo·seen·*gee*·zee
slice ⓝ *slaisi* sla·*ee*·see
slide film *filamu ya slaidi* fee·*la*·moo ya sla·*ee*·dee
slow *taratibu* ta·ra·*tee*·boo
slowly *polepole* poh·lay·*poh*·lay
small *-dogo* ·*doh*·goh
smaller *-dogo zaidi* ·*doh*·goh za·*ee*·dee
smallest *-dogo kabisa* ·*doh*·goh ka·*bee*·sa
smart *hodari* hoh·*da*·ree
smell ⓝ *harufu* ha·*roo*·foo
smile *-tabasamu* ·ta·ba·*sa*·moo
smoke *-vuta sigara* ·*voo*·ta see·*ga*·ra
snack *kumbwe* *koom*·bway
snail *konokono* koh·noh·*koh*·noh
snake *nyoka* *nyoh*·ka
snow *theluji* thay·*loo*·jee
soap *sabuni* sa·*boo*·nee
soccer *soka* *soh*·ka
social welfare *ustawi wa jamii* oo·*sta*·wee wa ja·*mee*
socialist *soshalisti* soh·sha·*lee*·stee
socks *soksi* *sohk*·see
soft drink *soda* *soh*·da
soft-boiled egg *yai lililochemshwa kidogo* *ya*·ee lee·lee·loh·*chaym*·shwa kee·*doh*·goh
soldier *askari* a·*ska*·ree
Somalia *Somalia* soh·*ma*·lee·a
some *kadhaa* ka·*dha*
someone *fulani* foo·*la*·nee
something *kitu* *kee*·too
sometimes *wakati mwingine* wa·*ka*·tee mween·*gee*·nay
son *mwana* *mwa*·na
song *wimbo* *weem*·boh
soon *sasa hivi* sa·sa *hee*·vee
sore *mwenye kuuma* *mway*·nyay koo·*oo*·ma
soup *supu* *soo*·poo
sour cream *malai ya maziwa ya mtindi* ma·*la*·ee ya ma·*zee*·wa ya m·*teen*·dee
south *kusini* koo·*see*·nee
South Africa *Afrika ya Kusini* a·*free*·ka ya koo·*see*·nee
souvenir *kumbukumbu* koom·boo·*koom*·boo
souvenir shop *duka la kumbukumbu* *doo*·ka la koom·boo·*koom*·boo
soy milk *maziwa ya soya* ma·*zee*·wa ya *soh*·ya
soy sauce *mchuzi wa soya* m·*choo*·zee wa *soh*·ya
(outer) space *angani* an·*ga*·nee
Spain *Uhispania* oo·hee·*spa*·nee·a
speak *-sema* ·*say*·ma
special *maalum* ma·*a*·loom
specialist *mtaalamu* m·ta·a·*la*·moo
speed (velocity) *mwendo* *mwayn*·doh
speed limit *kikomo cha mwendo* kee·*koh*·moh cha *mwayn*·doh
speedometer *spidomita* spee·doh·*mee*·ta
spider *buibui* boo·ee·*boo*·ee
spinach *mchicha* m·*chee*·cha
spoilage *uharibifu* oo·ha·ree·*bee*·foo
spoke *spoki* *spoh*·kee
spoon *kijiko* kee·*jee*·koh
sport *michezo* mee·*chay*·zoh
sports shop *duka la vifaa vya michezo* *doo*·ka la vee·*fa* vya mee·*chay*·zoh
sportsperson *mwanamichezo* mwa·na·mee·*chay*·zoh
sprain *mteguko* m·tay·*goo*·koh
spring (coil) *springi* *spreen*·gee
spring (season) *majira ya kuchipua* ma·*jee*·ra ya koo·chee·*poo*·a
square (town) *uwanja* oo·*wan*·ja
stadium *uwanja wa michezo* oo·*wan*·ja wa mee·*chay*·zoh
stairway *ngazi* n·*ga*·zee
stale *ya zamani* ya za·*ma*·nee
stamp *stempu* *staym*·poo
stand-by ticket *tiketi kutumia kama nafasi ikipatikana* tee·*kay*·tee koo·too·*mee*·a *ka*·ma na·*fa*·see ee·kee·pa·tee·*ka*·na
star *nyota* *nyoh*·ta
start ⓝ *mwanzo* *mwan*·zoh
start ⓥ *-anza* ·*an*·za
station *stesheni* stay·*shay*·nee
stationer *duka la vifaa vya ofisi* *doo*·ka la vee·*fa* vya o·*fee*·see
statue *sanamu* sa·*na*·moo
stay (at a hotel) *-kaa* ·ka
stay (in one place) *-baki* ·*ba*·kee
steak (beef) *mnofu* m·*noh*·foo
steal *-iba* ·*ee*·ba
steep *ya mwinuko mkali* ya mwee·*noo*·koh m·*ka*·lee
step *hatua* ha·*too*·a

S

english–swahili

stereo *stirio* stee·*ree*·oh
still water *maji baridi* *ma*·jee ba·*ree*·dee
stockings *soksi ndefu* *sohk*·see n·*day*·foo
stolen *ya kuibwa* ya koo·*ee*·bwa
stomach *tumbo* *toom*·boh
stomachache *maumivu ya tumbo* ma·oo·*mee*·voo ya *toom*·boh
stone *jiwe* *jee*·way
stoned (drugged) *-lewa* ·*lay*·wa
stop (bus, etc) ⓝ *kituo* kee·*too*·oh
stop (cease) ⓥ *-simama* ·see·*ma*·ma
stop (prevent) ⓥ *-zuia* ·zoo·*ee*·a
storm *dhoruba* dho·*roo*·ba
story *hadithi* ha·*dee*·thee
stove *jiko* *jee*·koh
straight *moja kwa moja* *moh*·ja kwa *moh*·ja
strange *ya kigeni* ya kee·*gay*·nee
stranger *mgeni* m·*gay*·nee
stream *kijito* kee·*jee*·toh
street *njia* n·*jee*·a
street children *watoto wa mtaani* wa·*toh*·toh wa m·ta·*a*·nee
street hawker *mchuuzi* m·choo·*oo*·zee
street market *soko la mtaani* *soh*·koh la m·ta·*a*·nee
strike *mgomo* m·*goh*·moh
string *uzi* *oo*·zee
stroke (health) *kiharusi* kee·ha·*roo*·see
stroller (pram) *kigari cha mtoto* kee·*ga*·ree cha m·*toh*·toh
strong *madhubuti* ma·dhoo·*boo*·tee
stubborn *mbishi* m·*bee*·shee
student *mwanafunzi* mwa·na·*foon*·zee
studio *studio* stoo·*dee*·oh
stupid *pumbavu* poom·*ba*·voo
style *mtindo* m·*teen*·doh
subtitles *maandishi chini* ma·an·*dee*·shee *chee*·nee
suburb *pembezoni mwa mji* paym·bay·*zoh*·nee mwa *m*·jee
Sudan *Sudan* soo·*dan*
sugar *sukari* soo·*ka*·ree
suitcase *mzigo* m·*zee*·goh
sultanas *zabibu nyeupe zilizokaushwa* za·*bee*·boo nyay·*oo*·pay zee·lee·zoh·ka·*oosh*·wa
summer *majira ya joto* ma·*jee*·ra ya *joh*·toh
sun *jua* *joo*·a
sunblock *dawa la kukinga jua* *da*·wa la koo·*keen*·ga *joo*·a
sunburn *kuchomwa kwa jua* koo·*chom*·wa kwa *joo*·a
Sunday *Jumapili* joo·ma·*pee*·lee
sunglasses *miwani ya jua* mee·*wa*·nee ya *joo*·a
sunny *ya jua* ya *joo*·a
sunrise *macheo* ma·*chay*·oh
sunset *machweo* ma·*chway*·oh
sunstroke *ugonjwa wa kuchomwa kwa jua* oo·*gohn*·jwa wa koo·*chohm*·wa kwa *joo*·a
supermarket *duka kubwa* *doo*·ka *koob*·wa
superstition *ushirikina* oo·shee·ree·*kee*·na
supporter (politics) *mwungaji mkono* mwoon·*ga*·jee m·*koh*·noh
supporter (sport) *mshabiki* m·sha·*bee*·kee
surface mail (land) *barua kwa lori* ba·*roo*·a kwa *loh*·ree
surface mail (sea) *barua kwa meli* ba·*roo*·a kwa *may*·lee
surfboard *ubao wa kutelezea* oo·*ba*·oh wa koo·tay·lay·*zay*·a
surfing *kuteleza* koo·tay·*lay*·za
surname *jina la baba* *jee*·na la *ba*·ba
surprise *mshangao* m·shan·*ga*·oh
sweater *sweta* *sway*·ta
Sweden *Uswidi* oo·*swee*·dee
sweet ⓐ *tamu* *ta*·moo
sweets *peremende* pay·ray·*mayn*·day
swelling *uvimbe* oo·*veem*·bay
swim *-ogelea* ·oh·gay·*lay*·a
swimming (sport) *kuogelea* koo·oh·gay·*lay*·a
swimming pool *bwawa la kuogelea* *bwa*·wa la koo·oh·gay·*lay*·a
swimsuit *vazi la kuogelea* *va*·zee la koo·oh·gay·*lay*·a
Switzerland *Uswisi* oo·*swee*·see
synagogue *kanisa ya kiyahudi* ka·*nee*·sa ya kee·ya·*hoo*·dee
synthetic *ya usanisia* ya oo·sa·nee·*see*·a
syringe *sindano* seen·*da*·noh

T

table *meza* *may*·za
tablecloth *kitambaa cha meza* kee·tam·*ba* cha *may*·za
table tennis *mpira wa meza* m·*pee*·ra wa *may*·za
tail *mkia* m·*kee*·a
tailor *mshonaji* m·shoh·*na*·jee

take *-chukua* ·choo·*koo*·a
take a photo *-piga picha* ·pee·ga *pee*·cha
talk *-sema* ·*say*·ma
tall *mrefu* m·*ray*·foo
tampon *sodo* *soh*·doh
tanning lotion *dawa la kugeuza rangi kwenye jua* *da*·wa la koo·gay·*oo*·za *ran*·gee *kway*·nyay *joo*·a
Tanzania *Tanzania* tan·za·*nee*·a
tap *bomba* *bohm*·ba
tap water *maji ya bomba* *ma*·jee ya *bohm*·ba
tasty *tamu* *ta*·moo
tax *kodi* *koh*·dee
taxi *teksi* *tayk*·see
taxi stand *kituo cha teksi* kee·*too*·oh cha *tayk*·see
tea *chai* *cha*·ee
teacher *mwalimu* mwa·*lee*·moo
team *timu* *tee*·moo
teaspoon *kijiko cha chai* kee·*jee*·koh cha *cha*·ee
technique *mbinu* m·*bee*·noo
teeth *meno* *may*·noh
telecom centre *telekom* *tay*·lay·kohm
telegram *telegramu* tay·lay·*gra*·moo
telephone ⓝ *simu* *see*·moo
telephone ⓥ *-piga simu* ·*pee*·ga *see*·moo
telephone box *kibanda cha simu* kee·*ban*·da cha *see*·moo
telephone centre *kituo cha simu* kee·*too*·oh cha *see*·moo
telescope *darubini* da·roo·*bee*·nee
television *televisheni* tay·lay·vee·*shay*·nee
tell *-ambia* ·am·*bee*·a
temperature (fever) *homa* *hoh*·ma
temperature (weather) *halijoto* ha·lee·*joh*·toh
temple *hekalu* hay·*ka*·loo
tennis *tenesi* tay·*nay*·see
tennis court *kiwanja cha tenesi* kee·*wan*·ja cha tay·*nay*·see
tent *hema* *hay*·ma
tent peg *banzi la hema* *ban*·zee la *hay*·ma
terrible *mbaya sana* m·*ba*·ya *sa*·na
test *mtihani* m·tee·*ha*·nee
thank *-shukuru* ·shoo·*koo*·roo
that (person) *huyo* *hoo*·yoh
that (thing) *hiyo* *hee*·yoh
theatre *ukumbi wa maonyesho* oo·*koom*·bee wa ma·oh·*nyay*·shoh
their *yao* *ya*·oh
there *huko* *hoo*·koh
they *wao* *wa*·oh
thick *-zito* ·*zee*·toh
thief *mwizi* *mwee*·zee
thin *mwembamba* mwaym·*bam*·ba
think *-fikiri* ·fee·*kee*·ree
third *ya tatu* ya *ta*·too
(to be) thirsty *(-sikia) kiu* (·see·*kee*·a) *kee*·oo
this (person) *huyu* *hoo*·yoo
this (thing) *hii* hee
thread *uzi* *oo*·zee
throat *koo* koh
thrush (health) *ugonjwa wa upele* oo·*gohn*·jwa wa oo·*pay*·lay
thunderstorm *dhoruba ya radi* dhoh·*roo*·ba ya *ra*·dee
Thursday *Alhamisi* al·ha·*mee*·see
ticket *tiketi/tikiti* tee·*kay*·tee/tee·*kee*·tee
ticket collector *mkusanyaji wa tiketi* m·koo·sa·*nya*·jee wa tee·*kay*·tee
ticket machine *mashine ya tiketi* ma·*shee*·nay ya tee·*kay*·tee
ticket office *ofisi ya tiketi* o·*fee*·see ya tee·*kay*·tee
tide *maji ya kujaa na kupwa* *ma*·jee ya koo·*ja* na *koop*·wa
tight *ya kubana* ya koo·*ba*·na
time *saa* sa
time difference *tofauti ya wakati* to·fa·*oo*·tee ya wa·*ka*·tee
timetable *ratiba* ra·*tee*·ba
tin (can) *mkebe/kopo* m·*kay*·bay/*koh*·poh
tin opener *kifungua kopo* kee·foon·*goo*·a *koh*·poh
tiny *ndogo sana* n·*doh*·goh *sa*·na
tip (gratuity) *bakshishi* bak·*shee*·shee
tire *tairi* *ta*·ee·ree
tired *ya kuchoka* ya koo·*choh*·ka
tissues *karatasi za shashi* ka·ra·*ta*·see za *sha*·shee
to *hadi* *ha*·dee
toast *slaisi* sla·*ee*·see
toaster *mashine ya kubanika mkate* ma·*shee*·nay ya koo·ba·*nee*·ka m·*ka*·tay
tobacco *tumbaku* toom·*ba*·koo
tobacconist *duka la tumbaku* *doo*·ka la toom·*ba*·koo
today *leo* *lay*·oh
toe *kidole cha mguu* kee·*doh*·lay cha m·*goo*
together *pamoja* pa·*moh*·ja
toilet *choo* choh

toilet paper *karatasi ya choo* ka·ra·*ta*·see ya choh
tomato *nyanya nya*·nya
tomato sauce *mchuzi wa nyanya* m·*choo*·zee wa *nya*·nya
tomorrow *kesho kay*·shoh
tomorrow afternoon *kesho mchana* *kay*·shoh m·*cha*·na
tomorrow evening *kesho jioni* *kay*·shoh jee·*oh*·nee
tomorrow morning *kesho asubuhi* *kay*·shoh a·soo·*boo*·hee
tongue *ulimi* oo·*lee*·mee
tonight *usiku huu* oo·*see*·koo hoo
too (expensive etc) *mno m*·noh
tooth *jino jee*·noh
toothache *maumivu ya jino* ma·oo·*mee*·voo ya *jee*·noh
toothbrush *mswaki* m·*swa*·kee
toothpaste *dawa la meno* *da*·wa la *may*·noh
toothpick *kijiti cha meno* kee·*jee*·tee cha *may*·noh
torch (flashlight) *tochi toh*·chee
touch *-gusa ·goo*·sa
tour *safari ya kutalii* sa·*fa*·ree ya koo·ta·*lee*
tourist *mtalii* m·ta·*lee*
tourist office *ofisi ya watalii* o·*fee*·see ya wa·ta·*lee*
towards *kuelekea* koo·ay·lay·*kay*·a
towel *taulo* ta·*oo*·loh
tower *mnara* m·*na*·ra
toxic waste *taka za sumu* *ta*·ka za *soo*·moo
toy shop *duka la vitu vya kuchezea* *doo*·ka la *vee*·too vya koo·chay·*zay*·a
track (path) *njia* n·*jee*·a
track (sport) *michezo ya kukimbia* mee·*chay*·zoh ya koo·keem·*bee*·a
trade *biashara* bee·a·*sha*·ra
tradesperson *mfanyabiashara* m·fa·nya·bee·a·*sha*·ra
traffic *magari mengi* ma·*ga*·ree *mayn*·gee
traffic light *taa ya barabarani* *ta* ya ba·ra·ba·*ra*·nee
trail *njia* n·*jee*·a
train *treni tray*·nee
train station *stesheni ya treni* stay·*shay*·nee ya *tray*·nee
transit lounge *chumba cha kupumzikia kwa wanaosafiri choom*·ba cha koo·poom·zee·*kee*·a kwa wa·na·oh·sa·*fee*·ree
translate *-tafsiri* ·taf·*see*·ree
transport *usafirishaji* oo·sa·fee·ree·*sha*·jee
travel *-safiri* ·sa·*fee*·ree
travel agency *uwakala wa safari* oo·wa·*ka*·la wa sa·*fa*·ree
travellers cheque *hundi ya msafiri* *hoon*·dee ya m·sa·*fee*·ree
travel sickness *kichefuchefu cha safari* kee·chay·foo·*chay*·foo cha sa·*fa*·ree
tree *mti m*·tee
trip (journey) *safari* sa·*fa*·ree
trousers *suruali* soo·roo·*a*·lee
truck *lori loh*·ree
trust *-amini* ·a·*mee*·nee
try (attempt) *-jaribu* ·ja·*ree*·boo
try (taste) *-onja ·ohn*·ja
T-shirt *tishati tee*·sha·tee
tube (tyre) *tyubu tyoo*·boo
Tuesday *Jumanne* joo·ma·*n*·nay
tumour *uvimbe* oo·*veem*·bay
tuna *jodari* joh·*da*·ree
tune *wimbo weem*·boh
turkey *bata mzinga ba*·ta m·*zeen*·ga
turn *-geuza* ·gay·*oo*·za
TV *televisheni* tay·lay·vee·*shay*·nee
tweezers *twiza twee*·za
twice *mara mbili ma*·ra m·*bee*·lee
twin beds *vitanda viwili* vee·*tan*·da vee·*wee*·lee
twins *mapacha* ma·*pa*·cha
two *mbili* m·*bee*·lee
type *aina* a·*ee*·na
typical *ya mfano hasa* ya m·*fa*·noh *ha*·sa
tyre *tairi ta*·ee·ree

U

Uganda *Uganda* oo·*gan*·da
ultrasound *kupiga picha ya mtoto tumboni* koo·*pee*·ga *pee*·cha ya m·*toh*·toh toom·*boh*·nee
umbrella *mwamvuli* mwam·*voo*·lee
uncomfortable *bila raha bee*·la *ra*·ha
understand *-elewa* ·ay·*lay*·wa
underwear *chupi choo*·pee
unemployed *asiye na kazi* a·*see*·yay na *ka*·zee
unfair *jeuri* jay·*oo*·ree
uniform ⓝ *nguo rasmi* n·*goo*·oh *ras*·mee
universe *ulimwengu* oo·lee·*mwayn*·goo
university *chuo kikuu* choo·oh kee·*koo*
unleaded *isiyo na risasi* ee·*see*·yoh na ree·*sa*·see

unsafe *ni hatari* nee ha·*ta*·ree
until *mpaka* m·*pa*·ka
unusual *siyo kawaida* *see*·yoh ka·wa·*ee*·da
up *juu* joo
uphill *mwinuko* mwee·*noo*·koh
urgent *muhimu sana* moo·*hee*·moo *sa*·na
urinary infection *ambukizo la mfumo wa mkojo* am·boo·*kee*·zoh la m·*foo*·moh wa m·*koh*·joh
USA *Marekani* ma·ray·*ka*·nee
useful *yenye manufaa* *yay*·nyay ma·noo·*fa*

V

vacancy *nafasi* na·*fa*·see
vacant *tupu* *too*·poo
vacation *likizo* lee·*kee*·zoh
vaccination *chanjo* *chan*·joh
vagina *kuma* *koo*·ma
validate *-thibitisha* ·thee·bee·*tee*·sha
valley *bonde* *bohn*·day
valuable *ya thamani* ya *tha*·ma·nee
value (price) *thamani* *tha*·ma·nee
veal *nyama ya ndama* *nya*·ma ya n·*da*·ma
vegetable *mboga* m·*boh*·ga
vegetarian *mlaji wa mboga za majani tu* m·*la*·jee wa m·*boh*·ga za ma·*ja*·nee too
vein *mshipa* m·*shee*·pa
venereal disease *ugonjwa wa zinaa* oo·*gohn*·jwa wa zee·*na*
venue *mahali* ma·*ha*·lee
very *sana* *sa*·na
video recorder *kemra ya video* *kaym*·ra ya vee·*day*·oh
video tape *mkanda wa video* m·*kan*·da wa vee·*day*·oh
view *mandhari* man·*dha*·ree
village *kijiji* kee·*jee*·jee
vine (grape) *mzabibu* m·za·*bee*·boo
vinegar *siki* *see*·kee
vineyard *shamba la mizabibu* *sham*·ba la mee·za·*bee*·boo
virus *virusi* vee·*roo*·see
visa *viza/visa* *vee*·za/*vee*·sa
visit *-tembelea* ·taym·bay·*lay*·a
vitamins *vitamini* vee·ta·*mee*·nee
voice *sauti* sa·*oo*·tee
volleyball (sport) *mpira wa wavu* m·*pee*·ra wa *wa*·voo
volume (sound) *sauti* sa·*oo*·tee
vote *-piga kura* ·*pee*·ga *koo*·ra
vulture *tumbusi* toom·*boo*·see

W

wage *mshahara* m·sha·*ha*·ra
wait *-subiri* ·soo·*bee*·ree
wait for *-ngojea* ·n·goh·*jay*·a
waiter *mhudumu* m·hoo·*doo*·moo
waiting room *chumba cha wanaosubiri* *choom*·ba cha wa·na·oh·soo·*bee*·ree
wake up *-amka* ·*am*·ka
wake someone up *-amsha* ·*am*·sha
walk *-tembea* ·taym·*bay*·a
wall (outer) *ukuta* oo·*koo*·ta
want *-taka* ·*ta*·ka
war *vita* *vee*·ta
wardrobe *kabati ya nguo* ka·*ba*·tee ya n·*goo*·oh
warm *ya joto* ya joh·toh
warn *-onya* ·*oh*·nya
wash (oneself) *-oga* ·*oh*·ga
wash (something) *-osha* ·*oh*·sha
wash cloth (flannel) *kitambaa cha uso* kee·tam·*ba* cha *oo*·soh
washing machine *mashine ya kufulia* ma·*shee*·nay ya koo·foo·*lee*·a
watch *saa* sa
watch *-tazama* ·ta·*za*·ma
water *maji* *ma*·jee
water bottle (hot) *chupa ya maji (ya moto)* *choo*·pa ya *ma*·jee (ya *moh*·toh)
waterfall *maporomoko ya maji* ma·poh·roh·*moh*·koh ya *ma*·jee
watermelon *tikiti maji* tee·*kee*·tee *ma*·jee
waterproof *kutopenyesha maji* koo·to·pay·*nyay*·sha *ma*·jee
wave *wimbi* *weem*·bee
way *njia* n·*jee*·a
we *sisi* *see*·see
weak *hafifu* ha·*fee*·foo
wealthy *tajiri* ta·*jee*·ree
wear *-vaa* ·va
weather *hali ya hewa* *ha*·lee ya *hay*·wa
wedding *arusi* a·*roo*·see
wedding cake *keki ya arusi* *kay*·kee ya a·*roo*·see
wedding present *zawadi ya arusi* za·*wa*·dee ya a·*roo*·see
Wednesday *Jumatano* joo·ma·*ta*·noh
week *wiki* *wee*·kee
weekend *wikendi* wee·*kayn*·dee
weigh *-pima uzito* ·*pee*·ma oo·*zee*·toh
weight *uzito* oo·*zee*·toh

welcome *-karibisha* ·ka·ree·*bee*·sha
welfare *ustawi* oo·*sta*·wee
well *vizuri* vee·*zoo*·ree
west *magharibi* ma·gha·*ree*·bee
West Afrika *Afrika ya Magharibi* a·*free*·ka ya mag·ha·*ree*·bee
wet ⓐ *-bichi* ·*bee*·chee
what *nini* *nee*·nee
wheel *gurudumu* goo·roo·*doo*·moo
wheelchair *kiti cha magurudumu* *kee*·tee cha ma·goo·roo·*doo*·moo
when *wakati* wa·*ka*·tee
when *lini* *lee*·nee
where *wapi* *wa*·pee
which *gani* *ga*·nee
white *nyeupe* nyay·*oo*·pay
who *nani* *na*·nee
why *kwa nini* kwa *nee*·nee
wide *pana* *pa*·na
wife *mke* m·kay
wildebeest *nyumbu* *nyoom*·boo
win *-shinda* ·*sheen*·da
wind *upepo* oo·*pay*·poh
window *dirisha* dee·*ree*·sha
windscreen *kiwambo upepo* kee·*wam*·boh oo·*pay*·poh
windsurfing *kuteleza na tanga* koo·tay·*lay*·za na *tan*·ga
wine *mvinyo* m·*vee*·nyoh
wings *mabawa* ma·*ba*·wa
winner *mshindi* m·*sheen*·dee
winter *majira ya baridi* ma·*jee*·ra ya ba·*ree*·dee
wire *waya* *wa*·ya
wish *-tumaini* ·too·ma·*ee*·nee
with *na* na
without *bila* *bee*·la
woman *mwanamke* mwan·*am*·kay
wonderful *ya ajabu* ya a·*ja*·boo
wood *mbao* m·*ba*·oh
woodcarver's market *soko la wachonga vinyago* *soh*·koh la wa·*chohn*·ga vee·*nya*·goh
wool *sufu* soo·foo
word *neno* *nay*·noh
work ⓝ *kazi* *ka*·zee
work ⓥ *-fanya kazi* ·*fa*·nya *ka*·zee
work experience *uzoefu wa kazi* oo·zoh·*ay*·foo wa *ka*·zee
workout *mazoezi* ma·zoh·*ay*·zee
work permit *ruhusa ya kazi* roo·*hoo*·sa ya *ka*·zee
workshop (place) *karakana* ka·ra·*ka*·na
workshop (meeting) *warsha* *war*·sha
world *dunia* doo·*nee*·a
World Cup *Kombe la Dunia* *kohm*·bay la doo·*nee*·a
worms *minyoo* mee·*nyoh*
worried *mwenye wasiwasi* *mway*·nyay wa·see·*wa*·see
worship *-abudu* ·a·*boo*·doo
wrist *kiwiko* kee·*wee*·koh
write *-andika* ·an·*dee*·ka
writer *mwandishi* mwan·*dee*·shee
wrong *kosa* *koh*·sa

x-ray *eksirei* ayk·see·*ray*·ee

Y

year *mwaka* *mwa*·ka
yellow *manjano* man·*ja*·noh
yes *ndiyo* n·*dee*·yoh
yesterday *jana* *ja*·na
yogurt *maziwa ganda* ma·*zee*·wa *gan*·da
you sg *wewe* *way*·way
you pl *nyinyi* *nyee*·nyee
young *ya kijana* ya kee·*ja*·na
your sg *yako* *ya*·koh
your pl *yenu* *yay*·noo
youth hostel *hosteli ya vijana* hoh·*stay*·lee ya vee·*ja*·na

Z

Zaire *Jamhuri ya Kidemokrasia ya Kongo* jam·*hoo*·ree ya kee·day·moh·kra·*see*·a ya *kohn*·goh
Zambia *Zambia* *zam*·bee·a
Zanzibar City *Mji Mkongwe* *m*·jee m·*kohn*·gway
Zanzibar Island *Unguja* oon·*goo*·ja
zebra *punda milia* *poon*·da mee·*lee*·a
zip/zipper *zipu* *zee*·poo
zodiac *zodiaki* zoh·dee·*a*·kee
zoo *hifadhi ndogo ya wanyama* hee·*fa*·dhee n·*doh*·goh ya wa·*nya*·ma

Verbs are shown in the dictionary in their root forms, with a hyphen in front. To express a series of functions in a sentence, the verb can have several prefixes, infixes and suffixes. Some adjectives will also have a hyphen in front as they take different prefixes depending on certain characteristics of the thing being described. For more details on verbs and adjectives, see the **phrasebuilder**. You'll also find words marked as adjective ⓐ, noun ⓝ, verb ⓥ, singular sg, plural pl, adverb adv and preposition prep where necessary. A Swahili dictionary is also available online at www.kamusiproject.org.

A

a/c ay·*see air conditioning*
abiria a·bee·*ree*·a *passenger*
-abudu ·a·*boo*·doo *worship*
-acha ·*a*·cha *quit*
achari a·*cha*·ree *pickles*
adapta a·*dap*·ta *adaptor*
afadhali a·fa·*dha*·lee *better*
afya *af*·ya *health*
-agiza ·a·*gee*·za *order* ⓥ
agizo a·*gee*·zoh *order* ⓝ
— **la daktari** la dak·*ta*·ree *prescription*
-ahidi ·a·*hee*·dee *promise*
aibu a·*ee*·boo *embarrassment*
aina a·*ee*·na *type*
— **ya damu** ya *da*·moo *blood group*
aiskrimu a·ee·*skree*·moo *ice cream*
ajali a·*ja*·lee *accident*
akaunti a·ka·*oon*·tee *account*
— **ya benki** ya *bayn*·kee *bank account*
akiba za chakula a·*kee*·ba za cha·*koo*·la *food supplies*
alama a·*la*·ma *score • sign*
Alhamisi al·ha·*mee*·see *Thursday*
aliyestaafu a·lee·yay·sta·*a*·foo *retired*
almasi al·*ma*·see *shiny*
amana a·*ma*·na *deposit (bank)*
amani a·*ma*·nee *peace*
-ambia ·am·*bee*·a *tell*
ambukizo am·boo·*kee*·zoh *infection*
— **la mfumo wa mkojo** la m·*foo*·moh wa m·*koh*·joh *urinary infection*
amekufa a·may·*koo*·fa *dead*
-amini ·a·*mee*·nee *trust*
-amka ·*am*·ka *wake up*
-amsha ·*am*·sha *wake someone up*
-amua ·a·*moo*·a *decide*
anasa a·*na*·sa *luxury*
-andaa ·an·*da prepare*
-andika ·an·*dee*·ka *write*
-angalia ·an·ga·*lee*·a *look*
angani an·*ga*·nee *airspace • outer space*
-anguka ·an·*goo*·ka *fall (down)*
anwani an·*wa*·nee *address*
-anza ·*an*·za *start*
ardhi *ar*·dhee *land*
arusi a·*roo*·see *wedding*
asali a·*sa*·lee *honey*
asante a·*san*·tay *thank you*
asilimia a·see·lee·*mee*·a *per cent*
asiye na hatia a·*see*·yay na ha·*tee*·a *innocent*
asiye na kazi a·*see*·yay na *ka*·zee *unemployed*
askari a·*ska*·ree *soldier*
aspirini a·spee·*ree*·nee *aspirin*
asubuhi a·soo·*boo*·hee *morning*
au *a*·oo *or*

B

baa ba *bar (pub)*
baada ya ba·*a*·da ya *after*
baadaye ba·a·*da*·yay *later*
baba *ba*·ba *father*
babamkwe ba·ba·*m*·kway *father-in-law*
babu *ba*·boo *grandfather*
-badilisha ·ba·dee·*lee*·sha *exchange*
— **hela** *hay*·la *change (money)*
bado *ba*·doh *not yet*
bafu *ba*·foo *bath*

bafuni ba·*foo*·nee *bathroom (for bathing) • shower*
bahari ba·*ha*·ree *ocean • sea*
bahasha ba·*ha*·sha *envelope*
bahati ba·*ha*·tee *luck*
baisikeli ba·ee·see·*kay*·lee *bicycle*
— **kwenye gia** *kway*·nyay *gee*·a *mountain bike*
— **ya mashindano** ya ma·sheen·*da*·noh *racing bike*
bajeti *ba*·jay·tee *budget*
-baka ·*ba*·ka *rape*
-baki ·*ba*·kee *stay (in one place)*
bakshishi bak·*shee*·shee *tip (gratuity)*
bakuli ba·*koo*·lee *bowl*
balbu ya taa *bal*·boo ya *ta light bulb*
balozi ba·*loh*·zee *ambassador*
balungi ba·*loon*·gee *grapefruit*
bandari ban·*da*·ree *harbour • port (sea)*
bangi *ban*·gee *hash • marijuana • pot (dope)*
bango *ban*·goh *poster*
banzi la hema *ban*·zee la *hay*·ma *tent peg*
bao la kukatia *ba*·oh la koo·ka·*tee*·a *chopping board*
barabara ba·ra·*ba*·ra *avenue • highway • motorway • road*
— **kuu** *koo main road*
barabara ba·*ra*·ba·ra *excellent*
barafu ba·*ra*·foo *ice*
baridi ba·*ree*·dee *cold* ⓐ
barua ba·*roo*·a *letter • mail*
— **kwa haraka** kwa ha·*ra*·ka *(by) express mail*
— **kwa lori** kwa *loh*·ree *surface mail (land)*
— **kwa meli** kwa *may*·lee *surface mail (sea)*
— **kwa ndege** kwa n·*day*·gay *airmail*
— **pepe** *pay*·pay *email*
— **ya rejista** ya *ray*·jee·sta *(by) registered mail/post*
basi *ba*·see *bus (intercity) • coach*
bata *ba*·ta *duck*
— **mzinga** m·*zeen*·ga *turkey*
-beba ·*bay*·ba *carry*
bega *bay*·ga *shoulder*
bei bay *price*
— **ya kuingia** ya koo·een·*gee*·a *cover charge • admission (price)*
bekoni bay·*koh*·nee *bacon*
bendera bayn·*day*·ra *flag*
benki *bayn*·kee *bank*
betri *bay*·tree *battery*
Bi bee *Mrs • Madam*
bia *bee*·a *beer*
biashara bee·a·*sha*·ra *business • trade*
bibi *bee*·bee *grandmother*
Bibi *bee*·bee *Ms • Miss*
Biblia beeb·*lee*·a *Bible*
-bichi ·*bee*·chee *fresh • raw • wet*
bila *bee*·la *without*
— **nyumba** *nyoom*·ba *homeless*
— **raha** *ra*·ha *uncomfortable*
bili *bee*·lee *cheque (bill)*
biliadi bee·lee·*a*·dee *pool (game)*
bima *bee*·ma *insurance*
binafsi bee·*naf*·see *private*
binti *been*·tee *daughter*
biri *bee*·ree *cigar*
biringani bee·reen·*ga*·nee *aubergine • eggplant*
-bisha ·*bee*·sha *argue*
biskuti bee·*skoo*·tee *biscuit • cookie*
bizari bee·*za*·ree *curry*
blanketi blan·*kay*·tee *blanket*
blue bandi bloo·*ban*·dee *margarine*
boga *boh*·ga *pumpkin*
bogi la kulia chakula *boh*·gee la koo·*lee*·a cha·*koo*·la *dining car*
bomba *bohm*·ba *faucet • tap*
bonde *bohn*·day *valley*
boti *boh*·tee *boat*
brandi *bran*·dee *brandy*
breki *bray*·kee *brakes*
bubu *boo*·boo *mute*
bucha *boo*·cha *butcher • butcher's shop*
buibui boo·ee·*boo*·ee *spider*
buking *boo*·keeng *reservation • booking*
buluu boo·*loo blue*
bunduki boon·*doo*·kee *gun*
bunge *boon*·gay *parliament*
-buni ·*boo*·nee *guess*
burashi boo·*ra*·shee *brush*
— **ya nywele** ya *nyway*·lay *hairbrush*
bure *boo*·ray *complimentary (free)*
burudani boo·roo·*da*·nee *fun*
bustani boo·*sta*·nee *garden*
— **ya kibotania** ya kee·boh·ta·*nee*·a *botanic garden*
busu *boo*·soo *kiss*
-busu ·*boo*·soo *kiss*
Bwana *bwa*·na *Mr • Sir*
bwawa la kuogelea *bwa*·wa la koo·oh·gay·*lay*·a *swimming pool*

C

chache *cha*·chay *few • less • little (not much)*
chafu *cha*·foo *dirty*
-chagua ·cha·*goo*·a *choose*
chai *cha*·ee *tea*
— **ya asubuhi** ya a·soo·*boo*·hee *breakfast*
chakula cha·*koo*·la *dish • food*
— **cha jioni** cha jee·*oh*·nee *dinner*
— **cha mchana** cha m·*cha*·na *lunch*
— **cha mtoto mchanga** cha m·*toh*·toh m·*chan*·ga *baby food*
chama *cha*·ma *party (politics)*
chandarua chan·da·*roo*·a *mosquito net*
-changanyika ·chan·ga·*nyee*·ka *mix*
chanjo *chan*·joh *vaccination*
chanuo cha·*noo*·oh *comb*
chavua cha·*voo*·a *pollen*
chawa *cha*·wa *lice*
chaza *cha*·za *oyster*
-cheka ·*chay*·ka *laugh*
chekechea chay·kay·*chay*·a *kindergarten*
chenji *chayn*·jee *change*
chenza *chayn*·za *mandarin*
cheti *chay*·tee *certificate*
— **cha kuzaliwa** cha koo·za·*lee*·wa *birth certificate*
-cheza ·*chay*·za *play (guitar, cards etc)*
-cheza densi ·*chay*·za *dayn*·see *dance*
chini *chee*·nee *below • bottom (position) • down • low*
chokoleti choh·koh·*lay*·tee *chocolate*
-choma sindano ·*choh*·ma seen·*da*·noh *inject*
chombo cha kusaidia kusikia *chohm*·boh cha koo·sa·ee·*dee*·a koo·see·*kee*·a *hearing aid*
chombo cha majivu *chohm*·boh cha ma·*jee*·voo *ashtray*
chomboni chohm·*boh*·nee *aboard*
choo choh *bathroom (toilet)*
— **cha hadhara** cha *ha*·dha·ra *public toilet*
choroa choh·*roh*·a *oryx*
-choshwa ·*choh*·shwa *bored*
chui *choo*·ee *leopard*
-chukua ·choo·*koo*·a *take*
chumba *choom*·ba *room*
— **cha dobi** cha *doh*·bee *laundry (room)*
— **cha kubadilisha nguo** cha koo·ba·dee·*lee*·sha n·*goo*·oh *changing room (in shop)*
— **cha kulala** cha koo·*la*·la *bedroom*
— **cha kupumzikia kwa wanaosafiri** cha koo·poom·zee·*kee*·a kwa wa·na·oh·sa·*fee*·ree *transit lounge*
— **cha kuwekea mizigo** cha koo·way·*kay*·a mee·*zee*·goh *left-luggage office*
— **cha makoti** cha ma·*koh*·tee *cloakroom*
— **cha mali ya kuokota** cha *ma*·lee ya koo·oh·*koh*·ta *lost property office*
— **cha wanaosubiri** cha wa·na·oh·soo·*bee*·ree *waiting room*
— **kwa watu wawili** kwa *wa*·too wa·*wee*·lee *double room*
— **kwa mtu mmoja** kwa *m*·too m·*moh*·ja *single room*
chumvi *choom*·vee *salt*
chungu *choon*·goo *bitter* ⓐ *• pot (ceramics)* ⓝ
chuo *choo*·oh *college*
— **kikuu** kee·*koo* *university*
chupa *choo*·pa *bottle • jar*
— **ya maji (ya moto)** ya *ma*·jee (ya *moh*·toh) *water bottle (hot)*
chupi *choo*·pee *boxer shorts • underwear*

D

dada *da*·da *sister*
dadu *da*·doo *dice*
daftari daf·*ta*·ree *notebook*
dagaa da·*ga* *sardine*
daima da·*ee*·ma *always*
dakika da·*kee*·ka *minute*
daktari dak·*ta*·ree *doctor*
— **wa akina mama** wa a·*kee*·na *ma*·ma *gynaecologist*
— **wa macho** wa *ma*·choh *optometrist*
— **wa meno** wa *may*·noh *dentist*
daladala Tan da·la·*da*·la *bus (city)*
damu *da*·moo *blood*
daraja da·*ra*·ja *bridge*
— **la kwanza** la *kwan*·za *first class*
— **la pili** la *pee*·lee *second class*
— **la tatu** la *ta*·too *economy class*
— **la wafanyabiashara** la wa·fa·nya·bee·a·*sha*·ra *business class*

darubini da·roo·*bee*·nee *binoculars • telescope*
dau *da*·oo *bet*
dawa *da*·wa *drug • medicine*
— **la kuendesha** la koo·ayn·*day*·sha *laxative*
— **la kugeuza rangi kwenye jua** la koo·gay·*oo*·za *ran*·gee *kway*·nyay *joo*·a *tanning lotion*
— **la kukinga jua** la koo·*keen*·ga *joo*·a *sunblock*
— **la kukohoa** la koo·koh·*hoh*·a *cough medicine*
— **la meno** la *may*·noh *toothpaste*
— **la midomo** la mee·*doh*·moh *lip balm*
— **la sindano** la seen·*da*·noh *injection*
— **la kuboresha nywele** la koo·boh·*ray*·sha *nyway*·lay *conditioner (hair)*
— **la kuongeza maji mwilini** la koo·ohn·*gay*·za *ma*·jee mwee·*lee*·nee *rehydration salts*
— **la kusafisha jeraha** la koo·sa·*fee*·sha jay·*ra*·ha *antiseptic* ⓝ
demokrasia day·moh·kra·*see*·a *democracy*
dengu *dayn*·goo *lentil*
densi *dayn*·see *dancing*
dhahabu dha·*ha*·boo *gold*
dhamana dha·*ma*·na *guarantee*
dharura dha·*roo*·ra *emergency*
dhidi ya nyuklia *dhee*·dee ya *nyoo*·klee·a *antinuclear*
dhoruba dho·*roo*·ba *storm*
— **ya radi** ya *ra*·dee *thunderstorm*
dini *dee*·nee *religion*
diodorani dee·oh·doh·*ra*·nee *deodorant*
dira *dee*·ra *compass*
dirisha dee·*ree*·sha *window*
disketi dees·*kay*·tee *disk (floppy)*
diski *dee*·skee *disk (CD-ROM)*
disko *dees*·koh *disco*
dobi *doh*·bee *launderette*
-dogo ·*doh*·goh *small*
— **kabisa** ka·*bee*·sa *smallest*
— **zaidi** za·*ee*·dee *smaller*
dola *doh*·la *dollar*
dozi kubwa mno ya dawa *doh*·zee *koob*·wa m·*noh* ya *da*·wa *overdose*
duara doo·*a*·ra *round*
duka *doo*·ka *shop*
— **kubwa** *koob*·wa *supermarket*
— **la aiskrimu** la a·ee·*skree*·moo *ice-cream parlour*
— **la baisikeli** la ba·ee·see·*kay*·lee *bike shop*
— **la bidhaa mbalimbali** la bee·*dha* m·ba·lee·m·*ba*·lee *convenience store*
— **la bidhaa za umeme** la bee·*dha* za oo·*may*·may *electrical store*
— **la dawa** la *da*·wa *chemist • pharmacy*
— **la fedha** la *fay*·dha *silver shop*
— **la keki** la *kay*·kee *cake shop*
— **la kemra** la *kaym*·ra *camera shop*
— **la kumbukumbu** la koom·boo·*koom*·boo *souvenir shop*
— **la magazeti** la ma·ga·*zay*·tee *newsstand*
— **la maua** la ma·*oo*·a *florist*
— **la mboga** la m·*boh*·ga *greengrocer*
— **la mitumba** la mee·*toom*·ba *second-hand shop*
— **la mkate** la m·*ka*·tay *bakery*
— **la muziki** la moo·*zee*·kee *music shop*
— **la nguo** la n·*goo*·oh *clothing store*
— **la pombe kali** la *pohm*·bay *ka*·lee *bottle shop • liquor store*
— **la samaki** la sa·*ma*·kee *fish shop*
— **la tumbaku** la toom·*ba*·koo *tobacconist*
— **la viatu** la vee·*a*·too *shoe shop*
— **la vifaa vya kambi** la vee·*fa* vya *kam*·bee *camping store*
— **la vifaa vya michezo** la vee·*fa* vya mee·*chay*·zoh *sports store*
— **la vifaa vya ofisi** la vee·*fa* vya o·*fee*·see *stationer (shop)*
— **la vifaa vya ujenzi** la vee·*fa* vya oo·*jayn*·zee *hardware store*
— **la vipuli** la vee·*poo*·lee *jewellery store*
— **la vitabu** la vee·*ta*·boo *bookshop*
— **la vitu vya kuchezea** la *vee*·too vya koo·chay·*zay*·a *toy shop*
— **lenye vitu vingi** *lay*·nyay *vee*·too *veen*·gee *department store*
duma *doo*·ma *cheetah*
Dunia doo·*nee*·a *Earth*
dunia doo·*nee*·a *world*

E

-egesha ·ay·*gay*·sha *park (a car)*
ekspres ayk·*sprays* *express* ⓐ
ekstasi *ayk*·sta·see *ecstacy (drug)*

elasto ay·*la*·stoh *Band-Aid*
-elekeza ·ay·lay·*kay*·za *point*
-elewa ·ay·*lay*·wa *understand*
elimu ay·*lee*·moo *education*
embe *aym*·bay *mango*
— **mafuta** ma·*foo*·ta *avocado*
-enda ·*ayn*·da *go*
— **dukani** doo·*ka*·nee *go shopping*
— **nje** *n*·jay *go out*
-endesha ·ayn·*day*·sha *drive*
eskaleta ays·ka·*lay*·ta *escalator*
euro ay·*oo*·roh *euro*
eutanasia ay·oo·ta·na·*see*·a *euthanasia*

F

-fa ·fa *die*
faida fa·*ee*·da *profit*
faini fa·*ee*·nee *fine (penalty)*
faksi *fak*·see *fax machine*
falaki fa·*la*·kee *horoscope*
familia fa·mee·*lee*·a *family*
-fanya ·*fa*·nya *do*
— **buking** *boo*·keeng *make a booking*
— **kazi** *ka*·zee *work*
farasi fa·*ra*·see *horse*
faulo fa·*oo*·loh *foul*
fedha *fay*·dha *cash • silver*
feni *fay*·nee *fan (machine)*
fenicha fay·*nee*·cha *furniture*
figili fee·*gee*·lee *radish*
figo *fee*·goh *kidney*
-fika ·*fee*·ka *arrive*
-fikiri ·fee·*kee*·ree *think*
-fikisha ·fee·*kee*·sha *deliver*
filamu fee·*la*·moo *film (cinema)*
— **ya hali halisi** ya *ha*·lee ha·*lee*·see *documentary (film)*
— **ya slaidi** ya sla·*ee*·dee *slide film*
fisi *fee*·see *hyena*
fleti *flay*·tee *flat (apartment)*
fluu floo *flu (influenza)*
forodha foh·*roh*·dha *customs*
foronya foh·*roh*·nya *pillowcase*
friji *free*·jee *fridge*
-fuata ·foo·*a*·ta *follow*
fulana ya ndani foo·*la*·na ya n·*da*·nee *singlet*
fulani foo·*la*·nee *someone*
fundi *foon*·dee *mechanic*
funga *foon*·ga *close*
-funga kwa ufunguo ·*foon*·ga kwa oo·foon·*goo*·oh *lock*
fungate foon·*ga*·tay *honeymoon*
-fungua ·foon·*goo*·a *open*
fupi *foo*·pee *short (height)*
-furahia ·foo·ra·*hee*·a *enjoy (oneself) • have fun*
fursa sawa *foor*·sa *sa*·wa *equal opportunity*
furushi foo·*roo*·shee *package*
-futa ·*foo*·ta *cancel*
futbol ya kimarekani *foot*·bohl ya kee·ma·ray·*ka*·nee *American football*
fuvu *foo*·voo *skull*

G

-ganda ·*gan*·da *freeze*
gani *ga*·nee *which*
gari *ga*·ree *car*
— **la hospitali** la hoh·spee·*ta*·lee *ambulance*
— **la vitanda** la vee·*tan*·da *sleeping car*
-gawa ·*ga*·wa *deal (cards)*
-gawana ·ga·*wa*·na *share (a dorm etc)*
gazeti ga·*zay*·tee *magazine • newspaper*
gereji gay·*ray*·jee *garage (to park a car)*
gereza gay·*ray*·za *jail*
gesti *gay*·stee *guesthouse • hotel • motel*
-geuza ·gay·*oo*·za *turn*
ghali *ga*·lee *expensive*
gharama ga·*ra*·ma *cost*
— **kwa mpigiwa simu** kwa m·pee·*gee*·wa *see*·moo *collect call*
ghorofa go·*ro*·fa *floor • storey*
giza *gee*·za *dark*
glesi *glay*·see *glass*
godolo goh·*doh*·loh *mattress*
goli *goh*·lee *goal*
goti *goh*·tee *knee*
gramu *gra*·moo *gram*
gundi *goon*·dee *glue*
-gundua ·goon·*doo*·a *find*
gurudumu goo·roo·*doo*·moo *wheel*
-gusa ·*goo*·sa *touch*

H

habari ha·*ba*·ree *news*
hadhi ya kindoa *ha*·dhee ya kee·n·*doh*·a *marital status*
hadi *ha*·dee *to*
hadithi ha·*dee*·thee *story*
— **kama riwaya** *ka*·ma ree·*wa*·ya *drama*

hafifu ha·*fee*·foo *weak*
haiwezekani ha·ee·way·zay·*ka*·nee *impossible*
haki ya kisheria ya mmiliki wa gari *ha*·kee ya kee·shay·*ree*·a ya m·mee·*lee*·kee wa *ga*·ree *car owner's title*
haki za binadamu *ha*·kee za been·a·*da*·moo *civil rights • human rights*
-hakikisha (buking) ·ha·kee·*kee*·sha (*boo*·keeng) *confirm (a booking)*
hakimu ha·*kee*·moo *judge*
hakuna ha·*koo*·na *none*
— **kitu** *kee*·too *nothing*
— **nafasi** na·*fa*·see *booked out • no vacancy*
— **sigara** see·*ga*·ra *nonsmoking*
halali ha·*la*·lee *halal • kosher • legal*
hali asili *ha*·le a·*see*·lee *nature*
hali ya hewa *ha*·lee ya *hay*·wa *weather*
halijoto ha·lee·*joh*·toh *temperature (weather)*
halisi ha·*lee*·see *pure*
hamna *ham*·na *none*
hapa *ha*·pa *here*
hapana ha·*pa*·na *no • not*
hapo jirani *ha*·poh jee·*ra*·nee *nearby*
hapo karibuni *ha*·poh ka·ree·*boo*·nee *nearby*
hariri ha·*ree*·ree *silk*
harufu ha·*roo*·foo *smell*
hatari ha·*ta*·ree *dangerous • risk*
hatua ha·*too*·a *step*
hedhi *hay*·dhee *menstruation*
hekalu hay·*ka*·loo *temple*
hela *hay*·la *money*
helmeti hayl·*may*·tee *helmet*
hema *hay*·ma *tent*
herini hay·*ree*·nee *earrings*
heroe hay·*roh*·ay *flamingo*
heroini hay·roh·*ee*·nee *heroin*
-hesabu ·hay·*sa*·boo *count*
hewa *hay*·wa *air (outside) • atmosphere*
hifadhi hee·*fa*·dhee *park*
— **ndogo ya wanyama** n·*doh*·goh ya wa·*nya*·ma *zoo*
— **ya wanyama** ya wa·*nya*·ma *game park • national park*
hii hee *it • this (thing)*
-hisi ·*hee*·see *feel (touch)*
hisia hee·*see*·a *feeling (physical) • feelings*
historia hee·stoh·*ree*·a *history*
-hitaji ·hee·*ta*·jee *need*
hivi karibuni *hee*·vee ka·ree·*boo*·nee *recently*
hiyo *hee*·yoh *that (thing)*
hodari hoh·*da*·ree *brilliant (smart)*
hoki ya barafuni *hoh*·kee ya ba·ra·*foo*·nee *ice hockey*
homa *hoh*·ma *fever (temperature)*
— **ya matezi** ya ma·*tay*·zee *glandular fever*
— **ya mzio** ya m·*zee*·oh *hay fever*
hongera hohn·*gay*·ra *congratulations*
honi *hoh*·nee *horn*
hospitali hoh·spee·*ta*·lee *hospital*
hosteli ya vijana hoh·*stay*·lee ya vee·*ja*·na *youth hostel*
huduma hoo·*doo*·ma *service*
huko *hoo*·koh *there*
hundi *hoon*·dee *cheque (banking)*
— **ya msafiri** ya m·sa·*fee*·ree *travellers cheque*
huru *hoo*·roo *free (not bound)*
husuni hoo·*soo*·nee *castle*
huyo *hoo*·yoh *that (person)*
huyu *hoo*·yoo *this (person)*

I

-iba ·*ee*·ba *rob*
ijayo ee·*ja*·yoh *next*
Ijumaa ee·joo·*ma* *Friday*
-imba ·*eem*·ba *sing*
imevunjika ee·may·voon·*jee*·ka *out of order*
-ingia ·een·*gee*·a *enter*
ini *ee*·nee *liver*
injini een·*jee*·nee *engine*
intanet kafe een·ta·*nayt* ka·*fay* *Internet café*
-ishi ·*ee*·shee *live (somewhere)*
isiyo na risasi ee·*see*·yoh na ree·*sa*·see *unleaded*
-ita ·*ee*·ta *call*

J

-ja ·ja *come*
jaketi ja·*kay*·tee *jacket*
— **la kuokolea** la koo·oh·koh·*lay*·a *life jacket*
jamhuri jam·*hoo*·ree *republic*
jamu *ja*·moo *jam*
— **ya machungwa** ya ma·*choon*·gwa *marmalade*

jana *ja*·na *yesterday*
jangwa *jan*·gwa *desert*
jani *ja*·nee *leaf*
-jaribu ·ja·*ree*·boo *try (attempt)*
-jaza ·*ja*·za *fill*
-jenga ·*jayn*·ga *build*
jengo *jayn*·goh *building*
jeraha jay·*ra*·ha *bruise* • *injury*
— **la moto** la *moh*·toh *burn*
jeshi *jay*·shee *military*
jeuri jay·*oo*·ree *unfair*
jibini jee·*bee*·nee *cheese*
jibu *jee*·boo *answer*
-jiburudisha ·jee·boo·roo·*dee*·sha *relax*
jicho *jee*·choh *eye*
-jifunza ·jee·*foon*·za *learn*
jiko *jee*·koh *kitchen* • *stove*
jina *jee*·na *name*
— **la baba** la *ba*·ba *surname*
— **la familia** la fa·mee·*lee*·a *family name*
— **la kwanza** la *kwan*·za *Christian name*
— **la utani** la oo·*ta*·nee *nickname*
jino *jee*·noh *tooth*
jinsia jeen·*see*·a *sex (gender)*
jinzi *jeen*·zee *jeans*
jioni jee·*oh*·nee *evening*
jipi *jee*·pee *jeep*
jirani jee·*ra*·nee *beside* • *near*
jiwe *jee*·way *rock* • *stone*
jodari joh·*da*·ree *tuna*
joko *joh*·koh *oven*
— **la mikrowevu** la mee·kroh·*way*·voo *microwave (oven)*
joto *joh*·toh *heat* ⓝ • *heating* ⓝ • *hot* ⓐ
jua *joo*·a *sun*
-jua ·*joo*·a *know*
jukwaa *joo*·kwa *platform*
Jumamosi joo·ma·*moh*·see *Saturday*
Jumanne joo·ma·*n*·nay *Tuesday*
Jumapili joo·ma·*pee*·lee *Sunday*
Jumatano joo·ma·*ta*·noh *Wednesday*
Jumatatu joo·ma·*ta*·too *Monday*
jumba *joom*·ba *palace*
— **la opera** la *oh*·pay·ra *opera house*
jumuiya ya masista joo·moo·*ee*·ya ya ma·*see*·sta *convent*
jusi *joo*·see *juice*
juu joo *high* • *up*
juu ya joo ya *above* ⓐ • *on* adv
juzi *joo*·zee *day before yesterday*

K

-kaa ·ka *sit* • *stay (at a hotel)*
-kaanga ·ka·*an*·ga *fry*
kabati ka·*ba*·tee *cupboard*
— **ya nguo** ya n·*goo*·oh *wardrobe*
kabichi ka·*bee*·chee *cabbage*
kabla *ka*·bla *before*
kaburi ka·*boo*·ree *grave*
kabuti ka·*boo*·tee *overcoat*
kadhaa ka·*dha* *several* • *some*
kadi ya benki *ka*·dee ya *bayn*·kee *credit card*
kadi ya simu (ya mikononi) *ka*·dee ya *see*·moo (ya mee·koh·*noh*·nee) *SIM card*
kadi ya simu za vibandani *ka*·dee ya *see*·moo za vee·ban·*da*·nee *phonecard*
-kagua ·ka·*goo*·a *check*
kahawa ka·*ha*·wa *coffee*
kahawia ka·ha·*wee*·a *brown*
kaka *ka*·ka *brother*
kakao ka·*ka*·oh *cocoa*
kalamu ka·*la*·moo *pen (ballpoint)*
kalenda ka·*layn*·da *calendar*
kama *ka*·ma *if*
-kamata ·ka·*ma*·ta *arrest*
kamba *kam*·ba *prawn* • *rope*
— **ya kukausha nguo** ya koo·ka·*oo*·sha n·*goo*·oh *clothesline*
— **za viatu** za vee·*a*·too *laces*
kamili ka·*mee*·lee *exactly* adv • *perfect* ⓐ
kamisheni ka·mee·*shay*·nee *commission*
kampuni kam·*poo*·nee *company*
— **ya ndege** ya n·*day*·gay *airline*
kamusi ka·*moo*·see *dictionary*
kamwe *kam*·way *never*
kanda *kan*·da *cassette*
— **ya musiki** ya moo·*zee*·kee *musical recording*
kando ya *kan*·doh ya *next to*
kanisa ka·*nee*·sa *church*
— **kuu** koo *cathedral*
— **ya kiyahudi** ya kee·ya·*hoo*·dee *synagogue*
kansa *kan*·sa *cancer*
kapera ka·*pay*·ra *single (person)*
kaptura kap·*too*·ra *shorts*
karakana ka·ra·*ka*·na *workshop (to make things)*
karanga ka·*ran*·ga *groundnut* • *peanut*
karani ka·*ra*·nee *secretary*

karantini ka·ran·*tee*·nee *quarantine*
karata ka·*ra*·ta *playing cards*
karatasi ka·ra·*ta*·see *paper*
— **ya choo** ya choh *toilet paper*
— **za shashi** za *sha*·shee *tissues*
-karibisha ·ka·ree·*bee*·sha *invite* • *welcome*
karibu ka·*ree*·boo *close (near)*
— **na** na *almost*
— **zaidi** za·*ee*·dee *nearest*
karoti ka·*roh*·tee *carrot*
kasha la fedha *ka*·sha la *fay*·dha *safe (for money)*
kasino ka·*see*·noh *casino*
kaskazini kas·ka·*zee*·nee *north*
-kata ·*ka*·ta *cut*
-kataa ·ka·*ta* *refuse*
katika ka·*tee*·ka *in*
— **muda wa (saa moja)** *moo*·da wa (*sa moh*·ja) *within (an hour)*
katikati ka·tee·*ka*·tee *between* adv • *centre* ⓝ
— **ya mji** ya *m*·jee *city centre*
katoni ka·*toh*·nee *carton*
kaunta ka·*oon*·ta *counter (at bar)*
-kausha ·ka·*oo*·sha *dry*
kavu *ka*·voo *dry*
kawaida ka·wa·*ee*·da *ordinary*
kazi *ka*·zee *job* • *work*
— **kwenye baa** *kway*·nyay ba *bar work*
— **ya mikono** ya mee·*koh*·noh *handicrafts*
— **ya nyumbani** ya nyum·*ba*·nee *housework*
— **ya ukarani** ya oo·ka·*ra*·nee *paperwork*
kebo za kuwashia *kay*·boh za koo·wa·*shee*·a *jumper leads*
kejekeje kay·jay·*kay*·jay *loose*
keki *kay*·kee *cake*
— **ya arusi** ya a·*roo*·see *wedding cake*
kemra *kaym*·ra *camera*
keshia kay·*shee*·a *cashier*
kesho *kay*·shoh *tomorrow*
— **asubuhi** a·soo·*boo*·hee *tomorrow morning*
— **jioni** jee·*oh*·nee *tomorrow evening*
— **kutwa** *koot*·wa *the day after tomorrow*
— **mchana** m·*cha*·na *tomorrow afternoon*
kiambato kee·am·*ba*·toh *ingredient*
kiasi gani kee·*a*·see *ga*·nee *how much*
kiatu kee·*a*·too *shoe*
kiazi kee·*a*·zee *potato*
kiazisukari kee·a·zee·soo·*ka*·ree *beetroot*
kibali kee·*ba*·lee *permit*
kibanda cha simu kee·*ban*·da cha *see*·moo *telephone box*
kibandiko cha chupi kee·ban·*dee*·koh cha *choo*·pee *panty liners*
kibarua kee·ba·*roo*·a *casual work* • *part-time*
kibiriti kee·bee·*ree*·tee *lighter (match)*
kibofu kee·*boh*·foo *bladder*
kiboko kee·*boh*·koh *hippopotamus*
kibole kee·*boh*·lay *appendix (body)*
kichapishi kee·cha·*pee*·shee *keyboard*
kichefuchefu kee·chay·foo·*chay*·foo *nausea*
— **cha asubuhi** cha a·soo·*boo*·hee *morning sickness*
— **cha baharini** cha ba·ha·*ree*·nee *seasickness*
— **cha safari** cha sa·*fa*·ree *travel sickness*
kichwa *keech*·wa *head*
kidole kee·*doh*·lay *finger*
— **cha mguu** cha m·*goo* *toe*
kidonge kee·*dohn*·gay *pill*
— **cha kuzuia mimba** cha koo·zoo·*ee*·a *meem*·ba *the pill*
kifafa kee·*fa*·fa *epilepsy*
kifaru kee·*fa*·roo *rhinoceros*
kifiko kee·*fee*·koh *destination*
kifungo kee·*foon*·goh *button*
kifungua chupa kee·foon·*goo*·a *choo*·pa *bottle opener*
kifungua kopo kee·foon·*goo*·a *koh*·poh *tin opener*
kifurushi kee·foo·*roo*·shee *parcel*
kigari cha mtoto kee·*ga*·ree cha m·*toh*·toh *stroller* • *pram*
kiharusi kee·ha·*roo*·see *stroke (health)*
Kiingereza kee·een·gay·*ray*·za *English (language)*
kijani kee·*ja*·nee *green*
kijiji kee·*jee*·jee *village*
kijiko kee·*jee*·koh *spoon*
— **cha chai** cha *cha*·ee *teaspoon*
kijitabu kee·jee·*ta*·boo *brochure*
kijiti cha meno kee·*jee*·tee cha *may*·noh *toothpick*
kijiti cha pamba safi kee·*jee*·tee cha *pam*·ba *sa*·fee *cotton buds*
kijito kee·*jee*·toh *stream*
kijivu kee·*jee*·voo *grey*
kikaango kee·ka·*an*·goh *frying pan*
kikapu kee·*ka*·poo *basket*

kikohozi kee·koh·*hoh*·zee *cough*
kikokotoo kee·koh·koh·*toh*·oh *calculator*
kikombe kee·*kohm*·bay *cup*
kikomo cha mwendo kee·*koh*·moh cha *mwayn*·doh *speed limit*
kikundi kee·*koon*·dee *band (music)*
kila *kee*·la *each • every*
kila kitu *kee*·la *kee*·too *everything*
kila siku *kee*·la *see*·koo *daily*
kilainishio kee·la·ee·nee·*shee*·oh *lubricant*
kilele kee·*lay*·lay *peak (mountain)*
kilema kee·*lay*·ma *paraplegic*
kilevi kee·*lay*·vee *alcohol*
kilimo kee·*lee*·moh *agriculture*
— **cha bustani** cha boo·*sta*·nee *gardening*
kilio kee·*lee*·oh *funeral*
kilo *kee*·loh *kilogram*
kilomita kee·loh·*mee*·ta *kilometre*
-kimbia ·keem·*bee*·a *run*
kimo *kee*·moh *altitude*
-kinga ·*keen*·ga *protect*
kingamimba keen·ga·*meem*·ba *contraceptives*
kinururishi kee·noo·roo·*ree*·shee *radiator*
kinyozi kee·*nyoh*·zee *barber*
kinyume kee·*nyoo*·may *opposite*
kinywaji kee·*nywa*·jee *drink*
kiondoa maumivu kee·ohn·*doh*·a ma·oo·*mee*·voo *painkiller*
kiongozi kee·ohn·*goh*·zee *guide (person) • leader*
kionyeshi kee·oh·*nyay*·shee *indicator*
kioo kee·*oh mirror*
kioski kee·*oh*·skee *kiosk*
kipa *kee*·pa *goalkeeper*
kipandauso kee·pan·da·*oo*·soh *migraine*
kipande kee·*pan*·day *piece*
— **cha namba ya gari** cha *nam*·ba ya *ga*·ree *numberplate*
kipasha moto kee·*pa*·sha *moh*·toh *heater*
kipepeo kee·pay·*pay*·oh *butterfly*
kipima mwanga kee·*pee*·ma *mwan*·ga *light meter*
kipimo cha damu kee·*pee*·moh cha *da*·moo *blood test*
kipindi cha baridi kidogo kee·*peen*·dee cha ba·*ree*·dee kee·*doh*·goh *fall (autumn)*
kiplefti keep·*layf*·tee *roundabout*
kipodozi kee·poh·*doh*·zee *make-up*
kipofu kee·*poh*·foo *blind*
kirekebisho moyo kee·ray·kay·*bee*·shoh *moh*·yoh *pacemaker*
kemra ya video *kaym*·ra ya vee·*day*·oh *video recorder*
kiroboto kee·roh·*boh*·toh *flea*
kisanduku cha huduma ya kwanza kee·san·*doo*·koo cha hoo·*doo*·ma ya *kwan*·za *first-aid kit*
kishota cha kukatia barafu kee·*shoh*·ta cha koo·ka·*tee*·a ba·*ra*·foo *ice axe*
kisiwa kee·*see*·wa *island*
kisu *kee*·soo *knife*
— **cha mfukoni** cha m·foo·*koh*·nee *penknife • pocket knife*
kisukari kee·soo·*ka*·ree *diabetes*
kitabu kee·*ta*·boo *book*
— **cha kumbukumbu** cha koom·boo·*koom*·boo *diary*
— **cha misemo** cha mee·*say*·moh *phrasebook*
— **cha mwongozo** cha mwohn·*goh*·zoh *guidebook*
— **cha namba za simu** cha *nam*·ba za *see*·moo *phone book*
kitambaa kee·tam·*ba fabric*
— **cha meza** cha *may*·za *tablecloth*
— **cha mkono** cha m·*koh*·noh *face cloth • handkerchief • napkin*
— **cha uso** cha *oo*·soh *wash cloth (flannel)*
kitambulisho kee·tam·boo·*lee*·shoh *identification • identification card (ID)*
kitanda kee·*tan*·da *bed*
— **cha watu wawili** cha *wa*·too wa·*wee*·lee *double bed*
— **katika behewa** ka·*tee*·ka bay·*hay*·wa *sleeping berth*
kitani kee·*ta*·nee *linen (material)*
kitanzi cha kuzuia kuzaa kee·*tan*·zee cha koo·zoo·ee·a koo·*za IUD*
kiti *kee*·tee *chair • seat (place)*
— **cha magurudumu** cha ma·goo·roo·*doo*·moo *wheelchair*
— **cha mtoto** cha m·*toh*·toh *child seat*
— **juu cha mtoto** joo cha m·*toh*·toh *highchair*
kitindamlo kee·teen·da·*m*·loh *dessert*
kitobosha kee·toh·*boh*·sha *pastry*
kitu *kee*·too *something*
kitunguu kee·toon·*goo onion*
— **saumu** sa·*oo*·moo *garlic*

K

kituo kee·*too*·oh *stop (bus etc)*
— **cha basi** cha *ba*·see *bus stop*
— **cha mafuta** cha ma·*foo*·ta *petrol station*
— **cha petroli** cha pay·*troh*·lee *service station*
— **cha polisi** cha poh·*lee*·see *police station*
— **cha simu** cha *see*·moo *telephone centre*
— **cha teksi** cha *tayk*·see *taxi stand*
— **cha ukaguzi** cha oo·ka·*goo*·zee *checkpoint*
(-sikia) kiu (·see·*kee*·a) *kee*·oo *(be) thirsty*
kiuavijasumu kee·oo·a·vee·ja·*soo*·moo *antibiotic*
kiungo kee·*oon*·goh *connection*
kivuko kee·*voo*·koh *ferry*
kivuli kee·*voo*·lee *shade • shadow*
kiwambo cha kizuia mimba kee·*wam*·boh cha kee·zoo·*ee*·a *meem*·ba *diaphragm (contraceptive)*
kiwambo upepo kee·*wam*·boh oo·*pay*·poh *windscreen*
kiwanda kee·*wan*·da *factory • industry*
kiwango cha kubadilishia fedha kee·*wan*·goh cha koo·ba·dee·lee·*shee*·a *fay*·dha *exchange rate*
kiwanja cha kupigia kambi kee·*wan*·ja cha kuu·pee·*gee*·a *kam*·bee *campsite*
kiwanja cha tenesi kee·*wan*·ja cha tay·*nay*·see *tennis court*
kiwashio kee·wa·*shee*·oh *cigarette lighter*
kiwiko kee·*wee*·koh *wrist*
— **cha mguu** cha m·*goo* *ankle*
kizibo kee·*zee*·boh *plug (bath)*
kizibuo kee·zee·*boo*·oh *corkscrew*
kizuizi kee·zoo·*ee*·zee *blockage*
kizunguzungu kee·zoon·goo·*zoon*·goo *dizzyness*
— **cha saa kutokana na kusafiri kwa ndege** cha sa koo·toh·*ka*·na na koo·sa·*fee*·ree kwa n·*day*·gay *jet lag*
klabu ya usiku *kla*·boo ya oo·*see*·koo *nightclub*
klachi *kla*·chee *clutch (car)*
koboko koh·*boh*·koh *cobra*
-kodi ·*koh*·dee *hire (rent)*
kodi *koh*·dee *tax*
— **ya mapato** ya ma·*pa*·toh *income tax*
— **ya mauzo** ya ma·*oo*·zoh *sales tax*
— **ya uwanja wa ndege** ya oo·*wan*·ja wa n·*day*·gay *airport tax*
kofia koh·*fee*·a *hat*
kokeini koh·kay·*ee*·nee *cocaine*
kokteli kohk·*tay*·lee *cocktail*
kokwa *kohk*·wa *nut*
koliflawa koh·lee·*fla*·wa *cauliflower*
Kombe la Dunia *kohm*·bay la doo·*nee*·a *World Cup*
kome *koh*·may *mussel*
kompyuta kohm·*pyoo*·ta *computer*
— **ya kubeba** ya koo·*bay*·ba *laptop*
komunyo koh·*moo*·nyoh *communion*
kona *koh*·na *corner*
kondom *kohn*·dohm *condom*
kondoo kohn·*doh* *sheep*
konokono koh·noh·*koh*·noh *snail*
koo koh *throat*
-kopa ·*koh*·pa *borrow*
kopo *koh*·poh *can • tin*
korosho koh·*roh*·shoh *cashew*
kosa *koh*·sa *(someone's) fault* ⓝ • *mistake* ⓝ • *wrong* ⓐ
-kosa ·*koh*·sa *miss (feel absence of)*
koti *koh*·tee *coat*
— **la mvua** la m·*voo*·a *raincoat*
kriketi kree·*kay*·tee *cricket (sport)*
krimu ya kulainisha ngozi *kree*·moo ya koo·la·ee·*nee*·sha n·*goh*·zee *moisturiser*
kuandikwa kitu kimoja kimoja koo·an·*deek*·wa *kee*·too kee·*moh*·ja kee·*moh*·jah *itemised*
kubadilisha hela koo·ba·dee·*lee*·sha *hay*·la *currency exchange*
-kubali ·koo·*ba*·lee *agree*
kubwa *koob*·wa *big (large)*
— **kabisa** ka·*bee*·sa *biggest*
— **sana** *sa*·na *huge*
— **zaidi** za·*ee*·dee *bigger*
kucha *koo*·cha *dawn*
kuchomwa kwa jua koo·*chom*·wa kwa *joo*·a *sunburn*
kuchuliwa koo·choo·*lee*·wa *massage*
kuelekea koo·ay·lay·*kay*·a *towards*
kufua koo·*foo*·a *chest (body)*
kufuli koo·*foo*·lee *lock • padlock*
— **ya baisikeli** ya ba·ee·see·*kay*·lee *bike lock*
kufungwa koo·*foon*·gwa *shut*
kuhara koo·*ha*·ra *diarrhoea*
kuharibu mimba koo·ha·*ree*·boo *meem*·ba *miscarriage*
kuharibu misitu koo·ha·*ree*·boo mee·*see*·too *deforestation*
kuhusu koo·*hoo*·soo *about*
kujeruhiwa koo·jay·roo·*hee*·wa *injured*

kukata nywele koo·*ka*·ta *nyway*·lay *haircut*
kukimbia koo·keem·*bee*·a *running*
— **taratibu** ta·ra·*tee*·boo *jogging*
kukodi gari koo·*koh*·dee *ga*·ree *car hire*
kuku *koo*·koo *chicken*
kulia koo·*lee*·a *right (direction)*
kuma *koo*·ma *vagina*
-kumbatia ·koom·ba·*tee*·a *hug*
kumbukumbu koom·boo·*koom*·boo *souvenir*
kumbwe *koom*·bway *snack*
kumi na mbili *koo*·mee na m·*bee*·lee *dozen*
kuna mawingu *koo*·na ma·*ween*·goo *cloudy*
kundekunde koon·day·*koon*·day *legume*
kundi ya roki *koon*·dee ya *roh*·kee *rock group*
kuni *koo*·nee *firewood*
kuogelea koo·oh·gay·*lay*·a *swimming (sport)*
kuondoka koo·ohn·*doh*·ka *departure*
kupanda baisikeli koo·*pan*·da ba·ee·see·*kay*·lee *cycling*
kupanda farasi koo·*pan*·da fa·*ra*·see *horse riding*
kupanda milima koo·*pan*·da mee·*lee*·ma *mountaineering*
kupatikana koo·pa·tee·*ka*·na *free (available)*
kupiga picha ya mtoto tumboni koo·*pee*·ga *pee*·cha ya m·*toh*·toh toom·*boh*·nee *ultrasound*
kupiga simu moja kwa moja koo·*pee*·ga *see*·moo *moh*·ja kwa *moh*·ja *direct-dial*
kupika koo·*pee*·ka *cooking*
kuponi koo·*pohn*·ee *coupon*
kurudisha pesa koo·roo·*dee*·sha *pay*·sa *refund*
kushambuliwa na maradhi ya moyo koo·sham·boo·*lee*·wa na ma·*ra*·dhee ya *moh*·yoh *heart attack*
kushoto koo·*shoh*·toh *left (direction)*
kusimama kwa mapigo ya moyo koo·see·*ma*·ma kwa ma·*pee*·goh ya *moh*·yoh *cardiac arrest*
kusini koo·*see*·nee *south*
kuskii koo·*skee skiing*
-kuta ·*koo*·ta *meet*
kutaamali koo·ta·a·*ma*·lee *meditation*
kutalikiwa koo·ta·lee·*kee*·wa *divorced*
kuteleza koo·tay·*lay*·za *surfing*
— **na tanga** na *tan*·ga *windsurfing*
kutembea porini koo·taym·*bay*·a poh·*ree*·nee *hiking*
kutengenezwa kwa mkono koo·tayn·gay·*nayz*·wa kwa m·*koh*·noh *handmade*
kutoa mimba koo·*toh*·a *meem*·ba *abortion*
kutoka koo·*toh*·ka *exit* ⓝ • *from* prep
kutopenyesha maji koo·to·pay·*nyay*·sha *ma*·jee *waterproof*
kutumikia jeshi koo·too·mee·*kee*·a *jay*·shee *military service*
-kuu ·koo *main*
kuuza madawa ya kulevya koo·*oo*·za ma·*da*·wa ya koo·*lay*·vya *drug trafficking*
kuvimba kibofu koo·*veem*·ba kee·*boh*·foo *cystitis*
kuvimbiwa koo·veem·*bee*·wa *indigestion*
kuvuna matunda koo·*voo*·na ma·*toon*·da *fruit picking*
kuvuta makasia koo·*voo*·ta ma·ka·*see*·a *rowing*
kuwahi koo·*wa*·hee *on time* • *early*
kuzamia koo·za·*mee*·a *diving*
kwa kwa *per (day)*
kwa haraka kwa ha·*ra*·ka *in a hurry*
kwa heri kwa *hay*·ree *goodbye*
kwa kuteremka kwa koo·tay·*raym*·ka *downhill*
kwa nini kwa *nee*·nee *why*
kwa sababu kwa sa·*ba*·boo *because*
kwa sauti kwa sa·*oo*·tee *loud*
kwa usiku mmoja kwa oo·*see*·koo m·*moh*·ja *overnight*
kwa wapenzi kwa wa·*payn*·zee *romantic*
kwenye *kway*·nyay *at* • *to*
— **a/c** ay·*see air-conditioned*

L

-la ·la *eat*
labda *lab*·da *maybe*
laiseni la·ee·*say*·nee *license*
lakini la·*kee*·nee *but*
-lala ·*la*·la *lie (not stand)*
-lalamika ·la·la·*mee*·ka *complain*
lalamiko la·la·*mee*·koh *complaint*
laza *la*·za *admit*
lazima la·*zee*·ma *necessary*
lengelenge layn·gay·*layn*·gay *blister*

lenzi mboni *layn*·zee m·*boh*·nee *contact lenses*
leo *lay*·oh *today*
leseni ya kuendesha gari lay·*say*·nee ya koo·ayn·*day*·sha *ga*·ree *drivers license*
-leta ·*lay*·ta *bring*
-lewa ·*lay*·wa *drunk* • *stoned (drugged)*
lifti *leef*·tee *lift* • *elevator* • *ride*
likizo lee·*kee*·zoh *holidays* • *vacation*
limau lee·*ma*·oo *lemon*
lindo *leen*·doh *lookout*
lini *lee*·nee *when*
-lipa ·*lee*·pa *pay*
-lipwa fedha kwa kutoa hundi ·*leep*·wa *fay*·dha kwa koo·*toh*·a *hoon*·dee *cash (a cheque)*
-lisha ·*lee*·sha *feed*
lori *loh*·ree *truck*
— **la wasafiri** la wa·sa·*fee*·ree *caravan*
losheni baada ya kunyoa ndevu loh·*shay*·nee ba·*a*·da ya koo·*nyoh*·a n·*day*·voo *aftershave*
lozi *loh*·zee *almond*
lugha *loo*·gha *language*

M

maakuli ma·a·*koo*·lee *provisions*
maalum ma·*a*·loom *special*
maandamano ma·an·da·*ma*·noh *demonstration* • *protest*
maandishi chini ma·an·*dee*·shee *chee*·nee *subtitles*
maarufu ma·a·*roo*·foo *famous*
mabaki ma·*ba*·kee *relic*
mabawa ma·*ba*·wa *wings*
mabuti ma·*boo*·tee *boots (footwear)*
— **ya kutembea porini** ya koo·taym·*bay*·a poh·*ree*·nee *hiking boots*
machela ma·*chay*·la *hammock*
macheo ma·*chay*·oh *sunrise*
macho *ma*·choh *eyes*
machumbwichumbwi ma·choom·bwee·*choom*·bwee *mumps*
machunda ma·*choon*·da *skim milk*
machweo ma·*chway*·oh *sunset*
madawa (ya kulevya) ma·*da*·wa (ya koo·*lay*·vya) *(illegal) drugs*
madhahabu ma·dha·*ha*·boo *altar*
madhubuti ma·dhoo·*boo*·tee *strong*
madukani ma·doo·*ka*·nee *shopping centre*
maelezo binafsi ya ujuzi ma·ay·*lay*·zoh bee·*naf*·see ya oo·*joo*·zee *CV* • *résumé*
mafuriko ma·foo·*ree*·koh *flood*
mafusha ya pamba ma·*foo*·sha ya *pam*·ba *cotton balls*
mafuta ma·*foo*·ta *gas (petrol)* • *oil*
— **ya taa** ya ta *gas (for cooking)*
— **ya zaituni** ya za·ee·*too*·nee *olive oil*
magari mengi ma·*ga*·ree *mayn*·gee *traffic*
magharibi ma·gha·*ree*·bee *west*
maglavu ma·*gla*·voo *gloves*
magofu ma·*goh*·foo *ruins*
mahadhi ma·*ha*·dhee *rhythm*
mahakama ma·ha·*ka*·ma *court (legal)*
mahali ma·*ha*·lee *place* • *venue*
— **pa kuzaliwa** pa koo·za·*lee*·wa *place of birth*
maharagwe ma·ha·*rag*·way *beans*
mahindi ma·*heen*·dee *corn*
mahojiano ma·hoh·jee·*a*·noh *interview*
maisha ma·*ee*·sha *life*
majaribio ya nyuklia ma·ja·ree·*bee*·oh ya *nyook*·lee·a *nuclear testing*
maji *ma*·jee *water*
— **baridi** ba·*ree*·dee *still water*
— **ya bomba** ya *bohm*·ba *tap water*
— **ya kujaa na kupwa** ya koo·*ja* na *koop*·wa *tide*
— **ya limau** ya lee·*ma*·oo *lemonade*
— **ya machungwa** ya ma·*choon*·gwa *orange juice*
— **ya madini** ya ma·*dee*·nee *mineral water*
— **ya moto** ya *moh*·toh *hot water*
majira ma·*jee*·ra *season*
— **ya baridi** ya ba·*ree*·dee *winter*
— **ya joto** ya *joh*·toh *summer*
— **ya kuchipua** ya koo·chee·*poo*·a *spring*
makaburini ma·ka·boo·*ree*·nee *cemetery*
makini ma·*kee*·nee *serious*
maktaba mak·*ta*·ba *library*
makumbusho ma·koom·*boo*·shoh *museum*
malai ya maziwa ya mtindi ma·*la*·ee ya ma·*zee*·wa ya m·*teen*·dee *sour cream*
malaya ma·*la*·ya *prostitute*
malazi ma·*la*·zee *accommodation*
malipo ma·*lee*·poh *payment*
— **ya huduma** ya hoo·*doo*·ma *service charge*

-maliza ·ma·*lee*·za *finish*
malkia mal·*kee*·a *queen*
mama *ma*·ma *mother*
mamamkwe ma·ma·*m*·kway *mother-in-law*
mamba *mam*·ba *crocodile*
mandari man·*da*·ree *picnic*
mandhari man·*dha*·ree *view*
manjano man·*ja*·noh *yellow*
maoni ma·*oh*·nee *opinion*
maonyesho ma·oh·*nyay*·shoh *exhibition*
mapacha ma·*pa*·cha *twins*
mapema ma·*pay*·ma *early*
mapenzi ma·*payn*·zee *sex (intercourse)*
— **salama** sa·*la*·ma *safe sex*
mapitio ma·pee·*tee*·oh *review*
mapokezi ma·poh·*kay*·zee *check-in (desk)*
maporomoko ya maji ma·poh·roh·*moh*·koh ya *ma*·jee *waterfall*
mapumziko ma·poom·*zee*·koh *intermission*
mara mbili *ma*·ra m·*bee*·lee *twice*
mara moja *ma*·ra *moh*·ja *once*
mara nyingi *ma*·ra *nyeen*·gee *often*
maradhi ma·*ra*·dhee *disease*
marashi ma·*ra*·shee *perfume*
marejeo ma·ray·*jay*·oh *reference*
Marekani ma·ray·*ka*·nee *USA*
masaa ya kufunguliwa ma·*sa* ya koo·foon·goo·*lee*·wa *opening hours*
mashariki ma·sha·*ree*·kee *east*
mashindano ya ubingwa ma·sheen·*da*·noh ya oo·*been*·gwa *championships*
mashine ma·*shee*·nay *machine*
— **ya kubanika mkate** ya koo·ba·*nee*·ka m·*ka*·tay *toaster*
— **ya kufulia** ya koo·foo·*lee*·a *washing machine*
— **ya kutolea pesa** ya koo·toh·*lay*·a *pay*·sa *automated teller machine (ATM)*
— **ya tiketi** ya tee·*kay*·tee *ticket machine*
mashuka ma·*shoo*·ka *linen (sheets etc)*
masikitiko ma·see·kee·*tee*·koh *sad*
maskini mas·*kee*·nee *poor*
mastadi ma·*sta*·dee *mustard*
matako ma·*ta*·koh *bottom (body)*
matatu ma·*ta*·too *bus (city)*
matibabu asilia ma·tee·*ba*·boo a·see·*lee*·a *naturopathy*
matone ya macho ma·*toh*·nay ya *ma*·choh *eye drops*
matope ma·*toh*·pay *mud*
matukio ya leo ma·too·*kee*·oh ya *lay*·oh *current affairs*
matunda yaliyokaushwa ma·*toon*·da ya·lee·yoh·ka·*oosh*·wa *dried fruit*
mauaji ma·oo·*a*·jee *murder*
maumivu ma·oo·*mee*·voo *pain*
— **ya jino** ya *jee*·noh *toothache*
— **ya kichwa** ya *keech*·wa *headache*
— **ya mwezini** ya mway·*zee*·nee *period pain*
maumivu ya tumbo ma·oo·*mee*·voo ya *toom*·boh *stomachache*
mawasiliano ma·wa·see·lee·*a*·noh *communications (profession)*
mawe za mizani *ma*·way za mee·*za*·nee *weights*
mayai yaliyovurugwa ma·*ya*·ee ya·lee·yoh·voo·*roog*·wa *scrambled eggs*
mayonezi ma·yoh·*nay*·zee *mayonnaise*
mazingira ma·zeen·*gee*·ra *environment*
maziwa ma·*zee*·wa *milk*
— **ganda** *gan*·da *yoghurt*
— **ya soya** ya *soh*·ya *soy milk*
mazoezi ma·zoh·*ay*·zee *workout*
mbali m·*ba*·lee *far* • *remote*
mbalimbali m·ba·lee·m·*ba*·lee *separate*
mbao m·*ba*·oh *wood*
mbaya m·*ba*·ya *bad* • *off (spoiled)*
mbaya sana m·*ba*·ya *sa*·na *awful* • *terrible*
mbele m·*bay*·lay *ahead*
— **ya** ya *in front of*
mbeleni m·bay·*lay*·nee *future*
mbili m·*bee*·lee *both* • *two*
mbilimbili m·bee·lee·m·*bee*·lee *double*
mbingu m·*been*·goo *sky*
mbinu m·*bee*·noo *technique*
mbishi m·*bee*·shee *stubborn*
mboga m·*boh*·ga *vegetable*
— **za majani** za ma·*ja*·nee *herbs*
mboni m·*boh*·nee *lens (eye)*
mboo m·*boh* *penis*
mbu *m*·boo *mosquito*
Mbudisti m·boo·*dee*·stee *Buddhist*
mbuni m·*boo*·nee *ostrich*
mbuzi m·*boo*·zee *goat*
mbwa *m*·bwa *dog*
— **wa kuongoza** wa koo·ohn·*goh*·za *guide dog*
mchana m·*cha*·na *afternoon*

M

swahili–english

mchanga m·*chan*·ga *sand*
mchele m·*chay*·lay *rice (uncooked)*
mchemuo m·chay·*moo*·oh *exhaust (car)*
mchezo m·*chay*·zoh *game (sport)*
— **kwenye kompyuta** *kway*·nyay kom·*pyoo*·ta *computer game*
— **wa kuigiza** wa koo·ee·*gee*·za *play (theatre)*
— **wa soka** wa *soh*·ka *football* • *soccer*
mchicha m·*chee*·cha *spinach*
mchonga vinyago m·*chohn*·ga vee·*nya*·goh *woodcarver*
mchuaji m·choo·*a*·jee *masseur/masseuse*
mchumba m·*choom*·ba *fiancé/fiancée*
mchuuzi m·choo·*oo*·zee *street hawker*
— **wa samaki** wa sa·*ma*·kee *fish monger*
mchuzi m·*choo*·zee *sauce*
— **wa nyanya** wa *nya*·nya *tomato sauce* • *ketchup*
— **wa pilipili hoho** wa pee·lee·*pee*·lee *hoh*·hoh *chilli sauce*
— **wa soya** wa *soh*·ya *soy sauce*
mdanganyi m·dan·*ga*·nyee *cheat*
mdomo m·*doh*·moh *mouth*
mdudu m·*doo*·doo *bug*
-mea ·*may*·a *grow*
mechi *may*·chee *match (sports)*
meli *may*·lee *ship*
mende *mayn*·day *cockroach*
meneja may·*nay*·ja *manager (restaurant, hotel)*
meno *may*·noh *teeth*
menyu *may*·nyoo *menu*
metali may·*ta*·lee *metal* ⓝ
meza *may*·za *table*
— **kujihudumia** koo·jee·hoo·doo·*mee*·a *buffet*
mfalme m·*fal*·may *king*
mfamasia m·fa·ma·*see*·a *chemist (person)* • *pharmacist*
mfano m·*fa*·noh *example*
mfanyabiashara m·fa·nya·bee·a·*sha*·ra *business person* • *tradesperson*
mfanyakazi m·fa·nya·*ka*·zee *employee* • *labourer*
— **ofisini** o·fee·*see*·nee *office worker*
— **wa kiwandani** kee·wan·*da*·nee *factory worker*
— **wa kutumia mikono** koo·too·*mee*·a mee·*koh*·noh *manual worker*
mfuko m·*foo*·koh *bag* • *pocket*
— **wa kiunoni** wa kee·oo·*noh*·nee *bumbag*
— **wa kulalia** wa koo·la·*lee*·a *sleeping bag*
mfumo wa matabaka m·*foo*·moh wa ma·ta·*ba*·ka *class system*
mfungwa m·*foon*·gwa *prisoner*
mfupa m·*foo*·pa *bone*
mgahawa m·ga·*ha*·wa *café* • *restaurant*
mganga wa madawa ya kienyeji m·*gan*·ga wa ma·*da*·wa ya kee·ay·*nyay*·jee *herbalist*
mgeni m·*gay*·nee *stranger*
mgomo m·*goh*·moh *strike*
mgongano m·gohn·*ga*·noh *crash*
mgongo m·*gohn*·goh *back (body)*
mgonjwa m·*gohn*·jwa *ill* • *sick*
mguu m·*goo foot* • *leg*
mhadhiri m·ha·*dhee*·ree *lecturer*
mhamisishaji m·ha·mee·see·*sha*·jee *activist*
mhandisi m·han·*dee*·see *engineer*
Mhindu m·*heen*·doo *Hindu*
mhudumu m·hoo·*doo*·moo *waiter* • *waitress*
mhuni m·*hoo*·nee *hoodlum*
mia *mee*·a *hundred*
miadi mee·*a*·dee *date (appointment)*
miche ya maharagwe *mee*·chay ya ma·ha·*rag*·way *beansprouts*
michezo mee·*chay*·zoh *sport*
— **ya kukimbia** ya koo·keem·*bee*·a *track (sport)*
— **ya riadha** ya ree·*a*·dha *athletics*
Michezo ya Olimpiki mee·*chay*·zoh ya oh·leem·*pee*·kee *Olympic Games*
midomo mee·*doh*·moh *lips*
mieleka mee·ay·*lay*·ka *martial arts*
mikutano mee·koo·*ta*·noh *conference (big)*
mila *mee*·la *custom*
milele mee·*lay*·lay *forever*
milimita mee·lee·*mee*·ta *millimetre*
milioni mee·lee·*oh*·nee *million*
mimi *mee*·mee *I* • *me*
minyoo mee·*nyoh worms*
misa *mee*·sa *mass (Catholic)*
mita *mee*·ta *metre*
mitumba mee·*toom*·ba *second-hand*
miwani mee·*wa*·nee *glasses (spectacles)*
— **ya jua** ya *joo*·a *sunglasses*
— **ya kuogelea** ya koo·oh·gay·*lay*·a *goggles (swimming)*

mizigo mee·*zee*·goh *baggage (luggage)*
— **iliyowekwa** ee·lee·yoh·*wayk*·wa *left luggage*
— **ziada** zee·*a*·da *excess baggage*
mjamzito m·ja·m·*zee*·toh *pregnant*
mjenzi m·*jayn*·zee *builder*
mji *m*·jee *city*
mjinga m·*jeen*·ga *idiot*
mjukuu m·joo·*koo* *grandchild*
mjusi m·*joo*·see *lizard*
mkalimani m·ka·lee·*ma*·nee *interpreter*
mkamba m·*kam*·ba *bronchitis*
mkanda wa feni m·*kan*·da wa *fay*·nee *fanbelt*
mkanda wa kiti m·*kan*·da wa *kee*·tee *seatbelt*
mkanda wa picha m·*kan*·da wa *pee*·cha *film (for camera)*
mkanda wa video m·*kan*·da wa vee·*day*·oh *video tape*
mkarimu m·ka·*ree*·moo *kind (nice)*
mkasi m·*ka*·see *scissors*
mkasi wa kucha m·*ka*·see wa *koo*·cha *nail clippers*
mkataba m·ka·*ta*·ba *contract*
mkate m·*ka*·tay *bread*
— **mkavu** m·*ka*·voo *cracker (biscuit)*
— **wa ngano asilia** wa n·*ga*·noh a·see·*lee*·a *wholemeal bread*
mke *m*·kay *wife*
— **anayekaa nyumbani** a·na·yay·*ka* nyoom·*ba*·nee *homemaker*
mkebe m·*kay*·bay *can • tin*
mkeka m·*kay*·ka *mat*
Mkesha wa Krismasi m·*kay*·sha wa krees·*ma*·see *Christmas Eve*
Mkesha wa Mwaka Mpya m·*kay*·sha wa *mwa*·ka *m*·pya *New Year's Eve*
mkia m·*kee*·a *tail*
mkimbizi m·keem·*bee*·zee *refugee*
mkoba m·*koh*·ba *briefcase • handbag • purse*
mkondo m·*kohn*·doh *current (electricity)*
mkono m·*koh*·noh *arm • hand*
mkopo m·*koh*·poh *credit*
Mkristo m·*kree*·stoh *Christian*
mkufu m·*koo*·foo *necklace*
mkulima m·koo·*lee*·ma *farmer*
mkurugenzi m·koo·roo·*gayn*·zee *director • manager*
mkusanyaji wa tiketi m·koo·sa·*nya*·jee wa tee·*kay*·tee *ticket collector*

mkutano m·koo·*ta*·noh *conference (small)*
— **wa hadhara** wa ha·*dha*·ra *rally • public meeting*
mlaji wa mboga za majani tu m·*la*·jee wa m·*boh*·ga za ma·*ja*·nee too *vegetarian* ⓝ
mlango m·*lan*·goh *door • gate (airport etc)*
— **wa kuondoka** wa koo·ohn·*doh*·ka *departure gate*
mlima m·*lee*·ma *hill • mountain*
mlio wa simu m·*lee*·oh wa *see*·moo *dial tone*
mlo *m*·loh *diet • meal*
mmea m·*may*·a *plant*
mnada m·*na*·da *fleamarket*
mnara m·*na*·ra *monument • tower*
mno *m*·noh *too (expensive etc)*
mnofu m·*noh*·foo *steak*
mnyama m·*nya*·ma *animal*
mnyororo m·nyoh·*roh*·roh *chain*
— **wa baisikeli** wa ba·ee·see·*kay*·lee *bike chain*
moja *moh*·ja *one*
— **kwa moja** kwa *moh*·ja *direct • straight*
motaboti moh·ta·*boh*·tee *motorboat*
moto *moh*·toh *fire*
— **ya mungu** ya *moon*·goo *shingles (illness)*
moyo *moh*·yoh *heart*
mpaka m·*pa*·ka *border* ⓝ • *until* prep
mpanda baisikeli m·*pan*·da ba·ee·see·*kay*·lee *cyclist*
mpenzi m·*payn*·zee *boyfriend • girlfriend • lover*
mpigapicha m·pee·ga·*pee*·cha *photographer*
mpira m·*pee*·ra *ball • chewing gum • gum*
— **wa gofu** wa *goh*·foo *golf ball*
— **wa kikapu** wa kee·*ka*·poo *basketball*
— **wa meza** wa *may*·za *table tennis*
— **wa mikono** wa mee·*koh*·noh *handball*
— **wa wavu** wa *wa*·voo *volleyball*
— **wa wavu ufukoni** wa *wa*·voo oo·foo·*koh*·nee *beach volleyball*
mpishi m·*pee*·shee *chef • cook*
mpya *m*·pya *new*
mradi m·*ra*·dee *program*
mrefu m·*ray*·foo *tall*

mrembo m·*raym*·boh *handsome*
mrengo wa kulia
m·*rayn*·goh wa koo·*lee*·a *right-wing*
mrengo wa kushoto
m·*rayn*·goh wa koo·*shoh*·toh *left-wing*
mruko m·*roo*·koh *flight (of a bird)*
msaada m·sa·*a*·da *help*
msagaji m·sa·*ga*·jee *lesbian*
msalaba m·sa·*la*·ba *cross (religious)*
msanifu wa majengo
m·sa·*nee*·foo wa ma·*jayn*·goh
architect
msanii m·sa·*nee* *artist*
— **wa rangi** wa *ran*·gee *painter*
msenge m·*sayn*·gay *gay (homosexual)*
mshabiki m·sha·*bee*·kee *fan (sport, etc)*
— **wa utawala huria**
wa oo·ta·*wa*·la hoo·*ree*·a *anarchist*
mshahara m·sha·*ha*·ra *salary* • *wage*
mshangao m·shan·*ga*·oh *surprise*
mshindi m·*sheen*·dee *winner*
mshipa m·*shee*·pa *vein*
mshonaji m·shoh·*na*·jee *tailor*
mshtuko wa ubongo m·*shtoo*·koh wa
oo·*bohn*·goh *concussion*
mshumaa m·shoo·*ma* *candle*
mshushio m·shoo·*shee*·oh *orgasm*
msichana m·see·*cha*·na *girl*
msikiti m·see·*kee*·tee *mosque*
msitu m·*see*·too *forest*
mstari m·*sta*·ree *queue*
msusi m·*soo*·see *hairdresser*
mswaki m·*swa*·kee *toothbrush*
mtaalamu m·ta·a·*la*·moo *specialist*
mtabiri m·ta·*bee*·ree *fortune teller*
mtakatifu m·ta·ka·*tee*·foo *saint*
mtalii m·ta·*lee* *tourist*
mtandao wa kompyuta
m·tan·*da*·oh wa kohm·*pyoo*·ta
Internet
mtawa m·*ta*·wa *monk*
mteguko m·tay·*goo*·koh *sprain*
mteja m·*tay*·ja *client*
mtembezi m·taym·*bay*·zee *pedestrian*
mti *m*·tee *tree*
mtihani m·tee·*ha*·nee *test*
mtindi m·*teen*·dee *cream*
mtindo m·*teen*·doh *fashion* • *style*
mto *m*·toh *pillow* • *river*
mtoto m·*toh*·toh *child*
— **mchanga** m·*chan*·ga *baby*
mtu *m*·too *person*
— **mzima** m·*zee*·ma *adult* ⓝ

mtumiaji wa madawa ya kulevya
m·too·mee·*a*·jee wa ma·*da*·wa ya
koo·*lay*·vya *drug user*
mtungi wa gesi m·*toon*·gee wa *gay*·see
gas cartridge
mtunza bustani m·*toon*·za boo·*sta*·nee
gardener
muhafidhina moo·ha·fee·*dhee*·na
conservative
muhimu moo·*hee*·moo *important*
— **sana** *sa*·na *urgent*
muhtasari mooh·*ta*·sa·ree *résumé (CV)*
mume *moo*·may *husband*
mumunye ya kula moo·*moo*·nyay ya
koo·la *courgette* • *zucchini*
Mungu *moon*·goo *God*
musuli moo·*soo*·lee *muscle*
muziki moo·*zee*·kee *music*
mvinyo m·*vee*·nyoh *wine*
— **mwenye povu** *mway*·nyay *poh*·voo
sparkling wine
mvivu m·*vee*·voo *lazy*
mvua m·*voo*·a *rain*
mvulana m·voo·*la*·na *boy*
mwajiri mwa·*jee*·ree *employer*
mwaka *mwa*·ka *year*
— **huu** hoo *this year*
mwalimu mwa·*lee*·moo
instructor • *teacher*
mwamba *mwam*·ba *cliff* • *ledge*
mwamuzi mwa·*moo*·zee *referee*
mwamvuli mwam·*voo*·lee *umbrella*
mwana *mwa*·na *son*
mwanachama mwa·na·*cha*·ma *member*
mwanafunzi mwa·na·*foon*·zee *student*
mwanakondoo mwa·na·kohn·*doh* *lamb*
mwanamichezo mwa·na·mee·*chay*·zoh
sportsperson
mwanamke mwan·*am*·kay *woman*
mwanamume mwa·na·*moo*·may *man*
mwanamuziki mwa·na·moo·*zee*·kee
musician
mwanasayansi mwa·na·sa·*yan*·see
scientist
mwanasesere mwa·na·say·*say*·ray *doll*
mwanasheria mwa·na·shay·*ree*·a *lawyer*
mwanasiasa mwa·na·see·*a*·sa *politician*
mwandishi mwan·*dee*·shee *writer*
— **wa habari** wa ha·*ba*·ree *journalist*
mwanga *mwan*·ga *light* ⓝ
mwanzo *mwan*·zoh *start*
mwasho *mwa*·shoh *itch*
mwema *mway*·ma *nice*

mwembamba mwaym·*bam*·ba *thin*
mwendo *mwayn*·doh *speed (velocity)*
— **wa mkanda** wa m·*kan*·da *film speed*
mwenye *mway*·nyay *owner*
— **bahati** ba·*ha*·tee *lucky*
— **choyo** *choh*·yoh *selfish*
— **furaha** foo·*ra*·ha *happy*
— **haiba** ha·*ee*·ba *charming*
— **hasira** ha·*see*·ra *angry*
— **hatia** ha·*tee*·a *guilty*
— **hisia** hee·*see*·a *emotional*
— **kichaa** kee·*cha* *crazy*
— **kuuma** koo·*oo*·ma *sore*
— **nyumba** *nyoom*·ba *landlady/landlord*
— **shughuli nyingi** shoo·*goo*·lee *nyeen*·gee *busy (person)*
— **shukrani** shook·*ra*·nee *grateful*
— **usingizi** oo·seen·*gee*·zee *sleepy*
— **wasiwasi** wa·see·*wa*·see *worried*
— **wivu** *wee*·voo *jealous*
mwenyekiti mway·nyay·*kee*·tee *mayor*
mwenzi *mwayn*·zee *companion*
— **wangu** *wan*·goo *colleague*
mwezi *mway*·zee *month • moon*
— **wa kuml** wa *koo*·mee *October*
— **wa kumi na mbili** wa *koo*·mee na m·*bee*·lee *December*
— **wa kumi na moja** wa *koo*·mee na *moh*·ja *November*
— **wa kwanza** wa *kwan*·za *January*
— **wa nane** wa *na*·nay *August*
— **wa nne** wa *n*·nay *April*
— **wa pili** wa *pee*·lee *February*
— **wa saba** wa *sa*·ba *July*
— **wa sita** wa *see*·ta *June*
— **wa tano** wa *ta*·noh *May*
— **wa tatu** wa *ta*·too *March*
— **wa tisa** wa *tee*·sa *September*
mwigizaji mwee·gee·*za*·jee *actor*
mwili *mwee*·lee *body*
mwimbaji mweem·*ba*·jee *singer*
— **barabarani** ba·ra·ba·*ra*·nee *busker*
mwingilio mween·gee·*lee*·oh *entry (access)*
mwinuko mwee·*noo*·koh *uphill*
mwisho *mwee*·shoh *end (finish)*
Mwislamu mwee·*sla*·moo *Muslim*
mwizi *mwee*·zee *thief*
mwombaji mwohm·*ba*·jee *beggar*
mwongo *mwohn*·goh *liar*
mwongozo (wa sauti) mwohn·*goh*·zoh (wa sa·*oo*·tee) *(audio) guide*
mwongozo wa burudani mwohn·*goh*·zoh wa boo·roo·*da*·nee *entertainment guide*
mwuguzi mwoo·*goo*·zee *nurse*
mwungaji mkono mwoon·*ga*·jee m·*koh*·noh *supporter (politics)*
mwuzaji wa chakula mwoo·*za*·jee wa cha·*koo*·la *food vendor*
mwuzaji wa madawa ya kulevya mwoo·*za*·jee wa ma·*da*·wa ya koo·*lay*·vya *drug dealer*
mwuzaji wa magazeti mwoo·*za*·jee wa ma·ga·*zay*·tee *newspaper vendor*
Myahudi m·ya·*hoo*·dee *Jewish*
myeyuko wa lenzi mboni m·yay·*yoo*·koh wa *layn*·zee m·*boh*·nee *contact lens solution*
mzabibu m·za·*bee*·boo *vine (grape)*
mzawa m·*za*·wa *descendent*
mzee m·*zay* *old person • pensioner*
mzigo m·*zee*·goh *suitcase*
mzio m·*zee*·oh *allergy*

N

na na *and • with*
nadra *na*·dra *rare (uncommon)*
nafaka na·*fa*·ka *cereal*
nafasi na·*fa*·see *chance • vacancy*
namba *nam*·ba *number*
— **ya chumba** ya *choom*·ba *room number*
— **ya gari** ya *ga*·ree *license plate number*
— **ya pasipoti** ya pa·see·*poh*·tee *passport number*
namna *nam*·na *how*
nanasi na·*na*·see *pineapple*
nani *na*·nee *who*
nauli na·*oo*·lee *fare*
nazi *na*·zee *coconut*
nchi *n*·chee *country*
— **za nje** za *n*·jay *abroad (overseas)*
ndala n·*da*·la *sandal*
ndani n·*da*·nee *indoor • inside*
— **yake** *ya*·kay *included*
ndefu n·*day*·foo *long*
ndege n·*day*·gay *airplane • bird • flight (scheduled)*
ndimu n·*dee*·moo *lime*
ndiyo n·*dee*·yoh *yes*

ndizi n·*dee*·zee *banana*
ndoa n·*doh*·a *marriage*
ndogo sana n·*doh*·goh *sa*·na *tiny*
ndondi n·*dohn*·dee *boxing*
ndoo n·*doh* *bucket*
ndoto n·*doh*·toh *dream*
ndovu n·*doh*·voo *elephant*
nene *nay*·nay *fat*
neno *nay*·noh *word*
nepi *nay*·pee *diaper • nappy*
neti *nay*·tee *net*
ng'ambo ng·*am*·boh *across*
ng'ombe ng·*ohm*·bay *cow*
ngamia n·ga·*mee*·a *camel*
ngazi n·*ga*·zee *stairway*
-ngoja ·n·*goh*·ja *wait*
-ngojea ·n·goh·*jay*·a *wait for*
ngoma n·*goh*·ma *drum*
— **ya kuigiza hadithi**
ya koo·ee·*gee*·za ha·*dee*·thee *ballet*
ngozi n·*goh*·zee *leather • skin*
— **ya kichwa** ya *keech*·wa *scalp*
ngumu n·*goo*·moo *hard (not soft)*
nguo n·*goo*·oh *clothing*
— **kufua** koo·*foo*·a *laundry (clothes)*
— **rasmi** *ras*·mee *uniform*
— **za kuogelea** za koo·oh·gay·*lay*·a *bathing suit*
nguruwe n·goo·*roo*·way *pig*
nguvu n·*goo*·voo *power*
ni hatari nee ha·*ta*·ree *unsafe*
nimechumbiwa nee·may·choom·*bee*·wa *(I'm) engaged*
nimeoa nee·may·*oh*·a *(I'm) married (man)*
nimeolewa nee·may·oh·*lay*·wa *(I'm) married (woman)*
nini *nee*·nee *what*
nishati ya nyuklia
nee·sha·tee ya *nyook*·lee·a *nuclear energy*
njaa n·*ja* *hunger*
nje *n*·jay *outside*
njegere n·jay·*gay*·ray *pea*
njia n·*jee*·a *aisle (on plane) • path • route • street • track • way*
— **mkato** m·*ka*·toh *shortcut*
— **ya baisikeli** ya ba·ee·see·*kay*·lee *bike path*
— **ya kupanda mlimani** ya koo·*pan*·da m·lee·*ma*·nee *mountain path*
— **ya kutembea porini**
ya koo·taym·*bay*·a poh·*ree*·nee *hiking route*
— **ya miguu** ya mee·*goo* *footpath*

noti *noh*·tee *banknote*
nukta *nook*·ta *point*
-nunua ·noo·*noo*·a *buy • shop*
nusu *noo*·soo *half*
nyama *nya*·ma *meat*
nyani *nya*·nee *baboon*
nyanya *nya*·nya *tomato*
nyasi *nya*·see *grass*
nyati *nya*·tee *buffalo*
nyekundu nyay·*koon*·doo *red*
nyepesi nyay·*pay*·see
light (not heavy) • quick
nyeupe nyay·*oo*·pay
light (of colour) • white
nyeusi nyay·*oo*·see *black • dark (of colour)*
— **na nyeupe** na nyay·*oo*·pay *B&W (film)*
nyika *nyee*·ka *countryside*
nyingi *nyeen*·gee *a lot • many*
nyingine nyeen·*gee*·nay *another • other*
nyinyi *nyee*·nyee *you* pl
-nyoa ·*nyoh*·a *shave*
nyoka *nyoh*·ka *snake*
-nyonyesha ·nyoh·*nyay*·sha *breast-feed*
nyonyo bandia *nyoh*·nyoh ban·*dee*·a
dummy • pacifier
nyota *nyoh*·ta *star*
nyuki *nyoo*·kee *bee*
nyuma *nyoo*·ma
back (position) • behind • rear (seat etc)
nyumba *nyoom*·ba *house*
— **ya sanaa** ya sa·*na* *art gallery*
— **ya utawa wa wanaume**
ya oo·*ta*·wa wa wa·na·*oo*·may *monastery*
— **ya wageni** ya wa·*gay*·nee
boarding house
nyumbani nyoom·*ba*·nee *home*
nyumbu *nyoom*·boo *wildebeest*
nyundo *nyoon*·doh *hammer*
nyuzi *nyoo*·zee *degrees (temperature)*
-nywa ·nywa *drink*
nywele *nyway*·lay *hair*
nzito n·*zee*·toh *heavy*
nzuri n·*zoo*·ree *fine • good*
— **kabisa** ka·*bee*·sa *best*
— **sana** *sa*·na *great (fantastic)*

O

-oa ·*oh*·a *marry (man)*
ofisi oh·*fee*·see *office*
— **ya tiketi** ya tee·*kay*·tee *ticket office*
— **ya watalii** ya wa·ta·*lee* *tourist office*

-oga ·*oh*·ga *wash (oneself)*
-ogelea ·oh·gay·*lay*·a *swim*
okestra oh·*kay*·stra *orchestra*
oksijeni ohk·see·*jay*·nee *oxygen*
-olewa ·oh·*lay*·wa *marry (woman)*
-omba ·*ohm*·ba *ask (for something)*
— **lifti** *leef*·tee *hitchhike*
ombi *ohm*·bee *petition*
omlet *ohm*·layt *omelette*
-ona ·*oh*·na *see*
-ondoka ·ohn·*doh*·ka *depart*
-onja ·*ohn*·ja *try (taste)*
-onya ·*oh*·nya *warn*
-onyesha ·oh·*nyay*·sha *show*
onyesho oh·*nyay*·shoh *gig (musical) • performance • show*
— **la muziki** la moo·*zee*·kee *concert*
opareta oh·pa·*ray*·ta *operator*
opena ya kopo *oh*·pay·na ya *koh*·poh *can opener*
opera *oh*·pay·ra *opera*
operesheni oh·pay·ray·*shay*·nee *operation (medical)*
-osha ·*oh*·sha *wash (something)*
ovari oh·*va*·ree *ovary*

P

-pa ·pa *give*
padri *pa*·dree *priest*
pafu *pa*·foo *lung*
paka *pa*·ka *cat*
pakiti pa·*kee*·tee *packet (general)*
palahala pa·la·*ha*·la *antelope*
pamba *pam*·ba *cotton*
pamoja pa·*moh*·ja *together*
pampu *pam*·poo *pump*
pana *pa*·na *wide*
pancha *pan*·cha *puncture*
-panda ·*pan*·da *board (a plane, ship etc) • climb*
— **baisikeli** ba·ee·see·*kay*·lee *cycle*
— **farasi** fa·*ra*·see *ride a horse*
pango *pan*·goh *cave*
panya *pa*·nya *mouse • rat*
Pasaka pa·*sa*·ka *Easter*
pasheni pa·*shay*·nee *passionfruit*
pasi *pa*·see *iron (for clothes)*
pasi ya kupanda ndege *pa*·see ya koo·*pan*·da n·*day*·gay *boarding pass*
pasipoti pa·see·*poh*·tee *passport*
-pata ·*pa*·ta *earn • get*
pauda kwa mtoto pa·*oo*·da kwa m·*toh*·toh *baby powder*
paundi pa·*oon*·dee *pound (money, weight)*
pea *pay*·a *pear*
pedeli pay·*day*·lee *pedal*
pekee pay·*kay* *alone*
-peleka ·pay·*lay*·ka *send*
pembezoni mwa mji paym·bay·*zoh*·nee mwa *m*·jee *suburb*
-penda ·*payn*·da *like • love*
-pendekeza ·payn·day·*kay*·za *recommend*
-pendelea ·payn·day·*lay*·a *prefer*
pensili payn·*see*·lee *pencil*
peremende pay·ray·*mayn*·day *sweets*
pesa *pay*·sa *change*
— **kichele** kee·*chay*·lay *loose change*
pete *pay*·tay *ring (on finger)*
pia *pee*·a *also*
picha *pee*·cha *painting (a work) • photo*
pichi *pee*·chee *peach*
-piga kambi ·*pee*·ga *kam*·bee *camp*
-piga kelele ·*pee*·ga kay·*lay*·lay *shout*
-piga kura ·*pee*·ga *koo*·ra *vote*
-piga picha ·*pee*·ga *pee*·cha *take a photo*
-piga risasi ·*pee*·ga ree·*sa*·see *shoot*
-piga simu ·*pee*·ga *see*·moo *ring (phone)*
-plga teke ·*pee*·ga *tay*·kay *kick*
pigano pee·*ga*·noh *fight*
-pika ·*pee*·ka *cook*
pikipiki pee·kee·*pee*·kee *motorcycle*
pilipili pee·lee·*pee*·lee *pepper*
— **hoho** pee·lee·*pee*·lee *hoh*·hoh *capsicum • chilli*
— **mbichi** pee·lee·*pee*·lee m·*bee*·chee *pepper (bell)*
-pima uzito ·*pee*·ma oo·*zee*·toh *weigh*
-plnda ·*peen*·da *turn*
-pinga ·*peen*·ga *protest*
pinki *peen*·kee *pink*
pipa la taka *pee*·pa la *ta*·ka *garbage can*
pipi *pee*·pee *candy (lollies)*
-pita ·*pee*·ta *pass*
plagi *pla*·gee *plug (electricity)*
plamu *pla*·moo *plum*
— **kavu** *ka*·voo *prune*
plasta *pla*·sta *bandage*
plastiki pla·*stee*·kee *plastic*
poda *poh*·da *powder*
polepole poh·lay·*poh*·lay *slowly*
polisi poh·*lee*·see *police • police officer*
pombe *pohm*·bay *drink (alcoholic)*
— **ya kienyeji** ya kee·ay·*nyay*·jee *home brew*

posho *poh*·shoh *dole*
posta *poh*·sta
mail (postal system) • *post office*
postikadi poh·stee·*ka*·dee *postcard*
-potea ·poh·*tay*·a *lose*
printa *preen*·ta *printer (computer)*
projekta proh·*jayk*·ta *projector*
pua *poo*·a *nose*
— **yenye makamasi**
yay·nyay ma·ka·*ma*·see *runny nose*
pumbavu poom·*ba*·voo *stupid*
pumu *poo*·moo *asthma*
-pumua ·poo·*moo*·a *breathe*
-pumzika ·poom·*zee*·ka *rest*
punda milia *poon*·da mee·*lee*·a *zebra*
punguzo poon·*goo*·zoh *discount*
pwani *pwa*·nee *coast*

R

rafiki ra·*fee*·kee *friend*
-rafikiana ·ra·fee·kee·*a*·na *go out with*
rafu *ra*·foo *shelf*
ragbi *rag*·bee *rugby*
rahisi ra·*hee*·see *cheap* • *easy* • *simple*
raia ra·*ee*·a *nationality*
rais ra·*ees* *president*
raketi ra·*kay*·tee *racquet*
ramani ra·*ma*·nee *map* • *road map*
rangi *ran*·gee *colour*
— **ya machungwa** ya ma·*choon*·gwa
orange (colour)
— **ya mdomo** ya m·*doh*·moh *lipstick*
rasimu ra·*see*·moo *design*
ratiba ra·*tee*·ba *timetable*
— **ya safari** ya sa·*fa*·ree *itinerary*
redio ray·*dee*·oh *radio*
-refu ·*ray*·foo *deep*
-rejeleza ·ray·jay·*lay*·za *recycle*
rejista ray·*gee*·sta *cash register*
-rekodi ·ray·*koh*·dee *record*
rimoti ree·*moh*·tee *remote control*
risiti ree·*see*·tee *receipt*
robo *roh*·boh *quarter*
roki *roh*·kee *rock (music)*
Romani roh·*ma*·nee
Catholic (denomination)
-rudi ·*roo*·dee *return (come back)*
ruhusa roo·*hoo*·sa *permission*
— **ya kazi** ya *ka*·zee *work permit*
-ruhusiwa ·roo·hoo·*see*·wa
can (have permission)
-ruka ·*roo*·ka *fly* • *jump*

S

saa sa *clock* • *hour* • *time* • *watch*
— **sita mchana** *see*·ta m·*cha*·na
midday (noon)
— **sita usiku** *see*·ta oo·*see*·koo
midnight
— **yenye kengele**
yay·nyay kayn·*gay*·lay *alarm clock*
sababu sa·*ba*·boo *reason*
sabuni sa·*boo*·nee *soap*
— **ya kunyolea** ya koo·nyoh·*lay*·a
shaving cream
safari sa·*fa*·ree *trip (journey)*
— **kwa biashara** kwa bee·a·*sha*·ra
business trip
— **ya kutalii** ya koo·ta·*lee* *tour*
— **yenye kiongozi**
yay·nyay kee·ohn·*goh*·zee
guided tour
safi *sa*·fee *clean*
-safiri ·sa·*fee*·ree *travel*
-safisha ·sa·*fee*·sha *clean*
safu ya milima *sa*·foo ya mee·*lee*·ma
mountain range
sahani sa·*ha*·nee *plate*
-sahau ·sa·*ha*·oo *forget*
sahihi sa·*hee*·hee *signature*
-saidia ·sa·ee·*dee*·a *help*
saizi sa·*ee*·zee *size (general)*
sakafu sa·*ka*·foo *floor*
sakitu sa·*kee*·too *frost*
sala *sa*·la *prayer*
salama sa·*la*·ma *safe*
-sali ·*sa*·lee *pray*
saloni sa·*loh*·nee *beauty salon*
samaki sa·*ma*·kee *fish*
-samehe ·sa·*may*·hay *forgive*
sana *sa*·na *very*
sanaa sa·*na* *art*
— **ya uchoraji wa rangi**
ya oo·choh·*ra*·jee wa *ran*·gee
painting (the art)
sanamu sa·*na*·moo *statue*
sanduku san·*doo*·koo *box*
— **la kuhifadhia mizigo**
la koo·hee·fa·*dhee*·a mee·*zee*·goh
luggage locker
— **la posta** la *poh*·sta *mailbox*
sarafu sa·*ra*·foo *change (coins)*
sarakasi sa·ra·*ka*·see *circus* • *gymnastics*
sarara sa·*ra*·ra *fillet*

sasa *sa*·sa *now • present (time)*
— **hivi** *hee*·vee *soon*
sataranji sa·ta·*ran*·jee *chess*
sauna sa·*oo*·na *sauna*
sauti sa·*oo*·tee *voice • volume (sound)*
sawa *sa*·wa *right (correct)*
sawasawa sa·wa·*sa*·wa *same*
sayansi sa·*yan*·see *science*
— **za jamii** za ja·*mee humanities*
sayari sa·*ya*·ree *planet*
sebule say·*boo*·lay *foyer*
sehemu say·*hay*·moo *part (component)*
— **ya kuchukulia mizigo** ya koo·choo·koo·*lee*·a mee·*zee*·goh *baggage claim*
— **ya kuegeshea magari** ya koo·ay·gay·*shay*·a ma·*ga*·ree *car park*
sekundi say·*koon*·dee *second (time unit)*
seli *say*·lee *sale*
-sema ·*say*·ma *say • speak • talk*
senti *sayn*·tee *cent*
sentimita sayn·tee·*mee*·ta *centimetre*
sera *say*·ra *policy*
seremala say·ray·*ma*·la *carpenter*
serikali say·ree·*ka*·lee *government*
shaba *sha*·ba *copper*
shairi pl sha·*ee*·ree *poetry*
shamba *sham*·ba *farm*
— **la mizabibu** la mee·za·*bee*·boo *vineyard*
shampeni sham·*pay*·nee *champagne*
shampuu sham·*poo shampoo*
shangazi shan·*ga*·zee *aunt*
shanta *shan*·ta *backpack*
shashi *sha*·shee *gauze*
shati *sha*·tee *shirt*
shayiri sha·*yee*·ree *oats*
sherehe shay·*ray*·hay *celebration • party (night out)*
sheria shay·*ree*·a *legislation • law (study, profession)*
shifta *sheef*·ta *derailleur*
-shinda ·*sheen*·da *win*
shindano sheen·*da*·noh *race (sport)*
shinikizo shee·nee·*kee*·zoh *pressure*
— **la damu** la *da*·moo *blood pressure*
shirika la habari shee·*ree*·ka la ha·*ba*·ree *newsagency*
-shirikiana ·shee·ree·kee·*a*·na *share (with)*
-shona ·*shoh*·na *sew*
shuka *shoo*·ka *bed linen • sheet*
— **na tandiko** na tan·*dee*·koh *bedding*
-shuka ·*shoo*·ka *get off (a train, etc)*

-shukuru ·shoo·*koo*·roo *thank*
shule *shoo*·lay *school*
— **ya msingi** ya m·*seen*·gee *high school*
shupavu shoo·*pa*·voo *brave*
siagi see·*a*·gee *butter*
siasa see·*a*·sa *politics*
sidiria see·dee·*ree*·a *bra*
sifa *see*·fa *quality*
— **za kielimu** za kee·ay·*lee*·moo *qualifications*
sigara see·*ga*·ra *cigarette*
siki *see*·kee *vinegar*
-sikia ·see·*kee*·a *hear*
-sikiliza ·see·kee·*lee*·za *listen*
-sikilizia ·see·kee·lee·*zee*·a *listen to*
sikio see·*kee*·oh *ear*
siku *see*·koo *day*
Siku ya Krismasi *see*·koo ya krees·*ma*·see *Christmas Day*
Siku ya Mwaka Mpya *see*·koo ya *mwa*·ka *m*·pya *New Year's Day*
sikukuu see·koo·*koo holiday*
— **ya kuzaliwa** ya koo·za·*lee*·wa *birthday*
-simama ·see·*ma*·ma *stop (cease)*
simba *seem*·ba *lion*
simbo ya posta *seem*·boh ya *poh*·sta *post code*
simu *see*·moo *telephone*
— **ya mkononi** ya m·koh·*noh*·nee *cell phone • mobile phone*
— **ya mtaani** ya m·*ta*·nee *public telephone*
sindano (ya dawa) seen·*da*·noh (ya *da*·wa) *needle (syringe)*
sindano (ya kushonea) seen·*da*·noh (ya koo·shoh·*nay*·a) *needle (sewing)*
sinema see·*nay*·ma *cinema*
-sinzia ·seen·*zee*·a *sleep*
sisi *see*·see *we*
sista *see*·sta *nun*
siyo kawaida *see*·yoh ka·wa·*ee*·da *unusual*
skafu *ska*·foo *scarf*
skati *ska*·tee *skirt*
-skii ·skee *ski*
skonzi *skohn*·zee *bread rolls*
slaidi sla·*ee*·dee *slide (film)*
soda *soh*·da *soft drink*
sodo *soh*·doh *sanitary napkin • tampon*
soga *soh*·ga *joke*
soka *soh*·ka *football (soccer)*

S

soko *soh*·koh *market*
— **la mtaani** la m·ta·*a*·nee *street market*
— **la wachonga vinyago** la wa·*chohn*·ga vee·*nya*·goh *woodcarver's market*
soksi *sohk*·see *socks* • *condom (slang)*
— **ndefu** n·*day*·foo *stockings*
-soma ·*soh*·ma *read*
somo *soh*·moh *reading*
soshalisti soh·sha·*lee*·stee *socialist*
spidomita spee·doh·*mee*·ta *speedometer*
spishi zilizo hatarini *spee*·shee zee·*lee*·zoh ha·ta·*ree*·nee *endangered species*
spishi zilizo hifadhiwa *spee*·shee zee·*lee*·zoh hee·fa·*dhee*·wa *protected species*
spoki *spoh*·kee *spoke*
springi *spreen*·gee *spring (coil)*
stempu *staym*·poo *postage* • *stamp*
stendi ya basi *stayn*·dee ya *ba*·see *bus station*
stesheni stay·*shay*·nee *station*
— **ya treni** ya *tray*·nee *railway station*
stirio *stee*·ree·oh *stereo*
studio *stoo*·dee·oh *studio*
-subiri ·soo·*bee*·ree *wait*
sufu *soo*·foo *wool*
sufuria soo·foo·*ree*·a *saucepan*
sukari soo·*ka*·ree *sugar*
-sukuma ·soo·*koo*·ma *push*
sungura soon·*goo*·ra *rabbit*
sungusungu soon·goo·*soon*·goo *ant*
supu *soo*·poo *soup*
surua soo·*roo*·a *measles*
suruali soo·roo·*a*·lee *pants (trousers)*
sururu soo·*roo*·roo *pickaxe*
swala *swa*·la *gazelle*
swalapala swa·la·*pa*·la *impala*
swali *swa*·lee *question*
sweta *sway*·ta *jumper (sweater)*

T

taa ta *light (lamp)*
— **ya barabarani** ya ba·ra·ba·*ra*·nee *traffic light*
— **za mbele** za m·*bay*·lay *headlights*
taarifa ta·a·*ree*·fa *information*
tabaka ta·*ba*·ka *class (category)*
— **la hewa ya ozoni** la *hay*·wa ya oh·*zoh*·nee *ozone layer*
-tabasamu ·ta·ba·*sa*·moo *smile*
tabibu wa maungo ta·*bee*·boo wa ma·*oon*·goh *chiropractor*
-tafsiri ·taf·*see*·ree *translate*
-tafuta ·ta·*foo*·ta *look for*
tairi *ta*·ee·ree *tyre*
tajiri ta·*jee*·ree *rich (wealthy)*
-taka ·*ta*·ka *want*
taka za sumu *ta*·ka za *soo*·moo *toxic waste*
takataka ta·ka·*ta*·ka *garbage*
— **za nyuklia** za *nyook*·lee·a *nuclear waste*
tamasha ta·*ma*·sha *festival*
tambalale tam·ba·*la*·lay *flat* ⓐ
tambi *tam*·bee *noodles* • *pasta*
tamu *ta*·moo *sweet* • *tasty*
tandiko tan·*dee*·koh *saddle*
tangazo tan·*ga*·zoh *advertisement*
tango *tan*·goh *cucumber*
tangu (Mei) *tan*·goo (*may*·ee) *since (May)*
taratibu ta·ra·*tee*·boo *slow*
tarehe ta·*ray*·hay *date (day)*
— **ya kuzaliwa** ya koo·za·*lee*·wa *date of birth*
taulo ta·*oo*·loh *towel*
taya *ta*·ya *jaw*
tayari ta·*ya*·ree *already* adv • *ready* ⓐ
-tazama ·ta·*za*·ma *watch*
teknolojia ya maarifa tayk·noh·loh·*jee*·a ya ma·a·*ree*·fa *IT*
teksi *tayk*·see *taxi*
telegramu tay·lay·*gra*·moo *telegram*
telekom *tay*·lay·kohm *telecom centre*
televisheni tay·lay·vee·*shay*·nee *television*
-teleza ·tay·*lay*·za *skate*
-tembea ·taym·*bay*·a *walk*
— **porini** poh·*ree*·nee *hike*
-tembelea ·taym·bay·*lay*·a *visit*
tembo *taym*·boh *elephant*
tena *tay*·na *again*
tende *tayn*·day *date (fruit)*
tenesi tay·*nay*·see *tennis*
-tengeneza ·tayn·gay·*nay*·za *make* • *repair*
tetekuwanga tay·tay·koo·*wan*·ga *chicken pox*

tetemeko la ardhi tay·tay·*may*·koh la *ar*·dhee *earthquake*
thamani *tha*·ma·nee *value (price)*
theluji thay·*loo*·jee *snow*
-thibitisha ·thee·bee·*tee*·sha *validate*
tiba ya harufu *tee*·ba ya ha·*roo*·foo *aromatherapy*
tiba ya kuchoma na sindano *tee*·ba ya koo·*choh*·ma na seen·*da*·noh *acupuncture*
tiketi tee·*kay*·tee *ticket*
— **kutumia kama nafasi ikipatikana** koo·too·*mee*·a *ka*·ma na·*fa*·see ee·kee·pa·tee·*ka*·na *stand-by ticket*
— **ya kwenda tu** ya *kwayn*·da too *one-way (ticket)*
— **ya kwenda na kurudi** ya *kwayn*·da na koo·*roo*·dee *return (ticket)*
— **ya mzigo** ya m·*zee*·goh *luggage tag*
tikiti tee·*kee*·tee *ticket*
timu *tee*·moo *team*
tini *tee*·nee *fig*
tishati *tee*·sha·tee *T-shirt*
titi *tee*·tee *breast (body)*
-toa rushwa ·*toh*·a *roosh*·wa *bribe*
tochi *toh*·chee *torch (flashlight)*
tofaa to·*fa apple*
tofauti to·fa·*oo*·tee *different*
— **ya wakati** ya wa·*ka*·tee *time difference*
treni *tray*·nee *train*
tu too *only*
-tulivu ·too·*lee*·voo *quiet*
-tumaini ·too·ma·*ee*·nee *wish*
tumbaku toom·*ba*·koo *tobacco*
tumbili toom·*bee*·lee *monkey*
tumbo *toom*·boh *stomach*
tumbusi toom·*boo*·see *vulture*
tunda *toon*·da *fruit*
-tunza ·*toon*·za *care (for someone)* • *look after*
tupu *too*·poo *empty* • *vacant*
twiga *twee*·ga *giraffe*
twiza *twee*·za *tweezers*
tyubu *tyoo*·boo *inner tube* • *tyre*

U

ua *oo*·a *flower*
-ua ·*oo*·a *murder*
ubaguzi oo·ba·*goo*·zee *discrimination*
— **wa kijinsia** wa kee·jeen·*see*·a *sexism*
— **wa rangi** wa *ran*·gee *racism*
ubakaji oo·ba·*ka*·jee *rape*
ubalozi oo·ba·*loh*·zee *embassy*
— **mdogo** m·*doh*·goh *consulate*
ubao wa kuteleza oo·*ba*·oh wa koo·tay·*lay*·za *skateboarding*
ubao wa kutelezea oo·*ba*·oh wa koo·tay·lay·*zay*·a *surfboard*
ubao wa matokeo oo·*ba*·oh wa ma·toh·*kay*·oh *scoreboard*
ubao wa sataranji oo·*ba*·oh wa sa·ta·*ran*·jee *chessboard*
ubaraza oo·ba·*ra*·za *balcony*
ubatizo oo·ba·*tee*·zoh *baptism*
ubavu oo·*ba*·voo *rib*
uchafuzi oo·cha·*foo*·zee *pollution*
uchaguzi oo·cha·*goo*·zee *election*
ucheleweshaji oo·chay·lay·way·*sha*·jee *delay*
uchongaji oo·chohn·*ga*·jee *sculpture*
uchumba oo·*choom*·ba *engagement*
udaktari oo·dak·*ta*·ree *medicine (study, profession)*
udobi oo·*doh*·bee *laundry (place)*
udongo oo·*dohn*·goh *clay*
uelekeo oo·ay·lay·*kay*·oh *direction*
ufinyanzi oo·fee·*nyan*·zee *ceramics*
ufukwe oo·*fook*·way *beach* • *seaside*
ufunguo oo·foon·*goo*·oh *key*
ugonjwa wa kuchomwa kwa jua oo·*gohn*·jwa wa koo·*chohm*·wa kwa *joo*·a *sunstroke*
ugonjwa wa moyo oo·*gohn*·jwa wa *moh*·yoh *heart condition*
ugonjwa wa upele oo·*gohn*·jwa wa oo·*pay*·lay *thrush (health)*
ugonjwa wa zinaa oo·*gohn*·jwa wa zee·*na venereal disease*
uhamiaji oo·ha·mee·*a*·jee *immigration*
uhandisi oo·han·*dee*·see *engineering*
uharibifu oo·ha·ree·*bee*·foo *spoilage*
uhusiano oo·hoo·see·*a*·noh *relationship*
— **wa jamii** wa ja·*mee public relations*
ujangili oo·jan·*gee*·lee *poached (game)*
ujao oo·*ja*·oh *next*
ujenzi oo·*jayn*·zee *architecture*
ujumbe oo·*joom*·bay *message*
ukarimu oo·ka·*ree*·moo *hospitality*
ukimwi oo·*keem*·wee *AIDS*
ukumbi oo·*koom*·bee *gym (place)*
— **wa maonyesho** wa ma·oh·*nyay*·shoh *theatre*
ukungu oo·*koon*·goo *fog*
ukurasa oo·koo·*ra*·sa *page*

ukurutu oo·koo·*roo*·too *eczema*
ukuta oo·*koo*·ta *wall (outer)*
Ulaya oo·*la*·ya *Europe*
ulezi wa mtoto oo·*lay*·zee wa m·*toh*·toh *childminding*
ulimi oo·*lee*·mee *tongue*
ulimwengu oo·lee·*mwayn*·goo *universe*
-uliza ·oo·*lee*·za *ask (a question)*
uma *oo*·ma *bite (dog, insect)* • *fork*
-uma ·*oo*·ma *hurt*
umaskini oo·ma·*skee*·nee *poverty*
umbo *oom*·boh *shape*
umeme oo·*may*·may *electricity*
umri *oom*·ree *age*
ungamo oon·*ga*·moh *confession*
ununuzi oo·noo·*noo*·zee *shopping*
uongezaji wa visa oo·ohn·gay·*za*·jee wa *vee*·sa *extension (visa)*
upandaji miamba oo·pan·*da*·jee mee·*am*·ba *rock climbing*
upande oo·*pan*·day *side*
upele oo·*pay*·lay *rash*
— **wa nepi** wa *nay*·pee *nappy rash*
upendo oo·*payn*·doh *love*
upepo oo·*pay*·poh *air (in a tyre)* • *wind*
upigaji picha oo·pee·*ga*·jee *pee*·cha *photography*
upimaji mimba oo·pee·*ma*·jee *meem*·ba *pregnancy test kit*
upungufu oo·poon·*goo*·foo *shortage*
— **wa damu** wa *da*·moo *anaemia*
uraia oo·ra·*ee*·a *citizenship*
urari oo·*ra*·ree *balance (account)*
usafi oo·*sa*·fee *cleaning*
usafirishaji oo·sa·fee·ree·*sha*·jee *transport*
usajili wa gari oo·sa·*jee*·lee wa *ga*·ree *car registration*
usawa oo·*sa*·wa *equality*
ushauri oo·sha·*oo*·ree *advice*
ushirikina oo·shee·ree·*kee*·na *superstition*
usiku oo·*see*·koo *night*
— **huu** hoo *tonight*
— **nje** *n*·jay *night out*
usimamizi oo·see·ma·*mee*·zee *administration*
uso *oo*·soh *face*
ustawi oo·*sta*·wee *welfare*
— **wa jamii** wa ja·*mee social welfare*
usukani pl oo·soo·*ka*·nee *handlebars*
usumbufu oo·soom·*boo*·foo *harassment*
utawala oo·ta·*wa*·la *rule*
utegemezi wa madawa ya kulevya oo·tay·gay·*may*·zee wa ma·*da*·wa ya koo·*lay*·vya *drug addiction*
utumiaji oo·too·mee·*a*·jee *exploitation*
uvimbe oo·*veem*·bay *inflammation* • *lump* • *swelling* • *tumour*
— **wa mboni** wa m·*boh*·nee *conjunctivitis*
— **wa ovari** wa oh·*va*·ree *ovarian cyst*
uvimbi wa ini oo·*veem*·bee wa *ee*·nee *hepatitis*
uvuvi oo·*voo*·vee *fishing*
uwakala wa safari oo·wa·*ka*·la wa sa·*fa*·ree *travel agency*
uwanda wa juu oo·*wan*·da wa joo *plateau*
uwanja oo·*wan*·ja *square (town)*
— **wa gofu** wa *goh*·foo *golf course*
— **wa kupigia kambi** wa kuu·pee·*gee*·a *kam*·bee *camping ground*
— **wa mbio** wa m·*bee*·oh *racetrack*
— **wa michezo** wa mee·*chay*·zoh *stadium*
— **wa ndege** wa n·*day*·gay *airport*
uwezo wa watu oo·*way*·zoh wa *wa*·too *human resources*
uwindaji oo·ween·*da*·jee *hunting*
uyabisi wa tumbo oo·ya·*bee*·see wa *toom*·boh *constipation*
uyoga oo·*yoh*·ga *mushroom*
-uza ·*oo*·za *sell*
uzi *oo*·zee *string* • *thread*
— **wa meno** wa *may*·noh *dental floss*
uzito oo·*zee*·toh *weight*
— **usiolipiwa** oo·see·oh·lee·*pee*·wa *baggage allowance*
uzoefu oo·zoh·*ay*·foo *experience*
— **wa kazi** wa *ka*·zee *work experience*
uzushi oo·*zoo*·shee *fiction*

V

-vaa ·va *wear*
vazi *va*·zee *dress*
— **la kuogelea** la koo·oh·gay·*lay*·a *swimsuit*
viatu vee·*a*·too *shoes*
vibiriti vee·bee·*ree*·tee *matches (for lighting)*
vidonge vya usingizi vee·*dohn*·gay vya oo·seen·*gee*·zee *sleeping pills*
vifaa vee·*fa equipment*
— **vya kuzamia** vya koo·za·*mee*·a *diving equipment*
vigumu vee·*goo*·moo *difficult*
vipengele vee·payn·*gay*·lay *details*
vipuli vee·*poo*·lee *jewellery*

virusi vee·*roo*·see *virus*
visa *vee*·sa *visa*
visu *vee*·soo *cutlery*
vita *vee*·ta *war*
vitamini vee·ta·*mee*·nee *vitamins*
vitanda viwili vee·*tan*·da vee·*wee*·lee *twin beds*
vitu vya sanaa *vee*·too vya sa·*na crafts*
viza *vee*·za *visa*
vizibo vya masikio vee·*zee*·boh vya ma·see·*kee*·oh *earplugs*
vizuri vee·*zoo*·ree *well*
-vunja ·*voon*·ja *break*
-vunjika ·voon·*jee*·ka *break down*
-vuta ·*voo*·ta *pull*
— **sigara** see·*ga*·ra *smoke*
VVU vee·vee·*yoo* *HIV*
vyakula vya·*koo*·la *groceries*
vyombo vya habari *vyohm*·boh vya ha·*ba*·ree *media*
vyombo vya udongo *vyohm*·boh vya oo·*dohn*·goh *pottery*

W

-wa ·wa *be*
— **marafiki** ma·ra·*fee*·kee *date (a person)*
— **mgonjwa** m·*gohn*·jwa *have a cold*
— **na** na *have*
— **na deni** na *day*·nee *owe*
wakala wa maeneo wa·*ka*·la wa ma·ay·*nay*·oh *real estate agent*
wakala wa shamba wa·*ka*·la wa *sham*·ba *estate agency*
wakati wa·*ka*·tee *when*
— **mwingine** mween·*gee*·nay *sometimes*
wala *wa*·la *neither*
wali *wa*·lee *rice (cooked)*
-wa na maumivu ya tumbo ·wa na ma·oo·*mee*·voo ya *toom*·boh *to have a stomachache*
wanaofika wa·na·oh·*fee*·ka *arrivals*
wao *wa*·oh *they* • *their*
wapi *wa*·pee *where*
warsha *war*·sha *workshop (meeting)*
wasiojiweza wa·see·oh·jee·*way*·za *disabled*
watoto wa·*toh*·toh *children*
— **wa mtaani** wa m·ta·*a*·nee *street children*
watu *wa*·too *people*
wawili wawili wa·*wee*·lee wa·*wee*·lee *pair (couple)*
waya *wa*·ya *wire*
wazazi wa·*za*·zee *parents*
wazi *wa*·zee *open (premises)*
wazimu wa·*zee*·moo *hallucination*
waziri mkuu wa·*zee*·ree m·*koo* *prime minister*
-weka ·*way*·ka *put*
wembe *waym*·bay *razor* • *razor blade*
wewe *way*·way *you* sg
-weza ·*way*·za *can (be able)*
wigo *wee*·goh *fence*
wikendi wee·*kayn*·dee *weekend*
wiki *wee*·kee *week*
— **iliyopita** ee·lee·yoh·*pee*·ta *last week*
— **mbili** m·*bee*·lee *fortnight*
wimbi *weem*·bee *wave*
wimbo *weem*·boh *song* • *tune*
wingu *ween*·goo *cloud*
wizi *wee*·zee *rip-off*
wote *woh*·tay *everyone*

Y

ya aibu ya a·*ee*·boo *shy*
ya ajabu ya a·*ja*·boo *wonderful*
ya awali ya *a*·wa·lee *original*
ya baridi ya ba·*ree*·dee *cool*
ya chujwa ya *chooj*·wa *filtered*
ya elimu kale ya ay·*lee*·moo *ka*·lay *archaeological*
ya hakika ya ha·*kee*·ka *positive*
ya jadi ya *ja*·dee *classical*
ya joto ya *joh*·toh *warm*
ya jua ya *joo*·a *sunny*
ya kabla ya *kab*·la *last (previous)*
ya kale ya *ka*·lay *ancient*
ya kasi ya *ka*·see *fast*
ya kidini ya kee·*dee*·nee *religious*
ya kienyeji ya kee·ayn·*nyay*·jee *local*
ya kigeni ya kee·*gay*·nee *foreign* • *strange*
ya kihistoria ya kee·hee·stoh·*ree*·a *historical*
ya kijana ya kee·*ja*·na *young*
ya kike ya *kee*·kay *female*
ya kimataifa ya kee·ma·ta·*ee*·fa *international*
ya kisasa ya kee·*sa*·sa *modern*
ya kuachwa ya koo·*ach*·wa *excluded*
ya kubana ya koo·*ba*·na *tight*

ya kuchekesha ya koo·chay·*kay*·sha *comedy • funny*
ya kuchelewa ya koo·chay·*lay*·wa *late*
ya kuchochea ashiki ya koo·choh·*chay*·a a·*shee*·kee *sexy*
ya kuchoka ya koo·*choh*·ka *tired*
ya kuchomwa ya koo·*chohm*·wa *burnt*
ya kuchosha ya koo·*choh*·sha *boring*
ya kufungwa ya koo·*foon*·gwa *closed • locked*
ya kugandwa ya koo·*gan*·dwa *frozen*
ya kuharibika ya koo·ha·ree·*bee*·ka *broken down*
ya kuibwa ya koo·*ee*·bwa *stolen*
ya kujaa ya koo·*ja* *full*
ya kujazana ya koo·ja·*za*·na *crowded*
ya kujiajiri ya koo·jee·a·*jee*·ree *self-employed*
ya kujihuduma ya koo·jee·hoo·*doo*·ma *self-service*
ya kukana ya koo·*ka*·na *negative*
ya kukaushwa ya koo·ka·*oosh*·wa *dried*
ya kula rushwa ya *koo*·la *roosh*·wa *corrupt*
ya kupendeza ya koo·payn·*day*·za *beautiful • pretty*
ya kupendwa ya koo·*payn*·dwa *popular*
ya kupotezwa ya koo·poh·*tayz*·wa *lost*
ya kurejeleza ya koo·ray·jay·*lay*·za *recyclable*
ya kutamanisha ya koo·ta·ma·*nee*·sha *sensual*
ya kutosha ya koo·*toh*·sha *enough*
ya kuumiza ya koo·oo·*mee*·za *painful*
ya kuvunjika ya koo·voon·*jee*·ka *broken*
— **kirahisi** kee·ra·*hee*·see *fragile*
ya kuvutia ya koo·voo·*tee*·a *interesting*
ya kuwezekana ya koo·way·zay·*ka*·na *possible*
ya kwanza ya *kwan*·za *first*
ya mfano hasa ya m·*fa*·noh *ha*·sa *typical*
ya mkoa ya m·*koh*·a *regional*
ya moto ya *moh*·toh *heated*
ya muda kamili ya *moo*·da ka·*mee*·lee *full-time*
ya mwinuko mkali ya mwee·*noo*·koh m·*ka*·lee *steep*
ya mwisho ya *mwee*·shoh *last (final)*
ya pili ya *pee*·lee *second* ⓐ
ya starehe ya sta·*ray*·hay *comfortable*
ya tatu ya *ta*·too *third*
ya thamani ya *tha*·ma·nee *valuable*
ya usanisia ya oo·sa·nee·*see*·a *synthetic*
ya zamani ya za·*ma*·nee *antique • old • stale*
yai *ya*·ee *egg*
yake *ya*·kay *her • his*
yako *ya*·koh *your* sg
yangu *yan*·goo *my*
yao *ya*·oh *their*
yaya *ya*·ya *babysitter*
yenu *yay*·noo *your* pl
yenye busara *yay*·nyay boo·*sa*·ra *sensible*
yenye kelele *yay*·nyay kay·*lay*·lay *noisy*
yenye kosa *yay*·nyay *koh*·sa *faulty*
yenye kufanana *yay*·nyay koo·fa·*na*·na *similar*
yenye manufaa *yay*·nyay ma·noo·*fa* *useful*
yenye sumu *yay*·nyay *soo*·moo *poisonous*
yenye uhalisi *yay*·nyay oo·ha·*lee*·see *realistic*
yetu *yay*·too *our*
yeye *yay*·yay *he • she*
yoyote yoh·*yoh*·tay *any*

Z

zabibu za·*bee*·boo *grapes*
— **kavu** *ka*·voo *raisin*
zaidi za·*ee*·dee *more*
zaituni za·ee·*too*·nee *olive*
-zalisha ·za·*lee*·sha *produce*
zamani za·*ma*·nee *past*
zambarau zam·ba·*ra*·oo *purple*
zao *za*·oh *crop*
zawadi za·*wa*·dee *present (gift)*
— **ya arusi** ya a·*roo*·see *wedding present*
zeze *zay*·zay *guitar*
ziara zee·*a*·ra *shrine*
zingizi zeen·*gee*·zee *premenstrual tension*
zipu *zee*·poo *zip/zipper*
-zito ·*zee*·toh *thick*
ziwa *zee*·wa *lake*
ziwi *zee*·wee *deaf*
zodiaki zoh·dee·*a*·kee *zodiac*
zote *zoh*·tay *all*
-zuia ·zoo·*ee*·a *stop (prevent)*
zulia zoo·*lee*·a *rug*

A

B

C

D

E

F

G

H

I

J

K

L

M

S

T

U

V

W

Z